D0930715

EARLY LUTHERAN
BAPTISMS AND MARRIAGES
IN
SOUTHEASTERN PENNSYLVANIA

Early Lutheran Baptisms and Marriages in Southeastern Pennsylvania

The Records of Rev. John Casper Stoever from 1730 to 1779

With an Index by Elizabeth P. Bentley

Originally published as *Records of Rev. John Casper Stoever,*
Harrisburg, Pennsylvania, 1896.
Reprinted under a new title and with an added index by
Genealogical Publishing Co., Inc.
Baltimore, 1982, 1984, 1988, 1998
Index copyright © 1982 by
Genealogical Publishing Co., Inc.
Baltimore, Maryland
All Rights Reserved
Library of Congress Catalogue Card Number 82-83232
International Standard Book Number 0-8063-1002-2
Made in the United States of America

EARLY LUTHERAN
BAPTISMS AND MARRIAGES
IN
SOUTHEASTERN PENNSYLVANIA

Rev. John Casper Stoever's Record of Baptisms and Marriages from 1730 to 1779.

PREFATORY.

For a translation of the Baptismal and Marriage records of one of the earliest divines of the Lutheran church in Pennsylvania, we are indebted to the Rev. F. J. F. Schantz, D. D., of Myerstown, Pa., who in forwarding it writes: "The original Record of Baptisms and Marriages of Rev. Johann Casper Stoever, containing also a sketch of his life, is in the possession of W. C. Stoever, Esq., Mt. Airy, Philadelphia, Pa., a son of the late Prof. M. L. Stoever, LL. D., of Pennsylvania College, Gettysburg, Pa. With his permission, at the request of Rev. H. E. Jacobs, D. D., LL. D., of the Theological Seminary at Mt. Airy, Pa., a copy of the record was made to be preserved in the archives of the Evangelical Lutheran Ministerium of Pennsylvania, &c. This translation of the record and permission for publication were secured also by the kind consent of Mr. Stoever. The original record of Johann Casper Stoever was written in German and contains many Latin phrases as well as a few English and French. The spelling of names of localities is generally given as in the original record. The biography of Johann Casper Stoever is given in the original record after the entries of the birth and baptism of his own children, and is placed in this publication at the beginning for convenient reference. As will be seen in a foot note added to the biography, Johann Casper Stoever, sr., and Johann Casper Stoever, jr., arrived in Pennsylvania on September 11th, 1728. The former labored in Spottsylvania, Va., and the latter in Pennsylvania, extending his labors to Virginia, as will be noticed in the record of his baptisms and marriages furnished for publication.

BIOGRAPHY.

Johann Casper Stoever, father of the children named above (in the record of baptisms), was born December 21st, 1707, in a place named Luedorff, in Solinger Amt, Duchy Berg, in Unter Pfaltz. His parents were Johann Caspar Stoever (a native of Frankenburg in Hesse and Gertraudt (family name not given), born in Amt Solingen. When he was six years of age he learned to read German perfectly in four weeks under his father's direction. After this he also commenced to study Latin under his father. Subsequently he received private instruction in Latin and Greek from four pastors successively named, H. Nicolaus Muentz, H. Samuel Bratschisch, H. Valentine Kraft and H. Antonius Pfaffman, and later in the languages named, as also in Hebrew and French, and likewise in theology from H. Knabel and finally from H. Special (Superintendent) Adolph Ruehfeld at Brumath, three hours (twelve miles), from Strassburg. Journeyed from Europe to America in 1728 on the Rhine and on an ocean vessel, preaching on Sundays. Arrived in Pennsylvania Sept. 29th and continued to preach; ordained on April 8th, 1733, by Christian Schultz, p. t. pastor in Philadelphia, and was married at the same time to Maria Catarina. They became the parents of the above named children (eleven named in record of baptisms.) His wife was born May 14th, 1715, at Lambesheim in Chur Pfaltz. Her sponsor was Catarina Ursula Schmidt. Her parents were Christian Merckling and his wife Catarina, nee Brucher.

November 2d, 1778—Whilst I am writing this cursum vitae, my age is by the grace and help of God 70 years, 10 months, 1 week and five days.

In the original record the following was added in a different handwriting: His full age—71 years, 4 months 3 weeks and 2 days.

Rev. Johann Casper Stoever died at his residence, west of Lebanon, Pa., May 13th, 1779, and was buried at Hill Church, north of west of Lebanon, Pa.—F. J. F. S.

September 29th is no doubt an error of memory at his advanced age. According to "Pennsylvania Archives, second series, vol. xvii, p. 15" and "Rupp's Collection of 30,000 names of Immigrants" no vessel arrived with immigrants in 1728, after September 11th, on which day the ship, James Goodwill, David Crocket, master, from Rotterdam, and the qualification of its passengers are reported. Among the names of its passengers are those of "Johann Casper Stoever, Missionaire," and "Johann Casper Stoever, S. S. Theol. Stud." (see Rupp's Collection, page 58.) "Johan Casper Steffer, sr., and Johan Casper Steffer, jr., (see Pennsylvania Archives, second series, vol. xvii, page 15.) In the State Library at Harrisburg, Pa., I saw the paper containing the names of foreigners who arrived September 11th, 1728. In this list are found the names "Johan Casper Steffer, sr., and Johan Casper Steffer, jr." Before the name of "Johan Casper Steffer, jr., "Minr." is written. Johann Casper Stoever, sr., labored 1733 as a minister in Spottsylvania, Va., went to Europe 1737 and died on board the vessel on his attempted return to America. (See Halle reports, new edition, 1886, page 686.) The record of baptisms and marriages given in this book is that of Johann Casper Stoever, jr.—F. J. F. S.

BAPTISMS.

WILHELM HEIM, (Coventry.)
Heim—John Christian, b. Oct. 1, 1731; bap. Oct. 24, 1731. Sponsor, John Christian Schunck.
—— John Casper, b. May 17, 1734; bap. May 22, 1734. Sponsor, John Casper Schunck.
—— Frantz Hugo, b. Sept. 17, 1738; bap. Jan. 10, 1739. Sponsors, Frantz Schunck and wife Elizabeth.

VALENTINE KUEHLER, (The Swamp.)
Kuehler—John Heinrich, b. Feb., 1731 bap. Oct. 24, 1731. Sponsors, Sebastian Miller and wife.

REES JONES, (Manatawny.)
Jones—Emma, b. Aug., 1731; bap. Oct. 30, 1731. Sponsors, John Williams and wife.

JOHN MICHAEL HENNINGER, (Maxatawny.)
Henninger—Maria Rosina, b. Nov. 21, 1731; bap. Nov. 27, 1731. Sponsors, Sebastian Zimmerman, Anna Elizabeth Levan and Anna Maria Levan.
—— John Michael, b. Sept. 30, 1736; bap. Oct. 29, 1736. Sponsors, Heinrich Christ and Eva Kuhn.

JOHN HEINRICH WOLF, (Oley.)
Wolf—John Adam, b. Nov. 2, 1731; bap. Nov. 28, 1731. Sponsors, John Adam Phibel and his wife.
—— John Heinrich, an adopted child of John Heinrich Wolf. Reputed father,

Isaac Leonhardt; mother, N. Scheidin, now married to John Callus, b. Nov., 1721; bap. Nov. 28, 1731. Sponsor, John Heinrich Wolf.
—— Johannes, b. Dec. 31, 1732; bap. Aug. 20, 1733. Sponsor, Johannes Messersmidt.

ABRAHAM LONG, (Oley.)
Long—Elizabeth, b. Nov. 14, 1731; bap. Nov. 28, 1731. Sponsors, Peter Long and wife Elizabeth.

THOMAS DOTSON, (French Creek.)
Dotson—Hannah, b. Dec. 7, 1727; bap. Dec. 3, 1731.
—— John William, b. Aug., 1729; bap. Dec. 3, 1731.
—— Richard, b. June 26, 1731; bap. Dec. 3, 1731.
Sponsors for the above Peter Richter and the parents.

THOMAS COOK, (The Swamp.)
Cook—Gratia, b. June, 1726; bap. Dec. 9, 1731. Sponsors, William Fell and wife, also Mary Porcks.

JOHN HOLDER, (Oley.)
Holder—Andreas Hugo, b. April 6, 1731; bap. Dec. 26, 1731. Sponsor, Karl Volck.

CHARLES FULCK, (Manatawny.)
Fulck—Johanna, b. Dec. 11, 1731. bap. Dec. 21, 1731. Sponsor, Maria Barbara Holderin.

JOHN ELLIS, (Manatawny.)
Ellis—Evans, b. Dec., 1724; bap. Feb.

24, 1732. Witness, William Richard.
—— John, b. Nov., 1726; bap. Jan. 24,
1732. Witnesses, Thomas Turner and
Susanna Turner.
ANTONY TURNER, (Manatawny.)
Turner—Antony, b. Jan. 21, 1732; bap.
Feb. 10, 1732. Sureties, John Ellis,
Thomas Turner and Susanna Turner.
MICHAEL SPON, (Maxatawney.)
Spon—Maria Barbara, b. Feb. 10, 1732;
bap. March 19, 1732. Sponsors, Jacob
Roth and wife.
—— Johann Adam, b. Nov. 1, 1735;
bap. Jan. 17, 1736. Sponsor, John
Adam Lueckenbuehl.
JOHN GEORGE KOELCHNER,
(Oley.)
Koelchner—George Adam, b. Sept. 20,
1732; bap. Jan. 20, 1733. Sponsors,
the parents.
JOHN GEORGE FROSCH,
(Conewago.)
Frosch—Johannes, b. Dec. 16, 1732;
bap. Feb. 4, 1733. Sponsors, John
Morgenstern and wife.
—— Catarina, b. July, 1735; bap. Nov.
5, 1735. Sponsors, John George Kuntz
and wife Catarina.
—— Maria Elizabetha, b. Sept. 21,
1738; bap. Nov. 25, 1738. Sponsors,
Jacob Kuntz and wife.
JOHANNES LISCHEER
(Providence.)
Lischeer—Abraham, b. Dec. 11, 1732;
bap. Feb. 11, 1733. Sponsors, the
parents.
ADAM WARTMAN,
(Falckner Schwamp.)
Wartman—Catarina, b. April 26, 1733;
bap. June 12, 1733. Sponsors, Mar-
tin Koeblinger and wife Catarina.
MICHAEL SCHMIDT,
(Falckner Schwamp.)
Schmidt—Maria Catarina, b. Feb. 29,
1733; bap. June 24, 1733. Sponsors,
Jacob Schwitzer and wife.
—— John Adam, b. Nov. 1, 1733; bap.
Jan. 13, 1734. Sponsors, Heinrich
Ganger and wife.
JOHN GEORGE EBERD,
(Falckner Schwamp.)
Eberd—Jacob, b. May 31, 1733; bap.
June 24, 1733. Sponsor, Jacob Her-
man.
THOMAS DEA, (Colebrook Dale.)
Dea—Sara, b. Feb., 1733; bap. Aug. 4,
1733. Evidence, Mary William.
ULRICH BOECKLE,
(Schifenthill.)
Boeckle—Margaretta Dorothea, b. June
11, 1733; bap. July 8, 1733. Sponsors,

John George Kleinhaus and wife Dor-
othea.
—— Catarina Charlotta, b. March 28,
1735; bap. April 7, 1735. Sponsors,
Jacob Mueller and wife.
VALENTINE BERNHAEUSZEL,
(Schifenthill.)
Bernhaeuszel — Susanna Catharina, b.
May 22, 1733; bap. July 15, 1733.
Sponsors, Andreas Beyer and wife.
JOHANNES JUNG'S Negro Children.
—— Sybilla, b. Sept. 3, 1723; bap. July
23, 1733. Sponsor, Johannes Jung.
—— Daniel, b. May 22, 1725; bap. July
23, 1733. Johannes Koeblinger.
—— Margaretha, b. April 18, 1727;
bap. July 23, 1733. Sponsors, Eliza-
beth Augin.
—— Ludwig, b. Feb. 2, 1729; bap. July
23, 1733. Sponsors, Ludwig Fisher
and Catharine Elizabeth Puls.
—— Jacob, b. Feb. 15, 1731; bap. July
23, 1733. Sponsors, John Nicolaus
Strauss and Anna Maria Kellerin.
—— Johannes, b. Feb. 15, 1733; bap.
July 23, 1733. Sponsors, John Nico-
laus Strauss and Anna Maria Kellerin.
MATTHEIS EGNER,
(Schifenthill.)
Egner—Johannes, b. June 15, 1733; bap.
Aug. 5, 1733. Sponsors, John Ehr-
man and Anna Maria Wipert.
—— Mattheis, b. June 2, 1735; bap.
Oct. 19, 1735. Sponsors, John Mat-
theis Schmidt and wife.
HEINRICH ZUBER,
(At the Schuylkill.)
Zuber—John Michael, b. Sept., 1726;
bap. Aug. 20, 1733. Sponsor, Michael
Fischer.
—— Maria Elizabetha, b. Nov. 6, 1730;
bap. Aug. 20, 1733. Sponsor, Maria
Elizabetha Bechtel.
—— John Peter Hugo, b. Feb. 25,
1734; bap. Oct. 7, 1734. Sponsors,
John Peter and Maria Elizabeth
Spenglein.
CHRISTIAN FREY, Oley Mountains,
(Colebrookdale.)
Frey—Maria Catharina, b. July 31,
1733; bap. Aug. 25, 1737. Sponsors,
John Frey, Anna Maria Junt and Anna
Catharina Henckle.
CHRISTOPH WITTMAN,
(Falckner Schwamp.)
Wittman—George Michael, b. July 13,
1733; bap. Sept. 3, 1733. Sponsors,
George Michael Meck and wife Maria
Barbara.
JOHN CUNRADT ROTH,
(Oley Mountains.)
Roth—John Jacob, b. Aug. 7, 1733;

bap. Sept. 20, 1733. Sponsors, John Jacob Roth and Elizabeth Ritter.

JOHN PETER GUENTHER,
(Oley Mountains.)
Guenther—John, b. Sept. 23, 1733; bap. Sept. 29, 1733. Sponsor, John Frederich Greinert.

—— Maria Margaretha, b. Dec. 29, 1734; bap. Dec. 29, 1734. Sponsors. Margaretha Nagle and Maria Magdalena Maess.

JOHN CHRISTOPH SPRECHER,
(Schifenthill.)
Sprecher—John George. b. Sept. 8, 1733; bap. Sept. 30, 1733. Sponsors, John Joseph Becker, Johannes Kepner and Elizabetha Kaercherin.

JONATHAN BAECKER,
Baecker—John Jonathan, b. Jan. 1, 1730; bap. Oct. 20, 1733. Sponsors, John Alstatt and wife.

HEINRICH KOEHLER,
(Colebrookdale.)
Koehler—Maria Catharine, b. Sept. 19, 1732; bap. Oct. 20, 1733. Sponsors, John Casper Reinhardt and Maria Cath. Greiner.

—— Maria Christina, b. April 18, 1734; bap. Aug. 11, 1734. Sponsors, Anna Cathlarina Henckelin and Maria Catharina Greinerin.

NICOLAUS ROEHBEN. (Merion.)
Roehben—Peter, b. Dec., 1732; bap. Oct. 28, 1733. Sponsor. Peter Richter.

—— Catarina Barbara, b. Feb. 18, 1734; bap. March 30, 1734. Sponsors, John Balthasar Steuber and wife, Maria Barbara.

—— Anna Margaretha, b. July 7, 1735; bap. June 28, 1736. Sponsors, the parents.

—— Nicolaus, b. Jan. 24, 1737; bap. Jan. 26, 1737. Sponsors, the parents.

MICHAEL RICHTER, (Riedge.)
Richter—Michael, b. Sept. 15, 1733; bap. Oct. 28, 1733. Sponsor, the father.

JOHN NICOLAUS LOESCHER,
(Skippack.)
Loescher—John Vincentz, b. Feb. 26, 1733; bap. Oct. 29, 1733. Sponsor, John Vincentz Meyer.

ADAM LAUER, (Skippack.)
Lauer—Peter, b. Oct. 2, 1733; bap. Oct. 29, 1733. Sponsors, John Peter Schneider and wife.

JOHN GEORGE HOEFFNER,
(Chestnut Hill.)
Hoeffner — John George, b. Nov. 20, 1733; bap. Nov. 25, 1733. Sponsors, John George Wriedner and wife.

JOHN MICHAEL EBERDT,
(Colebrookdale.)
Eberdt—Tobias, b. Nov. 13, 1733; bap. Dec. 2, 1733. Sponsor, Tobias Moser.

JOHN MICHAEL NOLDT,
(Oley Mountains.)
Noldt—Cornelius, b. Nov. 27, 1733; bap. Dec. 3, 1733. Sponsor, Cornelius Dress.

MATTHEIS JERGAN, (Oley.)
Jergan—John George, b. Oct. 18, 1733; bap. Dec. 10, 1733. Sponsors, John George Ohr and wife Elizabetha Gertrandt.

JOHN WOLFF BERLIDT, (Oley.)
Berlidt—Anna Catarina, b. Dec. 2, 1733; bap. Dec. 10, 1733. Sponsors, Gerhardt Henckel and wife.

LEONHARDT KUEFFER,
(Chestnut Hill.)
Kueffer—Margaretha Barbara, b. Nov. 19, 1733; bap. Dec. 16, 1733. Sponsors, Christoph Ollinger and Barbara Reugerin.

DAVID HOLTZEDER, (Germantown.)
Holtzeder—Anna Maria, b. Dec. 2, 1733; bap. Dec. 16, 1733. Sponsor, Anna Maria Renin.

MATTHEIS SCHMIDT,
(Chestnut Hill.)
Schmidt—Anna Elizabeth, b. Dec. 6, 1733; bap. Dec. 16. 1733. Sponsors, Mattheis Egner and wife.

—— Maria Ursula, b. Dec. 3, 1735; bap. Jan. 7, 1736. Sponsors, Balthasar Wott and wife Maria Ursula; also Maria Elizabeth Egnerin.

JOHN HELFFERICH, (Coventry.)
Helfferich—John Peter, b. Sept. 6, 1733; bap. Jan. 3, 1734. Sponsors, John Peter Steig and wife.

BERNHARDT WOLFFINGER,
(Chestnut Hill.)
Wolffinger—Anna Elizabeth, b. Jan. 1, 1733; bap. April 15, 1734. Sponsors, John Kepner and wife.

HEINRICH ACKER,
(Hanover.)
Acker—George Heinrich, b. Jan. 3, 1734; bap. Jan. 7, 1734. Sponsors, George Michael and wife.

CHRISTIAN BLASER, (Providence.)
Blaser—Juliana Catharina Margaretha, b. Dec. 31, 1733; bap. Jan., 1734. Sponsors, George Kuntz, Juliana Catharina Morgensternin and Anna Margaretha Gerhardtin.

JOHN JACOB BEBELER,
(Germantown.)
Bebeler—Anna Maria Barbara, b. Jan. 20, 1734; bap. Jan. 27, 1734. Sponsors,

Christoph and wife, Maria Barbara; also Maria Barbara Weifin.

PAULUS LINTZENBECHLER, (Hanover.)
Lintzenbechler—Johannes, b. Jan. 30, 1734; bap. Oct. 7, 1734. Sponsors, John Lichtenwallner and wife, Barbara.

JOHN LICHTENWALLNER, (Hanover.)
Lichtenwallner—Margaretha, b. Feb. 3, 1734; bap. Feb. 6, 1734. Sponsors, Tobias Moser and his wife Margaretha.

CASPER KRUEGER, (Oley Mountains.)
Krueger—George Valentine, b. Feb. 9, 1734; bap. March 2, 1734. Sponsor, John George Hoffert.

CARL VALENTINE MICHAEL SCHUETT, (Chestnut Hill.)
Schuett—Margaretha Elizabeth. b. Jan. 20, 1734; bap. March 10, 1734.
—— Maria Barbara, b. Jan. 20, 1734; bap. March 10, 1734.

ANDREAS KEPNER. (Hanover.)
Kepner—Catharina, b. Dec. 10, 1733; bap. Dec. 12, 1734. Sponsors, Benedict Kepner, Barbara Kepnerin and Catharina Eigster.

JOHANN CUNRADT SCHREIBER, (Hosensack.)
Schreiber—Anna Maria, b. Dec. 9, 1733; bap. March 25, 1734. Sponsors, John Valentine Grisemer and wife.

JOHN VALENTINE GRISZEMER, (Hosensack.)
Griszemer—Maria Elizabeth, b. Jan. 19, 1734; bap. March 25, 1734. Sponsor, Maria Elizabetha Steinmanerin.

JOHN MICHAEL FABIAN. (Hosensack.)
Fabian—Maria Barbara, b. Feb. 24, 1734; bap. March 25, 1734. Sponsors, Cunradt Kolb and wife Maria Barbara.

JOHN BALTHASER STUEBER, (Merion.)
Stueber—Maria Catharina Elizabetha, b. Feb. 13, 1734; bap. March 30, 1734. Sponsors, George Michael Meck and wife Maria Barbara.
—— Maria Catharina, b. Feb. 19, 1736; bap. June 28, 1736. Sponsors, George Michael Meck and wife Maria Barbara.
—— George Philipp, b. July 28, 1738; bap. July 26, 1739. Sponsors, George Michael Meck and Philipp Gutmann.

LEONHARDT OCHS, (Hanover.)
Ochs—John Leonhardt, b. March 11, 1734; bap. April 12, 1734. Sponsors,

Peter Rothermel and wife Anna Elizabeth.

LEONHARDT HERMAN, (Hanover.)
Herman—Maria Magdalena, b. April 8, 1734; bap. April 12, 1734. Sponsors, Mattheis Reuger and his wife.

CHRISTIAN STEINBACH, (Perkiomen.)
Steinbach—Maria Magdalena, b. Feb. 10, 1734; bap. Feb. 14, 1734. Sponsor, Michael Baumgartner.

JOHANNES NAGLE. (Germantown.)
Nagle—John, b. April 16, 1734; bap. May 19, 1734. Sponsors, John Ulrich Beckle and Susanna Margaretha Weipent.
—— Maria Margaretha, b. June 16, 1736; bap. June 28, 1736. Sponsors, John Adam Jaeger, Maria Margaretha Jaeger and Susanna Margaretha Weipentin.

ADAM ROESSHORN. (Chestnut Hill.)
Roesshorn—John Adam, b. June, 1733; bap. May 19, 1734. Sponsors, John Kaufman and wife Eva.

JOHANNES FREY, (Coventry.)
Frey—Maria Margaretha, b. April 26, 1734; bap. May 21, 1734. Sponsors, Heinrich Schnebele and his wife Appolonia.

SEBASTIAN MUELLER. (Providence.)
Mueller—Anna Maria Appolonia, b. Feb. 14, 1734; bap. May 23, 1734. Sponsors, Jacob Mueller and wife.

JACOB DELINGER, (Chestnut Hill.)
Delinger—Maria Barbara, b. Dec. 25, 1733; bap. Jan. 3, 1734. Sponsors, Andreas Klebsaddel and Elizabeth Kuefer.

JOHN MARTIN MOSER. (New Goshenhoppen.)
Moser—John Michael, b. May 30, 1734; bap. June 6, 1734. Sponsors, John Moser and wife Eva.

JOHN ALBRECHT, (Oley.)
Albrecht—Judith, b. June 1, 1734; bap. Aug. 9, 1734. Sponsors, John Altstatt and wife Judith.

PETER HILDEN, (Oley.)
Hilden—Catarina, b. May, 1734; bap. Aug. 9, 1734. Sponsors, Johannes Braun and wife.

MATHIAS LAEY, (Colebrookdale.)
Laey—Sybilla Margaretha, b. June 16, 1734; bap. Aug. 11, 1734. Sponsors, Sybilla Steinbrennerin and Anna Marg. Freiderich.

CUNRADT SEIBERT, (Coventry.)
Seibert—Elizabetha, b. Sept. 4, 1732;
bap. Oct. 5, 1734. Sponsor, Elizabeth
Tabernien.

MICHAEL FISCHER, (Schuylkill.)
Fischer—John Nicolaus, b. Sept. 16,
1734; bap. Oct. 7, 1734. Sponsors,
John Nicolaus Kintzer and wife.

JOHN SAENGER, (Perkiomen.)
Saenger—John Christian, b. Oct. 20,
1734; bap. Dec. 1, 1734. Sponsor, John
Christian Schmidt.

JOHN GEORGE KUNTZ, (Hanover.)
Kuntz—John Adam, b. Dec. 1, 1734; bap.
Dec. 4, 1734. Sponsors, John Adam
Ochs and wife.

ANDREAS LAUCK, (Germantown.)
Lauck—John David, b. Dec. 9, 1734;
bap. Dec. 16, 1734. Sponsor, John David Holtzeder.

RUDOLPH DOTTERER,
(Colebrookdale.)
Dotterer—John Michael, b. Jan., 1732;
bap. Dec. 29, 1734. Sponsor, John
Michael Dotterer.
—— John George, b. April 23, 1734;
bap. Dec. 29, 1734. Sponsors, George
Dotterer and wife.

MICHAEL GEBERT, (Coventry.)
Gebert—Johannes, b. Nov. 26, 1734; bap.
Jan. 10, 1735. Sponsors, John
Martin Heylmann and Christop En-
glerd.

JOHANNES VOGEL, (Germantown.)
Vogel—Andreas, b. Jan. 10, 1735; bap.
Jan. 12, 1735. Sponsors, Andreas
Schrack and wife Rosina.

CUNRADT REFIOR, (Coventry.)
Refior—Maria Appolonia, b. March 9,
1735; bap. April 23, 1735. Sponsors,
John Heinrich Schnaebele and wife.

CHRISTOPH AMBORN, (Coventry.)
Amborn—Anna Margaretha, b. Feb. 2,
1735; bap. March 23, 1735. Sponsors,
John George Klauer and wife.
—— John Wilhelm, b. Dec. 10, 1736;
bap. Jan. 22, 1737. Sponsors, John
Wilh. Hederling and wife.
—— John, b. July 6, 1741; bap. May 6,
1742. Sponsor, Johannes Hederling—
Locum otinebat pater.

CRISTOPH BAADER, (Moselem.)
Baader—Nicolaus, b. Feb. 2, 1735; bap.
April 3, 1735. Sponsors, John Nico-
laus Strauss and Anna Franzina
Merkling.

JOHANNES BOEHM,
(Colebrookdale.)
Boehm—John Heinrich, b. March 8,
1735; bap. April 4, 1735. Sponsors,

John Heinrich Koehler and wife Elizabetha.

JOHN FREDERICH HESSER,
(Germantown.)
Hesser—John George, b. Feb. 21, 1735;
bap. March 7, 1735. Sponsor, John
Frederich Haass.

GEORGE PETER BISZWANGER,
(Germantown.)
Biszwanger—Maria Barbara, b. Jan. 7,
1735; bap. April 7, 1735. Sponsors,
Jacob Mueller and Maria Barbara
Scheidter.

PETER REIFF, (Skippack.)
Reiff—George John, b. Jan. 2, 1735;
bap. April 8, 1735. Sponsors, John
Wendelwirbel and wife Sarah.

JACOB CARL, (Coventry.)
Carl—Anna Elizabetha, b. Jan. 28,
1735; bap. —— 19, 1735. Sponsors,
Melchior Koch and wife.
—— Maria Dorothea, b. June 10, 1738;
bap. Jan. 10, 1739. Sponsors, Carl
Krampf and wife Maria Dorothea.

HEINRICH KREBS, (Hanover.)
Krebs—Christiana Margaretha, b. Aug.
20, 1734; bap. April 20, 1735. Sponsor,
Eva Maria Sebastian.

JACOB AUMAN, (Schuylkill.)
Auman—Elizabetha, b. Jan. 29, 1735;
bap. April 29, 1735. Sponsors, John
Michael Staut and Elizabetha Brauerin.

JACOB SIKLES, (Opequon.)
Sikles—Zacharias, b. Oct. 8, 1734; bap.
May 16, 1735. Sponsors, Jost. Heydt
and wife and Abraham Weissman.

PETER STEPHAN, (Opequon.)
Stephan—John Heinrich, b. April 8,
1734; bap. May 16, 1735. Sponsor,
Heinrich Krauss.

ABRAHAM WEISSMAN. (Opequon.)
Weissman—Anna Christiana, b. April 15,
1735; bap. May 16, 1735. Sponsors,
Johannes Heydt and Anna Christina
Stephanin.

JACOB CHRISTMAN, (Opequon.)
Christman—Abraham, b. Oct. 15, 1735;
bap. May 16, 1735. Sponsor, John
Heydt.
—— Sara, b. Sept. 23, 1734; bap. May
16, 1735. Sponsor, Maria Baumaennin.
—— Anna Maria, b. Sept. 29, 1735;
bap. May 2, 1736. Sponsor, the mother.
—— Isaac, b. Nov. 9, 1736; bap. June
5, 1737. Sponsors, John Jost Heydt, his
son, Isaac, and his wife, Anna
Maria.

—— Johannes, b. March 9, 1739; bap. Apr. 29, 1739. Sponsors, Jno. Heydt and Sara.

GEORGE BAUMANN, (Opequon.)
Baumann—John George, b. Apr. 27, 1732 bap. May 16, 1735. Sponsor, Jost Heydt.

—— John Jacob, b. Dec. 2, 1733; bap. May 16, 1735. Sponsor, Jacob Christman.

—— Emma Maria, b. Nov. 9, 1735; bap. May 2, 1737. Sponsors, John Leewill and his spouse, Anna Christina Stephan.

—— Elizabetha, b. Jan. 5, 1735; bap. March 18, 1737. Sponsors, Paul Fromman and wife, Elisabetha.

—— Johannes, b. Dec. 19, 1738; bap. April 29, 1739. Sponsors, John Heydt and wife Sara.

PAUL FROMMAN, (Opequon.)
Fromman—Sarah, b. Nov. 16, 1732; bap. May 16, 1735. Sponsor, Susanna Weiszmaenn.

—— John Paul, b. Oct. 16, 1734; bap. May 16, 1735. Sponsor, Ludtwig Stephan.

—— Maria Christina, b. March 1, 1736; bap. May 2, 1736. Sponsors, Peter Stephan and wife Maria Christina.

—— Elisabetha, b. May 8, 1738; bap. June 4, 1738. Sponsors, George Baumann and wife Maria.

JOHN COLVERT, (Opequon.)
Colvert—Rebecca, b. Nov. 16, 1733; bap. May 16, 1735. Sponsor, Maria Baumaenin.

JOHANNES SCHNEPF, (Opequon.)
Schnepf—Anna Catharina, b. Sept. 28, 1734; bap. May 16, 1735. Sponsor, Anna Maria Kleesin.

—— Christina, b. May 15, 1737, bap. June 15, 1737. Sponsors, Philipp Schless and Barbara Burger.

JOHN PHILIPP KLEESZ, (Opequon.)
Kleesz—Maria Barbara, b. April 4, 1735; bap. May 16, 1735. Sponsor, Elizabetha Hartzenbuehler.

—— John George, b. Dec. 15, 1736; bap. June 5, 1737. Sponsor, Johannes Schepf.

—— Paulus, b. May 13, 1738; bap. June 4, 1738. Sponsors, Paul Fromman and wife.

JOHN ULRICH BUGER, (Opequon.)
Buger—Rosina, b. Feb. 9, 1735; bap. May 16, 1735. Sponsors, Jost Heydt, Susanna Weismaenn and Barbara Schnaeppin.

—— John, b. Nov., 1736; bap. June 5, 1737. Sponsors, Jost Heydt and wife Anna Maria, and John Schnepp.

—— Jacob, b. April 29, 1739; bap. April 29, 1739. Sponsors, Jost Heydt and Barbara Schneppin.

THEOBALDT JUNG, (Conewago.)
Jung—Maria Barbara, b. Sept. 1, 1734; bap. May 22, 1735. Sponsor, Anna Barbara Josin.

—— Catarina, b. 1736; bap. June 18, 1737. Sponsors, John George Kuntz and wife Catarina.

—— Anna Maria, b. Feb. 2, 1739; bap. June 6, 1739. Sponsors, Andreas Schreiber and wife Maria.

ANDREAS SCHREIBER, (Conewago.)
Schreiber—John Theobaldt, b. Apr. 28, 1735; bap. May 22, 1735. Sponsor, John Theobaldt Jung.

ANDREAS HERGER, (Conewago.)
Herger—Andreas, b. Aug. 22, 1734; bap. May 22, 1735. Sponsor, Andreas Schreiber.

—— Catarina, b. Jan. 24, 1739; bap. Apr. 19, 1739. Sponsors, George Kuntz and wife Catarina.

—— Anna Margaretha, b. Nov. 21, 1740; bap. Apr. 5, 1741. Sponsors, Geo. Spengel and wife.

—— Johannes, b. Oct. 24, 1742; bap. Nov. 23, 1742. Sponsors, John Morgenstern and wife.

PETER OHLER, (Conewago.)
Ohler—Andreas, b. Sept. 22, 1734; bap. May 22, 1735. Sponsor, Andreas Schreiber.

JOHANNES LEHMAN, (Conewago.)
Lehman—Johannes, b. April 22, 1734; bap. May 22, 1735. Sponsor, Johan Theobaldt Jung.

CUNRAD ECKERT, (Conewago.)
Eckert—Johannes, b. May 2, 1734; bap. May 22, 1735. Sponsor, Peter Mittelkauff.

—— Anna Dorothea, b. Nov. 11, 1738; bap. June 16, 1739. Sponsor, Ursala Ohlerin.

PETER MITTELKAUFF,
(Conewago.)
Mittelkauff—Catharina, b. Feb. 6, 1735; bap. May 22, 1735. Sponsors, Johan Theobaldt Jung and wife Catharina.

—— Leonhardt, b. Jan. 23, 1739; bap. Apr. 19, 1739. Sponsor, John Leonhardt Bernitz.

CASPER BERGHEIMER,
(Conewago.)
Bergheimer—Anna Eva, b. Sept. 30, 1734; bap. May 22, 1735. Sponsor, Anna Eva Kuntz.

—— John Ludwig, b. Dec. 8, 1735; bap. Apr. 27, 1736. Sponsors, John Ludwig Schreiber and wife.

—— Johann Leonhardt, b.Nov.13,1737; bap. May 23, 1738. Sponsors, John Leonhardt Bernitz, Johann Morgenstern and wife.

—— Maria Elisabetha, b. May 23, 1741; bap. June 25, 1741. Sponsor, Maria Elisabetha Morgenstern.

PHILIPP CARL JAEGER, (Schuylkill.)
Jaeger—Maria Philipena, b. Feb. 23, 1735; bap. May 30, 1735. Sponsors, John George Koch and Johanna Maria Messerschmidtin.

CHRISTOPH ENGELERDT, (Coventry.)
Engelerdt—Anna Catharina, b. June 1, 1735; bap. June 1, 1735. Sponsors, Valentine Pressel and Anna Catharina Schmidt.

WILLIAM TROTTER, (Swatara.)
Trotter—James, b. Aug. 31, 1735; bap. Oct. 7, 1735. Evidences, James Trotter, Jos. Reynolds and Hannah M. Carey.

—— Mary, b. Feb. 19, 1737; bap. May 19, 1737. Evidences, Jos. Reynolds, Anna Trotter and Elizabeth Trotter.

THOMAS ANDERSON, (Swatara.)
Anderson—His wife Mary, b. Oct. 1717, and a daughter, Mary; bap. Oct. 7, 1735. Evidences, Peter Von Beber and wife Anna and Sarah Reynolds.

(Swatara.)
Thomas Hui, b. Oct. 1714; bap. Oct. 17, 1735. Evidences, Joseph Von Beber and Joseph Reynolds.

JACOB WUERTZ, (Coventry.)
Wuertz—John Cunradt, b. Oct. 15, 1735; bap. Oct. 25, 1735. Sponsors, Reffior and wife.

—— Maria Catharina, b. Aug. 8, 1738; bap. Jan. 10, 1739. Sponsors, the parents.

—— Anna Margaretha, b. June 14, 1740; bap. Sep. 22, 1740. Sponsors, Ana. Margar. Spengler and Anna Cath. Kuntz.

CHRISTOPH SCHLAEGEL, (Conewago.)
Schlaegel—Heinrich, b. July, 1735; bap. Nov. 5, 1735. Sponsors, Henry Schmidt, John Geo. Kuntz and wife.

JOH. GEORGE DIETER, (Opequon.)
Dieter—Maria, b. May, 1734; bap. Nov. 5, 1735. Sponsors, Christoph Schlaegel and wife.

—— Susanna, b. Sept. 1736; bap. June 5, 1737. Sponsors, Jacob Christman and wife Magdalena.

—— John George, b. March 9, 1739; bap. April 29, 1739. Sponsors, George Bauman and wife Maria.

THOMAS CRYSOP, (Conojohela.)
Crysop—Daniel, b. Feb. 28, 1728; bap. July 21, 1735. Evidences, John Killis, Thomas Parry and Francis Foy.

—— Michael, b. Aug. 16, 1729; bap. July 21, 1735. Evidences, Phillip Ernest Gruber, Andrew McGill and Elisabetha Low.

—— Thomas, b. Feb. 28, 1733; bap. July 21, 1735. Evidences, Joseph Ogle, William Kanely and Mary McGill.

—— Robert, b. Jan. 17, 1735; bap. July 21, 1735. Evidences, Robert Paul, John Low and Charlotta Fredericka Gruber.

—— Elisabeth, b. Jan. 19, 1737; bap. Aug. 1, 1737. Evidence, Veronica Baseler.

JAMES MOOR, (Conojohela.)
Moor—Theodota, b. Aug. 28, 1734; bap. June 21, 1735. Evidences, John Killis and Mary Shepherd.

CHRISTIAN BLANCK, (Opequon.)
Blanck—A daughter, name not given, bap. June 5, 1737. Sponsors, Carl Ehrhardt and Theobaldt Gerlach and wives.

—— Johannes, b. March 28, 1737; bap. June 4, 1838. Sponsors Johannes Heydt and wife.

WILLIAM CANAAN, (Conojohela.)
Canaan—Charity, b. Dec. 24, 1728; bap. June 21, 1735. Witnesses, Nicolaus Josee and Mary McGill.

—— Lasenbury, b. Sept. 19, 1732; bap. June 21, 1735. Witnesses, Thomas Crysop and Francies Foy.

—— John, b. Jan. 19, 1735; bap. June 21, 1735. Witnesses, Parry, William and Elizabeth Low.

ROBERT CANAAN, (Conojohela.)
Canaan—Benjamin, b. March 22, 1732; bap. June 21, 1735. Evidences, Wil-Nolten, William Canaan and Francies Foy.

—— Francies, b. Sept. 23, 1733; bap. June 21, 1735. Evidences, William Low and Francies Foy.

—— Robert, b. Nov. 9, 1734; bap. June 21, 1735. Evidences, Robert Paul, Thomas Parry and Francies Canaan.

JOHN LOW, (Conojohela.)
Low—Elizabeth, b. June 16, 1726; bap. June 21, 1735. Sponsors, George Warren, Sara Ogle and Hannah Crysop.

EDWARD EVANS, (Conojohela.)
Evans—Edward, b. Aug., 1731; bap. Aug., 1735. Evidences, Thomas Queer. John Low and Elizabeth Low.

—— Daniel, b. Nov., 1732; bap. Aug., 1735. Evidences, Philipp Ernst Gruber and wife and Daniel Low.

—— Samuel, b. Oct., 1734; bap. Aug., 1735. Evidences, William Low, William Morgan and Francies Canaan.

—— Rachael, b. in Feb., 1730; bap. Aug., 1735. Evidences, Thomas Crysop and Elizabeth Groll.

JACOB HARRINGTON, (Conojohela.) Harrington—Sarah, b. May, 1735; bap. Aug., 1735. Evidences, Christian Groll and Charlotta Frederica Gruber.

BALTHASER FAUTH, (Monocacy.) Fauth—Catharina Barbara, b. Dec. 4, 1735; bap. April 28, 1736. Sponsors, Jacob Fauth and Barbara Teufersbiss.

JACOB FAUTH, (Monocacy.) Fauth—Balthaser, b. Mar. 1, 1736; bap. April 28, 1736. Sponsors, Batlhaser Fauth and wife.

—— Catharina, b. Sept. 30, 1738; bap. Nov. 24, 1738. Sponsor, Catharina Geiger.

JACOB DELINGER, (Opequon.) Delinger—6 Knaben and 2 Maegdlein, bap. May 3, 1736.

—— Maria Catharina, b. Nov. 22, 1737; bap. June 2, 1738. Sponsor, Maria Baumann.

MATTHIAS ROESSEL, (Monocacy.) Roessel—Catharina, b. May 1, 1736; bap. May 27, 1736. Sponsor, Catharina Barbara Teufersbissen.

JOHANNES MITTAG, (Monocacy.) Mittag—Susanna, b. Jan. 25, 1735; bap. May 14, 1735. Sponsor, Agnes Pattison.

GEORGE LATHLY, (Monocacy.) Lathly—Rachael, b. March 16, 1730; bap. May 17, 1736. Sponsors, Antonius Banckauf and Magdalena Lein.

JOHN JACOB HOOF, (Monocacy.) Hoof—Emma Maria, b. May 8, 1736; bap. May 16, 1736. Sponsors, John Jacob Matthias and wife Margaretha.

—— Jacob, b. Nov. 2, 1738; bap. Nov. 24, 1738. Sponsors, Samuel Bruschel and Eva Rosina Fauth.

ADAM BAKER, (Monocacy.) Baker—Elizabetha, b. Jan. 17, 1736; bap. May 17, 1736. Sponsor, Elizabeth Barbara Teufersbiss.

HENRY PREY, (Monocacy.) Prey—Anna Maria, b. April 15, 1733; bap. May 16, 1736. Sponsors, Anna Maria Bronnerin and Maria Barbara Bronner.

—— Susanna, b. March 10, 1735; bap. May 16, 1736. Sponsors, Dietrich Lehnich and Susanna Tauth.

—— Sarah, b. March 31, 1732; bap. June 5, 1737.

—— Catarina, b. April 26, 1737; bap. June 5, 1737.

—— Elizabetha, b. Nov. 3, 1739; bap. Sept. 21, 1740. Sponsors, George Schweinhardt and wife Maria Elizabetha.

JACOB KUNTZ, Conewago.) Kuntz,—John George, b. Oct., 1735; bap. April 27, 1736. Sponsors, John George Frosch and wife.

RUDI MAAG, (Opequon.) Maag—Elizabetha, b. Nov. 1, 1735; bap. May 2, 1736. Sponsors, Carl Ehrhardt and Susanna Barbara Buger.

WILLIAM CRISP, (Opequon.) Crisp—Sarah—b. July 2, 1728; bap. May 2, 1736. Sponsors, Paul Fromman and wife Elizabetha.

BERNHARDT TROSTEL, (Chestnut Hill.) Bernhardt—Adam Valentine John, b. May 3, 1736; bap. June 6, 1736. Sponsors, John Adam Kittler and John Valentine Schrielecker and wife.

JOHN PHILIP FAUST, (Moselem.) Faust—Emma Frantzina, b. March 26, 1736; bap. June 6, 1736. Sponsors, Michael Albrecht and wife Anna Frantzina.

PETER DUNCKELBERGER, (Moselem.) Dunckleberger — Anna Catharina, b. March 1, 1735; b. June 17, 1736. Sponsors, John Michael Ludwig and Catharina Hill.

ROBERT HUESTON, (Codorus.) Hueston—Sarah, b. in April, 1735; bap. Oct. 21, 1736. Evidences, Jacob Rudesilie and wife Elizabetha.

—— Andrew, b. Sept. 18, 1739; bap. May 20, 1740. Testes, Andrew McGill and his wife Mary.

DANIEL McLOUGHLIY, (Codorus.) McLoughly—John, b. in Feb., 1735; bap. Oct. 21, 1736. Evidences, John Heorkin and wife Bregille.

JOHN GEORGE STEUER, (Moselem.) Steuer—George Simon, b. Sept. 4, 1736; bap. Oct. 29, 1736. Sponsors, Adam Simon Kuhn and Anna Frantzina Merckling.

THOMAS GOWRINGER, (Ontelaunee.) Gowringer—Samuel, b. June 6, 1736; bap. Oct. 29, 1736. Sponsors, Michael Henninger and wife Anna Maria.

JAMES STUART, (Lebanon.) Stuart—Mary, b. Oct., 1736; bap. Feb. 19, 1737.

CARL EHRHARDT, (Opequon.) Ehrhardt — Theobaldt, bap. June 5, 1734. Sponsor, Theobaldt Gerlach.

JAMES McKNEES, (Opequon.)
McKnees—Henry, b. June 5, 1737; bap.
June 6, 1737. Evidences, his grand-
father and grandmother.
JOHN GEORGE GEIGER,
(Monocacy.)
Geiger—Maria Elizabetha, b. Dec. 11,
1736; bap.June 16, 1737. Sponsors,
Jacob F. Fauth and wife.
—— John Jacob, b. March 4, 1739;
bap. June 17, 1739. Sponsors,
Matheis Roessel and wife Maria Bar-
bara.
ANDREW BIRD, (Shenandoah.)
Bird—Rebecca, b. July 6, 1732; bap.
June 8, 1737. Evidences, James Gill
and Sarah Moor.
WILLIAM BREEDYES,
(Shenandoah.)
Breedyes—James, b. Oct. 1733; bap.
June 8, 1737.
—— Hanna, b. Aug., 1734; bap. June
8, 1737. Testes, the parents them-
selves.
RILIE MOOR, (Shenandoah.)
Moor—Terkis, b. Feb. 15, 1731; bap.
June 8, 1737. Testis, Catharine Ger-
lach.
—— Thomas, b. October, 1732; bap.
June 8, 1737. Testes, Theobaldt Ger-
lach and wife.
—— Jacob, b. Dec., 1734; bap. June 8,
1737. Testes, Andrew Bird.
—— John, b. Nov., 1736; bap. June 8,
1737. Testes, Charles Ehrhardt and
his wife Clara.
JAMES GUILL, (Shenandoah.)
Guill—Thomas, b. Sept. 15, 1728; bap.
June 8, 1737. Testis, John Dawbin.
—— James, b. Aug., 1732; bap. June 8,
1737. Testis, Elizabeth Dawbin.
—— Mary, b. Jan. 15, 1735; bap. June
8, 1737. Sponsor, the father himself.
—— John, b. May, 1737; bap. June 8,
1737. Sponsor, the father himself.
JOHN DAWBIN, (Shenandoah.)
Dawbin—Thomas, b. Nov. 8, 1736; bap.
June 8, 1737. Testes, James Guill.
JOHN HODGE, (Shenandoah.)
Hodge—David, b. Aug. 2, 1733; bap.
June 8, 1737.
—— Elizabeth, b. April 7, 1735; bap.
June 8, 1737.
—— Rohamy, b. May 8, 1738; bap.——
Testes, to the above baptisms, James
Guill and his wife and the parents
themselves.
WILLIAM WHITE, (Shenandoah.)
White—Ruth, b. Feb. 28, 1732; bap.
June, 1737.
—— Charity, b. March 6, 1734; bap.
June, 1737.

—— Benjamin, b. in Jan., 1736; bap.
June 1737. Sponsors, the parents
themselves.
DANIEL HOOLMAN, (Shenandoah.)
Hoolman, Isaac.
—— Rebecca.
Testes, James Guill and the
mother herself.
JOHN LEENWILL, (Shenandoah.)
Leenwill—Lewis, b. Feb. 20, 1737; bap.
June 7, 1737. Testis, Stephen Lewis.
JOHN LERCH, (Saucon.)
Lerch—John Michael, b. Aug. 2, 1737;
bap. Oct. 20, 1737. Sponsors, Jno.
George Marstellar, Michael Myer and
Barbara Brunner.
DAVID JONES, (Coventry.)
Jones—June, b. in Jan., 1737; bap. Oct.
22, 1737. Sponsor, Margareth Schmidt.
CUNRADT HAASZ, (Providence.)
Haasz—Anna Maria, b. Feb. 1, 1734;
bap. Feb. 10, 1734. Sponsors, Hein-
rich Michael and wife Anna Maria.
—— John, b. Dec. 27, 1735; bap. Jan.
9, 1736. Sponsors, John Jacob Tun-
steld and wife Anna Catarina.
—— Margaretha, b. Oct. 8, 1737; bap.
Oct. 22, 1737. Sponsor, Wintermuthin.
JAMES McCHEES, (Lebanon.)
McChees—Isaac, b. July, 1737; bap. Feb.
7, 1738. Testes, Peter Kucher and
wife Anna Barbara.
LUDWIG SCHREIBER, (Conewago.)
Schreiber—Catarina, b. March, 1738;
bap. May 23, 1738. Sponsors, Jno.
Geo. Kuntz and wife.
—— Anna Margaretha, b. Nov. 16,
1746; bap. Apr. 5, 1741. Sponsors,
Andreas Schreiber and Anna Marga-
retha Diehlin.
THEOBALDT GERLACH,
(Shenandoah.)
Gerlach—John George, b. Nov. 22, 1737;
bap. June 4, 1739. Sponsors, John
George Baumann and wife Maria.
GEORGE HENCKEL, (Monocacy.)
Henckel—John Balthasar, b. Dec. 25,
1737; bap. Jan. 7, 1738. Sponsors,
Balthasar Fauth and wife.
—— Philipp Christoph, b. May 7, 1740;
bap. May 21, 1740. Sponsors, John
Philipp Kuntz and wife.
HEINRICH FORTUNEE, (Monocacy.)
Susanna Catarina, b. Oct., 1737; bap.
Jun 7, 1738. Sponsors, John George
Gump and Susanna Fauthin.
—— John Heinrich, b. Dec. 31, 1739;
bap. Sept. 21, 1740. Sponsors, Leon-
hardt Lutz and Catarina Geiger.
JOSEPH MAYHEW, (Monocacy.)
Mayhew—William, b. Dec. 16, 1737; bap.
June 7, 1738. Testes George Schwein-

hardt and his wife, Balthasar Fauth and his wife.
—— Anna, b. May 1, 1740; bap. Sept. 21, 1740. Sponsors, Gabriel Schweinhardt and sister Susanna, and Anna Margaretha Goetz-Danner.

VALENTINE MUELLER,
(Monocacy.)
Mueller—Magdalena, b. Nov. 11, 1738; bap. Nov. 27, 1738. Sponsor, Magdalena Schweinhardt.
—— Catharina, b. April 21, 1740; bap. April 27, 1740. Sponsors, John Jacob Mattheis and wife Margaretha, and Catharina Geiger.

PHILIPP ERNST GRUEBER,
(Monocacy.)
Grueber—Maria Elisabetha, b. June 13, 1738; bap. Nov. 25, 1738. Sponsors, John George Lay and wife.

HENRY JONES, (Opequon.)
Jones—Anna, b. April 9, 1735; bap. April 29, 1739. Sponsors, Jacob Neuschwanger and Susan Weismannin.
—— David, b. Jan. 16, 1737; bap. April 29, 1739. Sponsors, Abraham Weissman and Maria Neuschwanger.

GEORGE SPENGEL, (Monocacy.)
Spengel—Johanna, b. Sept. 5, 1738; bap. Nov. 28, 1738. Sponsors, Augustus and Catharina Schreyer.

JOHN GEORGE RUESSER,
(Coventry.)
Ruesser—Agnes, b. May 2, 1738; bap. Feb. 18, 1739. Sponsor, Agnes Hylman.

JOHANNES SCHNAUBER,
(Coventry.)
Schnauber—John Christoph, b. Apr. 7, 1738; bap. Feb. 18, 1739. Sponsor, Christopher Wintermuth.

FRANTZ SCHUNCK, (Coventry.)
Schunck—Anna Barbara, b. Feb. 3, 1739; bap. Feb. 18, 1739. Sponsors, the parents.

CUNRADT WALTHER, (Coventry.)
Walther—Margaretha Barbara, b. Jan. 30, 1739; bap. Feb. 18, 1739. Sponsors, Nicolaus Coerper and wife Margaretha.

JACOB GEIGER, (Merion.)
Geiger—Anna Elizabeth, b. Feb. 23, 1738; bap. March 23, 1739. Sponsors, Barbara Stueber and Eva Margaretha Gutmaennin.

JOHN GEORGE SCHREYER,
(Conewago.)
Schreyer—John George, b. Feb. 24, 1739; bap. April 1, 1739. Sponsors, John George Soldner and Anna Marie Immler.

JOHN HEYDT (,Opequon.)
Heydt—Anna Maria, b. Dec. 25, 1738;

bap. April 29, 1739. Sponsors, Jost Heydt and wife.

JOHN DYART, (Opequon.)
Dyart—William, b. Aug. 11, 1736; bap. April 29, 1739. Testis, Lorentz Schnepf.

JOHN CUNTZ, (Opequon.)
Cuntz—John, b. March 26, 1739; bap. April 29, 1739. Sponsors, Caspar Stoever, Jacob Neuschwanger and Maria Baumann.

VALENTIN WENDEL, (Opequon.)
Wendel—Anna Elizabeth, b. Aug. 15, 1738; bap. April 27, 1739. Sponsor, Anna Elizabetha Stoecklin.

LORENTZ SCHNEPF, (Opequon.)
Schnepf—Johannes, b. Aug. 12, 1738; bap. April 19, 1739. Sponsors, Thomas Schnepp and wife.
—— Lorentz, b. Feb. 29, 1740; bap. April 29, 1740. Sponsors, Ulrich Buger and Barbara Schnepf.

JOHANN BROBAND, (Opequon.)
Broband—John, b. March 1, 1740; bap. April 29, 1740. Sponsors, John Cuntz and wife Anna Elizabetha Catharina.

PETER MAAG, (Opequon.)
Maag—Johannes, b. Nov. 25, 1739; bap. April 29, 1740. Sponsor, Abraham Weissmann.

JOHN TONDITH, (Monocacy.)
Tondith—Elizabetha, b. April 29, 1738; bap. May 2, 1740. Sponsors, Heinrich Bischoff and wife Elizabetha.

WILHELM DORN, (Monocacy.)
Dorn—Anna Catharina, b. May 26, 1739; bap. June 17, 1739. Sponsors, Matheis Roessel and wife Maria Barbara.

BERNHARDT WEINMAR,
(Monocacy.)
Weinmar—John Bernhardt, b. April 15, 1739; bap. June 17, 1739. Sponsors, Martin Wetzel and wife Maria Barbara.

ADAM MUELLER, (Shenandoah.)
Mueller—Catarina, b. Dec. 20, 1734; bap. May 1, 1739.
—— Adam, b. July 16, 1736; bap. May 1, 1739.
—— Anna Christina, b. Oct. 18, 1738; bap. May 1, 1739. Testes, pater, mater and Anna Christina Seltzer.

MICHAEL RHEINHARDT,
(Shenandoah.)
Rheinhardt—Emma Christina, b. Jan. 26, 1739; bap. May 1, 1739. Sponsor Anna Christina Seltzerin.

ANDREAS McGUILL, (Codorus.)
McGuill—James, b. May 22; bap. June 20, 1735. Testes, Joseph Ogle and wife Sarah.

JOSEPH OGLE, (Codorus.)
Ogle—Mary, b. April 15, 1735; bap. June
20, 1735. Testes, Andrew McGuill
and wife Mary.

JOHANNES WILDENSINN,
(Conewago.)
Wildensinn—George Carl, b. Jan. 6,
1740; bap. May 29, 1740. Sponsor,
George Carl Barnitz.

HEINRICH ENGELSCH,
(Antecessor in Thow.)
Engelsch—John Michael, b. March 25,
1737; bap. March 12, 1738. Sponsors,
John Michael Beyerle and wife.

LUDWIG SUESS, (Conewago.)
Suess—John Leonhardt, b. March 10,
1740; bap. May 20, 1740. Sponsor,
John Leonhardt Bernitz.
—— Maria Salome, b. —— ——; bap.
May 20, 1740. Sponsor, Maria Salome
Mittelkauf.

EDWARD DOVIES, (Conewago.)
Dovies—Martha, b. Feb. 2, 1740; bap.
May 20, 1740. Testes, Geo. Kuntz and
his wife.

JOHN ADLAM, (Conewago.)
Adlam—Mary, b. March 19, 1740; bap.
May 20, 1740. Testes, Edward Dovies
and Juliana Morgenstern.

FRANTZ KLEBSSADDEL,
(Conewago.)
Klebssaddel—Maria, b. Feb. 17, 1740;
bap. May 20, 1740. Sponsors, Christian
Schlaegel and wife Maria.

JOHANNES JOHO, (Conewago.)
Joho—Maria Christina, b. March 14,
1740; bap. May 22, 1740. Sponsors,
Janeslaus Wuchtel and Maria Chris.
Baumann.
—— Eva Catarina, b. May 26, 1741;
bap. June 25, 1741. Sponsors, Wentzel
Buchtrueckel and wife.

HENRY HENDRICKS, (Conewago.)
Hendricks—Jone, b. Oct. 6, 1739; bap.
May 22, 1740. Sponsors, Adam
Mueller and wife Christina.

MARTIN SCHAUB, an Immersionist,
(Conewago.)
Schaub—Anna, b. 1724; bap. May 21,
1740. Sponsors, Philip Kintz and wife,

PHILIPP MORGENSTERN,
(Conewago.)
Morgenstern—Johannes, b. June 16,
1740; bap. June 30, 1740. Sponsors,
John Morgenstern, Johann Ebert and
Cat. Kuntz.

JACOB STAMBACH, (Conewago.)
Stambach—Maria Catharina, b. Sept. 22,
1740; bap. Sept. 22, 1740. Sponsors,
John George Kuntz and daughter
Maria Catarina and Maria Elizabetha
Morgenstern.

JOHN GEORE HANSPACHER,
(Codorus.)
Hanspacher—Maria Eva. b. July 26,
1740; bap. Sept. 18, 1740. Sponsors,
Valeutin Schultz and wife Maria Eva.

DANIEL EARLY, (Codorus.)
Early—Catarina, b. April 18, 1740; bap.
Sept. 18, 1740. Sponsors, Balthasar
Knertzer and his wife.

JOHN HEARKEN, (Codorus.)
Hearken—Eleonora, b. March, 1740;
bap. Sept. 18, 1740. Sponsors, Tobias
Hanspacher and daughter Rebecca.

JCHN PHILIP ZIEGLER, (Codorus.)
Ziegler—Anna Christina, b. Sept. 7,
1740; bap. Spt. 18, 1740. Sponsors,
Jacob Ziegler and Agnes Schmidt.

SIMON MUELLER, (Conewago.)
Mueller—Anna Maria, b. Aug. 21, 1733;
bap. Sept. 30, 1733. Sponsors, Bern-
hardt Haessel and his wife.
—— Christian, b. Sept. 8, 1734; bap.
March 30, 1735. Sponsor, Christian
Kampf.

SIMON MUELLER, (Conewago.)
Mueller—Christina, b. May 1, 1740; bap.
Sept. 19, 1740. Sponsor, Christina
Nosseler.

JOHANNES HEIM, (Conewago.)
Heim—John Caspar, b. Sept. 9, 1740;
bap. Sept. 19, 1740. Sponsor, Caspar
Kuehner.

JOHN GEEMBEL, (Conewago.)
Geembel—William, b. Dec., 1738; bap.
Sept. 19, 1740. Sponsors, Michael
Carl, Edward Davis and Eve Morgen-
stern.

JOHN GEORGE BEER, (Monocacy.)
Beer—Catarina Barbara, b. May 16,
1740; bap. Sept. 21, 1740. Sponsors,
John George Lay and Catarina Barbara Ruesel.

HERMAN HARTMAN, (Monocacy.)
Hartman—Elisabetha, b. Sept. 5, 1740;
bap. Sept. 21, 1740. Sponsors, Heinrich Bischof and wife Elisabetha.

MICHAEL SCHAUFFLE,
(Monocacy.)
Schauffle—Eva Dorothea, b. March 9,
1740; bap. Aug. 10, 1740. Sponsors,
George Spengele and wife Margaretha,
and Sebastian Winterbauer.

JACOB HILL, (Moselem.)
Hill—Anna Maria, b. July 24, 1740; bap.
Oct. 22, 1740. Sponsors, John Hill and
Anna Maria Mercklingen.
—— Anna Catarina, b. Nov. 27, 1741;
bap. Dec. 8, 1741. Sponsors, Frederick
Sauer and Anna Catarina Kern.
—— John Jacob, b. Jan. 29, 1744; bap.
Feb. 24, 1744. Sponsor, Christian
Hausknecht.

—— John Christian, b. March 7, 1746; bap. May 1, 1746. Sponsor, Christian Hausknecht and his wife.

GOTTFRIED MANCK, (Codorus.) Manck—Eva Maria, b. Sept. 23, 1740; bap. Oct. 29, 1740. Sponsors, John Heinrich Wolf and Eva Catarina Israel.

JOHN MORRIS, (Kreutz Creek.) Morris——, b. 1732; bap. Nov. 27, 1740.

—— Jane, b. 1734; bap. Nov. 27, 1740.

—— William, b. 1736; bap. Nov. 27, 1740. Testes, Christian Groll and wife Elisabetha.

—— Mary, b. in 1738; bap. Nov. 27, 1740.

—— John, b. in 1740; bap. Nov. 27, 1740. Testes, Peter Gaertner and his wife.

JOHN NICOLAUS, (Lancaster.) Nicolaus—Ludwig Heinrich, b. Oct. 13, 1740; bap. Nov. 23, 1740. Sponsors, Ludw. Heinr. Detteborn and wife.

HEINRICH SCHULTZ, (Codorus.) Schultz—Fredericka, b. Nov. 13, 1740; bap. Nov. 24, 1740. Sponsors, Michael Walck and wife.

PAUL BURCKHART, (Codorus.) Burckhart—Maria Magdalena, b. Oct. 13, 1740; bap. Nov. 25, 1740. Sponsors, George Schwab, Jr., and his wife.

MATTHEIS SCHMEISSER, (Codorus.) Schmeisser—John Michael, b. Nov. 21, 1740; bap. Nov. 25, 1740. Sponsors, John George Schmeisser and his wife Barbara.

JACOB BAERLING,(Codorus.) Baerling—Jacob Cunradt, b. Nov. 16, 1740; bap. Nov. 25, 1740. Sponsors, Lau and his wife Anna Kunigunda.

—— John Frederick, b. April 3, 1742; bap. April 6, 1742. Sponsors, John Frederick Geelwuchs and his wife:.

JOHN GEORGE QUICKEL, (Conestoga.) Quickel—John George, b. Oct. 25, 1740; bap. Dec. 14, 1740. Sponsors, John George Hesset and his wife Anna.

DIETERICH MAYER, (Codorus.) Mayer—Anna Margaretha, b. Nov. 2, 1740; bap. Nov. 26, 1740. Sponsors, Philip Ziegler, Jr., and his wife Anna Margaretha.

LEONHARDT REBER, (Ontelaunee.) Reber—John George, b. Dec. 5, 1740; bap. Jan. 9, 1741. Sponsors, John George Kreamer and Eva Barbara Kuhn

CUNRADT HAUSSMAN, (Ontelaunee.) Haussmann—Anna Margaretha, b. Oct. 18, 1740; bap. Jan. 1741. Sponsors, Leonhardt Reber and wife Anna Margaretha.

MICHAEL REUSNER, (Monocacy.) Reusner—Catarina Barbara, b. Nov. 13, 1734; bap. Jan. 1, 1735. Sponsor, Anna Catarina Beyerlin.

—— Anna Elisabetha, b. Jan. 5, 1737; bap. Dec. 15, 1739. Sponsors, Michael Rausch and his wife.

—— Catarina Barbara, b. Oct. 29, 1738; bap. Jan. 29, 1739. Sponsors, Michael Boltz and his wife Catarina, Balthasar Ort and his wife Barbara.

ANASTASIUS UHLER, (Lebanon.) Uhler—Christopher, b. Feb. 2, 1741; bap. March 25, 1741. Sponsors, Balthasar Ort and his wife Barbara.

—— Anna Barbara, b. March 20, 1743; bap. March 27, 1743. Sponsors, Balthasar Ort and his wife Barbara.

—— John Martin, b. Sept. 24, 1744; bap. Oct. 28, 1744. Sponsors, Martin Kirstaetter and his wife.

—— Michael, b. April 23, 1743; bap. May 25, 1746. Sponsors, Michael Wagener and Margaretha Zoth.

PETER HEYLMAN, (Lebanon.) Heylman—Anna Maria, b. Nov. 14, 1739; bap. Dec. 6, 1739. Sponsors, Martin Kirstaetter and his wife Maria Dorothea.

PETER HEYLMANN, (Lebanon.) Heylmann—John Adam, b. Nov. 4, 1740; bap. March 25, 1741. Sponsors, John Adam Heylmann and wife.

—— Anastasius, b. March 3, 1742; bap. April 15, 1742. Sponsors, Anastasius Uhler and wife.

—— John Peter, b. May 16, 1743; bap. May 23, 1743. Sponsors, Superiores. Heylmann—Maria Magdalena, b. May 1, 1746; bap. June 24, 1746. Sponsors, Superiores.

JACOB BENTZ, (Swatara.) Bentz—John Jacob, b. Feb. 3, 1739; bap. April 15,1739. Sponsors,Peter Rousch and wife.

—— Maria Barbara, b. Oct. 29, 1740; bap. March 26, 1741. Sponsor, Maria Elizabetha Borst.

—— John George, b. April 9, 1743; bap. May 23, 1743. Sponsors, John George Kuntz and wife.

PETER KUCHER, (Lebanon.) Kucher—Rosina, b. March 20, 1741; bap. March 28, 1741. Sponsors, Christopher Meyer and wife Rosina.

GEORGE GLASSBRENNER,
(Lebanon.)
Glassbrenner—Maria Christiana Margaretha, b. Feb. 28, 1741; bap. March 25, 1741. Sponsors, Andreas Weltz and wife and Margaretha Glassbrenner.

MICHAEL KLEBER, (Swatara.)
Kleber—George Ludwig, b. July 4,1736; bap. Sept. 12, 1736. Sponsors, George Ludwig Friedle and wife.
—— Anna Maria, b. Sept. 4, 1738; bap. Jan. 30, 1739. Sponsors, Heinrich Klein and wife.
—— Michael, b. March 1, 1740; bap. March 26, 1741. Sponsors, Heinrich Klein and wife Anna Maria.
—— Barbara, b. Feb. 25, 1744; bap. March 18, 1744. Sponsors, Ottmar Schnabele and wife Barbara.
—— Susanna, b. Feb. 19, 1749; bap. March 19, 1749. Sponsors, Martin Speck and wife Susanna.

MARTIN KIRSTAETTER,
(Lebanon.)
Kirstaetter—John, b. Sept. 3, 1739; bap. Nov. 5, 1739. Sponsors, John Schmeltzer and his wife.
——Julianna, b. Jan. 25, 1741; bap. March 25, 1741. Sponsor, Julianna Umberger.

ANDREAS KRAEMER, (Swatara.)
Kraemer—Andreas, b. Feb. 8, 1741; bap. March 26, 1741. Sponsors, Martin Kappler and wife Margaretha.
—— John George, b. Feb. 12, 1746; bap. March 16, 1746. Sponsors, John George Einert and wife.

MICHAEL HAHN, (Conestoga.)
Hahn—John Michael, b. Jan. 31, 1741; bap. March 27, 1741. Sponsors, John Michael Quickel.

HEINRICH SCHAEFER, (Conestoga.)
Schaeffer—Anna Margaretha, b. Jan. 9, 1741; bap. March 27,1741. Sponsor, Anna Margaretha Budinger.

JACOB SPANNSEILER, (Lancaster.)
Spannseiler—Catarina, b. March 19, 1741; bap. March 27, 1741. Sponsor, CatarinaBerlin.

PETER HEYLMANN.
Heylmann—Johannes, b. Dec. 11, 1744; bap. Jan. 6, 1745. Sponsors, Anastasius Uhler and wife Dorothea.

STEPHEN TRAENCKEL,
(Lancaster.)
Traenckel—Catarina. Sponsors, Jacob Spannseiler and wife.

CHRISTIAN LOEFFEL,
(Conewago.)
Loeffel—Anna Margaretha, b. Feb. 28, 1738; bap. May 22, 1738. Sponsor, Catarina Baumann.

—— John Peter, b. Jan. 2, 1741; bap. April 5, 1741. Sponsors, John Peter Schultz and wife Anna Catarina.

HEINRICH MEYER, (Lebanon.)
Meyer—Christoph, b. Oct. 20, 1736; bap. Nov. 19, 1736. Sponsors, Christoph Meyer and wife Anna Rosina.

NICOLAUS KLEE, (Conewago.)
Klee—Anna Margaretha, b. March 9, 1741; bap. April 5, 1741. Sponsors, Jacob Beerling and wife Anna Margaretha Euler.

MARTIN ERNST, (Conewago.)
Ernst—Eva, b. Dec. 26, 1740; bap. April 5, 1741. Sponsors, Andreas Herger and wife Eva.

WILLIAM WILSON, (Conewago.)
Wilson—John, b. Nov. 6, 1740; bap.April 5, 1741. Sponsor, Philip Morgenstern.

JOHN OWEN, (Conewago.)
Owen—William, b. March 28, 1741; bap. April 5, 1741. Sponsors, Daniel Schlaegel and sister Catarina.

WILLIAM MORPHEW, (Conewago.)
Morphew—Henry, b. Nov. 25, 1740; bap. April 5, 1741. Sponsors, Christoph Schlaegel and his wife.

WILLIAM WELSH, (Codorus.)
Welsh—John Peter, b. Oct., 1740; bap. April 5, 1741. Sponsors,Jacob Welsch and wife.

JOHN DIETRICH ULRICH,
(Codorus.)
Ulrich—Rosina, b. Dec. 28, 1740; bap. April 5, 1741. Sponsors, John Adam Rupert and wife Anna Barbara.

JOHN FUNCK, (Codorus.)
Funck—Catarina, b. March 5, 1741; bap. April 5, 1741. Sponsor, Catarina Loewenstein.

JOHN WOLF, (Codorus.)
Wolf—Elizabetha, b. Dec. 9, 1740; bap. April 5, 1741. Sponsors, Carl Eisen and wife .

GEORGE LOEWENSTEIN,
(Codorus.)
Loewenstein—Maria Elizabetha, b. Nov. 27, 1740; bap. April 5, 1741. Sponsors, Daniel Diehl and his wife.

JOHN GEORGE MAEUNTZER,
(Lancaster.)
Maeuntzer — Elizabeth Catarina, b. April 13, 1741; bap. May 16, 1741. Sponsors, Jacob Spannseiler and his wife.
—— Anna, Catarina, b. May 23, 1742; bap. July 18, 1742. Sponsors, George Buerger and his wife.
—— George Jacob, b. Nov. 18, 1744; bap. Feb. 3, 1745. Sponsors, George Buerger and wife and Jacob Wolf.

—— Anna Dorothea, b. Nov. 17, 1746; bap. March 29, 1747. Sponsors, Jacob Wolf and his wife.

TOBIAS HEINRICH, (Codorus.)
Heinrich—John, b. Mch. 9, 1741; bap. May 17, 1741. Sponsors, John Wolf and his wife.

JACOB JUNGBLUT, (Conewago.)
Jungblut—John Jacob, b. Mch. 13, 1739; bap. Nov. 13, 1739. Sponsors, Leonhardt Bernitz, Casper Kuehner, Anna Catarina Kuntz and Hanna Jungblut.

ERASMUS HOLZAPFEL, (Codorus.)
Holzapfel—B. Aug. 25, 1740; bap. May 17, 1741. Sponsors, John Adam Rupert and his wife.

WEIRICH RUDIESIEL, (Codorus.)
Rudiesiel—Anna Johanna, b. Dec. 28, 1740; bap. May 17, 1741. Sponsors, Jacob Ottinger and Ana Johanna Igsin.

HEINRICH DEVIS, (Conewago.)
Devis—Catarina, b. Jan. 6, 1741; bap. May 18, 1741. Sponsors, Peter Schultz and his wife Catarina.

JOHN JACOB KLUND, (Conewago.)
Klund—John Adam, b. Feb. 11, 1741; bap. May 18, 1741. Sponsors, John Adam Soll and Catarina Elizabeth Speugel.

JOHN BIRDMAN, (Conewago.)
Birdman—Catarina, b. April 20, 1741; bap. May 18, 1741. Sponsors, Elias Daniel Bernitz and his wife, also Catarina Berghoester.

ANTONIUS HEUTELER, (Conewago.)
Heuteler—John Mattheis, b. Sept. 19, 1738; bap. Oct. 16, 1738. Sponsors, John Mattheis Maercker and his wife.

—— Antonius, b. April 5, 1741; bap. May 18, 1741. Sponsors, Daniel Speugel and Magdal. Winterbauer.

SEBASTIAN WINTERBAUER, (Conewago.)
Winterbauer—Maria Susanna, b. 1738; bap. 1738. Sponsors, Heinrich Vadis and Susanna Heissmann. .

—— Sybilla, b. Aug. 30, 1740; bap. May 18, 1741. Sponsors, Michael Schaeufle and Maria Sybilla Weiss.

PHILIPP BENTZ, (Kreutz Creek.)
Bentz—Christian, b. Mch. 30, 1741; bap. May 19, 1741. Sponsors, John Christian Groll, John Jost Sultzbach and Barbara Weller.

JACOB VERDRIESS, (Monocacy.)
Verdriess—Catarina, b. Mch., 1739; bap. June 24, 1741.

—— Johannes, b. April 27, 1741; bap. June 24, 1741. Sponsors, for both, Philipp Ernst Gruber and wife, and also John Valentin Verdriess.

JEREMIAS ELLRADT, (Monocacy.)
Ellradt—Elisabetha, b. April 16, 1741; bap. June 24, 1741. Sponsors, Dietrich Ellradt and his wife.

FREDERICH TRANBERG, (Conewago.)
Tranberg—Christina Barbara, b. Sept. 29, 1740; bap. June 25, 1741. Sponsors, Christian Loefel and Anna Christina Baumann.

NICOLAUS LAYENBERGER, (Conewago.)
Layenberger—John George, b. June 13, 1741; bap. June 25, 1741. Sponsors, Joh. George Kuntz and Catarina Baulinger.

FREDERICH KREUTER, (Conewago.)
Kreuter—Anna Margaretha, b. May 15, 1741; bap. June 25, 1741. Sponsors, Cunradt Euler and his wife.

JACOB WELSCH, (Codorus.)
Welsch—John Jacob, b. May 20, 1741; bap. June 26, 1741. Sponsors, John Jacob Ottinger and Hannah Jost.

MARTIN BAUER, (Codorus.)
Bauer—A son (name wanting), b. May 2, 1741; bap. June 26, 1741. Sponsors, John Peter Wolf, Jacob Welsch and Veronica Baseler.

ULRICH BUETZER, (Kreutz Creek.)
Buetzer—John Christian, b. Dec. 18, 1740; bap. June 26, 1741. Sponsors, John Christian Groll and his wife.

JOHN SCHMELTZER, (Swatara.)
Schmeltzer—John Peter, b. Dec. 8, 1738; bap. Jan. 30, 1739. Sponsors, Peter Kucher and his wife.

—— Johannes, b. April 11, 1741; bap. June 2, 1741. Sponsors, Peter Kucher and his wife Barbara.

—— Sabina, b. Sept. 2, 1746; bapt. Sept. 14, 1746. Sponsors, Thomas Kreugel and his wife Margaretha.

LEONHARD KNEDY, (Codorus.)
Knedy—Isaac, b. July 2, 1741; bap. Aug. 20, 1741. Sponsors, Isaac Laudenbusch and his wife.

JOST MOHR, (Codorus.)
Mohr—Eva Catarina, b. July 3, 1741; bap. Aug. 20, 1741. Sponsors, Marx Heus and Eva Catarina Iserlin.

JOSEPH BEREN, (Codorus.)
Beren—Frederick, b. July 20, 1741; bap. Aug. 20, 1741. Sponsors, John Frederich Baseler and wife Veronica.

MICHAEL KRUEGER, (Codorus.)
Krueger — Elias. Sponsor, Michael Rausch.

WILLIAM MORGON, (Codorus.)
Morgon—Elisabetha, b. Jan., 1741; bap.

Aug. 20, 1741. Sponsors, Christian Groll and his wife Elisabetha.

ULRICH BUEHLER, (Codorus.)
Buehler, Susanna, b. Feb. 17, 1741; bap. Aug. 21, 1741. Sponsors, George Baecker and his wife.

JACOB GANNEMER, (Codorus.)
Gannemer—Anna Maria, b. Feb. 17, 1741; bap. Aug. 1, 1741. Sponsors, Ulrich Buehler and his wife.

CASPER SCHMIDT, (Conewago.)
Schmidt—George Jacob, b. June 10,1741; bap. Aug. 21, 1741. Sponsor, Jacob Baerlinger.

MARX BIEGELER, (Conewago.)
Biegeler—Anna Maria, b.March 30.1741; bap. Aug. 21, 1741. Sponsors, Andreas Hill and Catarina Kuntz.

ALBINUS BEYER, (Codorus.)
Beyer—Maria Sophia Margaretha, b. Aug. 7, 1741; bap. Sept. 27, 1741. Sponsors, John Nicolaus Kau and his wife.

NICOLAUS KOGER.
Koger—John Jacob, b. Sept. 4, 1741; bap. Sept. 27, 1741. Sponsors, John Jacob Weller and his wife Barbara.

FREDERICH SCHULTZ, (Conewago.)
Schultz—Julia Catarina, b. Sept. 6, 1741; bap. Sept. 29, 1741. Sponsor, Juliana Catarina Morgenstern.

CHRISTOPH KAUFFELD, (Codorus.)
Kauffeld—John Christoph, b. July 15, 1741; bap. Oct. 1, 1741.
—— Maria Elisabetha, b. July 15,1741; bap. Oct. 1, 1741. Sponsors, Michael Rausch and Elisabetha Rausch.

MICHAEL BOLTZ, (Quitapahilla.)
Boltz—Elizabetha, b. May 10, 1741; bap. Oct. 9, 1741. Sponsors, George Berger and his wife.

GEORGE HEINRICH PETER, (Quitapahilla.)
Peter—Catarina, b. June, 1741; bap. Oct. 4, 1741. Sponsors, George Berger and his wife.

HEINRICH DUPS, (Swatara.)
Dups—Maria Sabina, b. Sept. 2, 1741; bap. Oct. 4, 1741. Sponsors, Ludwig Bors and Margaretha Kappler.

JOHN GEORGE KUENIG, (Swatara.)
Kuenig—George Jacob, b. Aug. 28, 1741; bap. Oct. 4, 1741. Sponsors, Sebastian Naess and Barbara Kuefer.

JOHN GEORGE VELTIN, (Swatara.)
Veltin—Maria Elisabetha, b. Sept. 4, 1741; bap. Oct. 4. 1741. Sponsors, Valentin Kuefer and his wife.

LAMPERT BUBAR, (Swatara.)
Bubar—Maria Catarina, b. July, 1740; bap. Oct. 4, 1741. Sponsors, Daniel Schui and his wife.

ANDREAS BORT.
Bort—Maria Barbara, b. July 20, 1741; bap. Nov. 28, 1741. Sponsors, Frantz Seip and Catarina Barbara Spaller.

ABRAHAM HAUSWIRTH, (Conewago.)
Hauswirth—John, b. Sept. 25, 1741; bap. Oct. 28, 1741. Sponsors, Johannes Morgenstern and his wife.

JACOB BIRCKEL, (Swatara.)
Birckel—John Jacob,b. Jan. 7, 1734; bap. April 28, 1734. Sponsors, Peter Gaertner and his wife.
—— Michael Leonhardt, b. Aug. 20, 1736; bap. Nov. 9, 1736. Sponsors, Leonhardt Billmeyer and spouse Ana Bart.
—— Anna Eva, b. May 8, 1739; bap. June 12, 1739. Sponsors, Adam Vollmar and his wife.
—— Maria Dorothea, b. Nov. 27, 1741; bap. Jan. 2, 1742. Sponsors, Frederich Haehle and wife Margaretha.

CHRISTOPH HOFMANN, (Lancaster.)
Hofmann—John Christoph, b. Feb. 21, 1734; bap. April 28, 1734. Sponsors, Anastasius Uhler and Christina Ziegeler.
—— Maria Margaretha, b. April 18, 1736; bap. May 23, 1736. Sponsors, John Wolf Allgeyer and wife Maria.

PETER RAUP, (Dorm Furnace.)
Raup—John Michael, b. Sept. 15, 1733; bap. April 28, 1734. Sponsors, John Martin Myle and his wife.

JOHN JACOB MATTHEIS, (Monocacy.)
Mattheis—Anna Margaretha, b. June 11, 1734; bap. June 23, 1734. Sponsors, Christian Kleeman and Anna Barbara Hoof.
—— Magdalena, b. Sept. 15, 1735; bap. April 28, 1736. Sponsors, John Jacob Hoof and Anna Barbara Teafersbiss.
—— John George, b. March 30, 1737; bap. June 16, 1737. Sponsors, John George Geyer and his wife.
—— Catarina, b. May 20, 1738; bap. June 7, 1738. Sponsers, Mattheis Roesal and Catarina Geiger.

JOHN DIETRICH KOBER, (Lebanon.)
Kober—Anna Elisabetha, b. May 12, 1734; bap. July 21, 1734. Sponsors, John Adam Heyl and his wife.
—— John Egidius, b. Dec. 18, 1738; bap. Dec. 24, 1738. Sponsors, Egidius Hoffmann.

—— George, b. Jan. 27, 1741; bap. Feb. 22, 1741. Sponsors, John Egidius Hoffmann and his wife.

—— Anna Margaretha, b. May 13, 1743; bap. May 23, 1743. Sponsors, Thomas Krevel and his wife.

—— John Michael , b. Nov. 30, 1748; bap. Nov. 27, 1749. Sponsors, David Fischer and his wife.

JOHN GEORGE DOERR, (Manheim.)
Doerr—Maria Juliana, b. Aug. 4, 1734; bap. Aug. 18, 1734. Sponsors, Johannes Herburger and wife Juliana.

—— Johannes, b. April 18. 1736; bap. May 23, 1736. Sponsors, John Bindtnagel.

—— Maria Urgina, b. Jan. 30, 1738; bap. April 30, 1738. Sponsors, John Bindtnagel and his wife.

JOHN MICHAEL GRAFF, (Tulpehocken.)
Graff—John Cunradt, b. Sept. 22, 1734; bap. Oct. 13, 1734. Sponsors, John Cunradt Fey and his wife.

—— George, b. April 6, 1739; bap. April 22, 1739. Sponsors, John George Graff, jr., and his wife.

MARTIN KAPPLER, (Swatara.)
Kappler—John Jacob, b. Sept. 20, 1734; bap. Nov. 10, 1734. Sponsors, Sebastian Ruhi and Elisabetha Kaiser.

—— Catarina Barbara, b. June 19. 1736; bap. Sept. 12, 1736. Sponsors, Cunradt Lang and his wife.

JOHN GEORGE MEYER, (Swatara.)
Meyer—Anna Barbara, b. Oct. 6, 1734; bap. Jan. 1, 1735. Sponsor, Anna Barbara Teufersbiss.

—— Veronica, b. Feb. 28, 1737; bap. Oct. 10, 1737. Sponsors, John Schmeltz and his wife.

—— Elisabetha, b. April 7, 1739; bap. June 12, 1739. Sponsors, Philip Schnaetterle and wife Sabina.

—— Anna Sabina, b. June 3, 1745; bap. 1745. Sponsors, Philip Schnaetterle and his wife.

FREDERICH GEBERT, (Shenandoah.)
Gebert—Susanna Catarina, b. June 27, 1736; bap. Aug. 29, 1736. Sponsor, Clara Strubel.

NICOLAUS BRINTZLER, (Shenandoah.)
Brintzler—John Frederick, b. Feb. 17, 1735; bap. March 31 1735. Sponsor, John Frederick Strubel.

—— Maria Elisabetha, b. Jan. 24, 1738; bap. April 9, 1738. Sponsors, the above.

JOHN BRECHBIEL.
Brechbiel—Maria Regina, b. May 15,

1739; bap. June 12, 1739. Sponsors, John Bindtnagel and his wife.

HEINRICH SINN, (Monocacy.)
Sinn—Susanna, b. May 2, 1735; bap. March 30, 1735. Sponsor, Susanna Rudiesielin.

—— Jacob Mattheis, b. Jan. 13, 1739; bap. May 23, 1739. Sponsor, Jacob Mattheis Mausser.

JOHN WOLF ALLGEYER, (Tulpehocken.)
Allgeyer—Maria Eva, b. April 25, 1736; bap. May 23, 1736. Sponsors, Wilhelm Albert and his wife.

GEORGE ADAM HEYL, (Moesenutten.)
Heyl—Elisabetha Barbara, b. May 19, 1736 bap. May 23, 1736. Sponsors, Peter Schmidt and Elisabetha Barbara Heyl.

—— Anna Maria, b. March 16 1738, bap. March 23, 1738. Sponsors, Peter Schmidt and Elisabetha Barbara Heyl.

—— John Adam, born July 7, 1739, bap. July 8, 1739. Sponsors, John Stephen Traenckel and John Adam Hambrecht and his wife.

PETER KUCHER, (Lebanon.)
Kucher—John Frantz, b. July 13, 1736; bap. Aug. 1, 1736. Sponsors, John Frantz Fuchs and his wife.

—— Anna Catarina, b. July 12, 1738; bap. Feb. 7, 1738. Sponsors, John George Graff, junior, and Catarina Kopfenhoefer.

—— Christoph, b. March 19, 1739; bap. April 22, 1739. Sponsors, Christoph Meyer and his wife.

—— Rosina, b. March 20, 1741; bap. March 25, 1741. Sponsors, Christoph Meyer and his wife.

—— John Peter, b. Feb. 12, 1743; bap. March 27, 1743. Sponsors, Albrecht Siechele and his wife.

PETER MUENCH, (Tulpehocken.)
Muench—John Michael, b. Jan. 2, 1738; bap. Jan. 24, 1738. Sponsors, John Michael Becker and his wife.

—— John Cunradt, b. Nov. 28, 1740; bap. September 5. 1742. Sponsors, Cunradt Scharf and his wife Appollonia.

MATTHEIS SELTZER, (Moesenutten.)
Seltzer—John Ludwig, b. Feb. 23, 1734; bap. April 28, 1734. Sponsors, Ludwig Stein and his wife.

—— Maria Catarina, b. Jan. 8, 1736; bap. May 6, 1736. Sponsors, parents.

—— John Heinrich, b. Sept. 12, 1737; bap. May 28, 1738. Sponsors, John Heinrich Schneid and Christoph Zimmerman.

—— Ana Christina, b. in 1741; bap. May 27, 1742. Sponsor, Elisabetha Heyl.

MICHAEL ADAM, (Moselem.)
Adam—John George, b. Aug. 28, 1741; bap. Dec. 8, 1741. Sponsor, John George Faust.

JOHN LUDWIG HUTZEL, (Trappe.)
Hutzel—John Mattheis, b. Sept. 26, 1741; bap. Dec. 11, 1741. Sponsors, John Mattheis Kuehnle and Anna Margaretha Buettel.

FREDERICK MARSTALLER, (Trappe.)
Marstaller—Philip Balthasar, b. Jan. 4, 1742; bap. Jan. 6, 1742. Sponsors, Philip Balthasar Croesman and wife Felicitas.

JOHN PETER STOBER, (Trappe.)
Stober—Anna Eva, b. Sept. 8, 1742; bap. Jan. 18, 1743. Sponsors, Ulrich Hartman and his wife.

DORST BRECKBIEL, (Swatara.)
Breckbiel—Elizabetha, b. June 3, 1739; bap. 1739. Sponsors, George Hauck and his wife.

—— John Peter, b. Nov,. 1750; bap. April 5, 1751. Sponsors, Johannes Bindnagel and his wife Regina.

DORST BRECKBIEL, (Swatara.)
Breckbiel—Johannes, b. Sept. 21, 1741; bap. Jan. 1, 1742. Sponsors, Frederick Kuehner and his wife.

ABRAHAM WILLIAMS, (Swatara.)
Williams—Isaac, b. Nov. 7, 1741; bap. Jan. 1, 1742. Sponsors, Frederick Deabi and his wife.

BENJAMIN CLARK, (Swatara.)
Clark—Jane, b. April 17, 1739; bap. June 12, 1739.

—— Mary, b. April 12, 1741; bap. Jan. 1, 1742. Sponsors, Abraham and Christian Williams.

—— Thomas, b. Dec. 7, 1746; bap. April 26, 1747. Sponsors, Thomas Kreuel and his wife Margaretha.

FREDERICK DEEBI, (Swatara.)
Deebi—Catarina, b. Nov. 6. 1741; bap. Jan. 1742. Sponsors, John Tittle and wife.

CARL SCHALLY, (Lebanon.)
Schally—John Peter, b. Sept. 29, 1741; bap. Jan. 3, 1742. Sponsors, John Peter Kucher and his wife.

PETER RUTH, (Lebanon.)
Ruth—Anna Catarina, b. Jan. 29, 1735; bap. June 29, 1735. Sponsor, Susanna Barbara Teuss.

—— Maria Catarina, b. Oct. 27, 1741; bap. Jan. 3, 1742. Sponsors, Michael Myer and his wife.

—— Barbara, b. Nov. 25, 1742; bap. Dec. 20, 1742. Sponsor, Jonh Immel.

JOHN ADAM KITTRING, (Lebanon.)
Kittring—George Michael, b. Dec. 11, 1741; bap. Jan. 3, 1742. Sponsors, Michael Boltz and his wife Maria Barbara.

—— Maria Margaretha, b. Aug. 4, 1743; bap. Nov. 15, 1743. Sponsors, The above.

—— Rosina Barbara, b. Mch. 18, 1745; bap. Apr. 28, 1745. Sponsors, the above.

GEORGE ADAM VOLLMAR, (Swatara.)
Vollmar—Anna Maria, b. Jan. 6, 1739; bap. June 3, 1739. Sponsors, Jacob Birckel and his wife Dorothea.

—— Maria Magdalena, b. Sept. 19, 1743; bap. Oct. 23, 1743. Sponsor, Maria Magdalena Kraemer.

VINCENS KUEFFER, (Successor in Thow.)
Kueffer—Catarina, b. March 11, 1747; bap. March 29, 1747. Sponsors, George Buerger and his wife Catarina.

JACOB HERMAN, (Swatara.)
Herman—Anna Maria, b. Aug. 29, 1737; bap. Nov. 5, 1739. Sponsors, George Bernhardt Mann and his wife.

—— Maria Elisabeth, b. Oct. 22, 1742; bap. Dec. 21, 1742. Sponsors, George Bernhardt Mann and his wife.

ADAM HEILMAN, (Lebanon.)
Heylman—Catarina, b. April 7, 1740; bap. May 26, 1740. Sponsors, Anastasius Uhler and his wife.

—— Anna Elizabeth, b. March 2, 1742; bap. April 15, 1742.

PHILIP SCHNATTERLE, (Swatara.)
Schnatterle—Sabina, b. July 13, 1735; bap. Oct. 7, 1735. Sponsors, Heinrich Dubs and the child's mother.

—— Heinrich, b. Dec. 23, 1738; bap. Jan. 30, 1739. Sponsors, Heinrich Kline and his wife Anna Maria.

—— John Michael, b. Mch. 12, 1740; bap. May 26, 1740. Sponsors, John Seigmund Haehnle and his wife.

—— Martin, b. Sept. 31, 1741; bap. Jan. 1, 1742. Sponsors, Heinrich Klein and his wife.

—— John Jacob, b. Feb. 22, 1744; bap. Mch 2, 1744. Sponsors, Heinrich Klein and his wife.

—— John George, b. Sept. 17, 1745; bap. Oct. 26, 1745. Sponsors, George Meyer and his wife.

—— Adam, b. April 4, 1747; bap. April 26, 1747. Sponsors, Adam Faber and wife of George Meyers.

PETER BAUMGAERTNER,
(Swatara.)
Baumgaertner—Johannes, b. May 13, 1740; bap. May 26, 1740. Sponsors, John Brechbiel and his wife.
—— John Dorst, b. May 9, 1742; bap. July 18, 1742. Sponsors, Dorst Brechtbill, Anna Barbara Brechbille, John Brechbill's wife.

LEONHARDT RAMLER,
(Tulphocken)
Ramler—Johannes, b. in May, 1725. His mother was a Menonite. After her death, when more than 17 years of age, he was baptized in the old Kirchen-Wanne on the day on which he was confirmed. He partook of the Lord's Supper on the following day.

GEORGE MEYER, (Lebanon.)
Meyer—Anna Catarina, b. July 11, 1740, bap. Aug. 10, 1740. Sponsors, Peter Ruth and his wife Catarina.
—— John Heinrich, b. Dec. 19, 1741; bap April 26, 1742. Sponsors, Heinrich Beyer and his wife
—— Michael, b. Feb 28. 1743; bap. May 23, 1743. Sponsor, Michael Meyer and his wife.
—— George Peter, b. Oct. 19, 1744; bap. April 28, 1745 Sponsors, Peter Marker, Ulrich Peter and Elizabeth Lutz.
—— John Jacob, b. Aug. 28, 1746; bap. Nov 9, 1746. Sponsors, John Jacob Schlauch and wife Ursula Elisabetha

JOHN MARTIN KITZMUELLER,
(Conewago.)
Kitzmueller—John Jacob, b. Feb. 28, 1731; bap. April 19, 1731. Sponsor, John Jacob Kitzmueller.
—— Johannes, b. Oct. 15, 1734; bap. Dec. 27, 1734. Sponsors, John Jacob Kitzmueller, senior, and his wife.
—— John George, b. Oct. 29, 1738; bap. Nov. 30, 1738. Sponsors, John Kuntz and his wife.

JOHN MICHAEL BOLTZ,
(Lebanon.)
Boltz—Anna Dorothea, b. Feb. 18, 1738; bap. March 30, 1738. Sponsors, Balthasar Ort and his wife
—— Catarina Barbara, b. June 23,1745; bap. Aug. 24, 1745. Sponsors, George Buerger and his wife.

JOHN HEINRICH CASSEL,
(Conewago.)
Cassel—John Jacob, b. Oct. 7, 1743; bap. March 9, 1735. Sponsors, John Jacob Beuskert.
—— Catarina, b. Oct., 1739; bap. May 3, 1740. Sponsor, Catarina Weyhmueller.

ISAAC WILLIAM, (Swatara.)
William—Isaac, b. Nov. 3, 1746; bap.Apr. 26, 1741. Sponsors, Philipp Schnatterle and his wife.
—— Jacob, b. March 23, 1753; bap.June 17, 1753. Sponsors, Valentine Gerhard and Mary Rosenbaum.
—— Mary Elisabetha, b. Jan. 27, 1755; bap. June 8, 1755. Sponsor, Veronica Meyer.
—— George, born in 1757; bap. Sept. 3, 1757. Sponsors, Anastasius Uhler and wife.

CHRISTOPH KNAUER,
(French Creek.)
Knauer—Anna Elisabetha, b. Jan. 16, 1742; bap. March 16, 1742. Sponsor, Anna Elisabetha Olin.

GEORGE LUDTWIG FRIEDTEL,
(Swatara.)
Friedtel—John George, b. March 31, 1737 (?); bap. Aug. 14, 1737 (?). Sponsors, John George Houck and his wife.
—— Maria Magdalena, b. April 28,1739; bap. June 11, 1739. Sponsors, Johannes Hohmann an dhis wife Maria Magdalena.

JOHN ALBRECHT SCHELL,
(Swatara.)
Schell—Christina Regina, b. Dec. 22, 1737; bap. Feb. 6, 1738. Sponsors, John Bindtnagel and his wife Regina.

JOHANNES DIRBI, (Lebanon.)
Dirbi—John George, b. Nov. 6,1734; bap. July 29, 1735. Sponsor, John George Steitz.
—— Maria Catharine, b. Sept., 1737; bap. Feb. 6, 1738. Sponsors, Maria Catharine and Johanna Catharine Blum.

JOHN MICHAEL CARL, (Conewago.)
Carl—Anna Maria, b. Feb. 2, 1738; bap. Feb. 7, 1738. Sponsors, Andreas Carl and his wife Anna Maria.
—— Maria Catarina, b. Sept. 24, 1729; bap. Nov. 13, 1739. Sponsors, Marx Birgler and his wife.

MICHAEL BORST, (Lebanon.)
Borst—Maria Elizabetha, b. March 9, 1735; bap. Aug. 29, 1735. Sponsors, Martin Kirstaetter and his wife.
—— Susanna, b. b. Dec. 8, 1736; bap. Sept. 11, 1737. Sponsor, Dorothea Kirstaetter.
—— Anna Dorothea, b. Dec. 25, 1738; bap. Jan. 29, 1739. Sponsors, Anastasius Uhler and wife Dorothea.

LEONHARD UMBERGER,
-(Successor in Thow.)
Johannes—b. Feb. 7, 1743; bap. March 27, 1743. Sponsors, Johannes Umberger and sister Elizabeth Dorothea.

PETER MARCKER, (Swatara.)
Marcker—Maria Elizabetha, b. April 21,
1743; bap. May 23, 1743. Sponsors,
Christoph Zimmer and his wife.
—— Julianna, b. Feb. 3, 1746; bap.
March 3, 1746. Sponsors, Adam Ul-
rich and his wife Juliana.
—— Catarina, b. Feb. 4, 1751; bap.
March 17, 1751. Sponsors, George
Mueller and his wife.

JOHN ADAM LOEFFLER,
(Lancaster.)
Loeffler—George Ludwig, b. April 4,
1742; bap. April 8, 1742. Sponsors,
George Graf and his wife, also Ludwig
Heinrich Dettborn.
MARTIN HOFFMANN, (Hempfield.)
Hoffman—John Andreas, b. March 14,
1742; bap. April 4, 1742. Sponsor, An-
dreas Hoffman.
JOHN TITTLE, deceased, (Swatara.)
Tittle—Peter, b. Sept. 20, 1742; bap.
April 27, 1747. Sponsors, George
Meyer and his wife.

JONAS WOLF, (Lebanon.)
Wolf—John Jacob, b. Jan. 4, 1742; bap.
April 15, 1742. Sponsors, John Jacob
Kaemmerling and his wife.
—— John Herman, b. Aug. 5, 1743;
bap. Aug. 28, 1743. Sponsors, Her-
man Trott and his wife.
—— Anna Maria, b. Jan. 7, 1745; bap.
Jan. 19, 1745. Sponsors, Herman
Trott and his wife.
—— Simon, b. Oct. 28, 1746; bap. Dec.
7, 1746. Sponsors, George Wagner
and wife Anna Elizabetha.
JOHN ALBRECHT SIECHELE,
(Lebanon.)
Siechele—John Peter, b. March 7, 1741;
bap. April 15, 1742. Sponsors, Peter
Kucher and his wife.
—— Eva Barbara, b. Oct. 2, 1744; bap.
Oct. 28, 1744. Sponsors, Peter Kucher
and his wife.
JACOB FROELICH, (Lebanon.)
Froelich—Anna Catarina, b. Oct., 1741;
bap. April 15,1742. Sponsors, Buerger
and his wife.
WILLIAM KALLY, (Lebanon.)
Kally—Sarah, b. April 6, 1742; bap.April
15, 1742. Sponsors,Andreas Wolf and
his wife.
HEINRICH WILHELM, (Swatara.)
Wilhelm—Maria, b. Dec. 4, 1741; bap.
April 16, 1742. Sponsor, Magdalena
Homann.
—— John Philipp, b. Jan. 28,1743; bap.
July 19, 1743. Sponsors, Philipp Lo-
rentz Houtz and wife.
MARTIN SPECK, (Swatara.)
Speck—Anna, Maria, b. Jan. 15, 1741;

bap. April 16, 1742. Sponsors, Sig-
mund Haehnle, jr., and Anna Maria
Becker.
—— Maria Catarina, b. Aug. 28, 1748;
bap. Sept. 4, 1748. Sponsors, Sigmund
Haehnle and his wife.
—— Johannes, b. Sept. 18, 1754; bap.
Oct. 7, 1754. Sponsors, Jacob Loresch
and his wife.

FRIEDERICH HAEHNLE,
(Swatara.)
Haehnle—Jacob Friederich, b.·March 12,
1742; bap. April 16, 1742. Sponsors,
Jacob Birckel and his wife.
—— John Michael, b. Oct. 12, 1743;
bap. Oct. 23, 1743. Sponsors, George
Frederich and his wife.
—— Anna Margaretha, b. Dec. 30,
1745; bap. March 12, 1746. Sponsors,
Wendel Heyl and wife Anna.
—— Maria Eva, b. March 5, 1747; bap.
March 29, 1747. Sponsors, Wendel
Heyl and wife Anna.
—— Elizabetha, b. Dec. 18, 1748; bap.
Dec. 25, 1748. Sponsors, Wendel Heyl
and wife Anna.

FREDERICH HAEHNLE,
(Swatara, continued.)
Haehnle—Eva Catarina, b.Jan.6,1751;
bap. Jan. 21, 1751. Sponsors, Veit
Kapf and wife Gertraudt.
—— Anna Barbara, b. Jan. 14, 1753;
bap. Feb. 25, 1753. Sponsors, Wendel
Heyl and wife Anna.
JOHN BROWN, (Swatara.)
Brown—Maria Regina, b. Feb. 26, 1742;
bap. April 16, 1742. Sponsors, John
Bindtnagle and wife.
—— Jacob, b. March 27, 1746; bap.
April 27, 1746. Sponsors, John Bindt-
nagle and wife.
—— Anna Barbara, b. April 6, 1755;
bap. June 15, 1755. Sponsors not
given.
ANTONIUS ROSENBAUM,
(Swatara.)
Rosenbaum—Susanna—b. May 3, 1739;
bap. April 16, 1742. Sponsors, Martin
Speck and is wife.
—— Salome, b. March, 1741; bap. April
16, 1742. Sponsors, Philip Dubs and
his wife.
JOHN GEORGE SCHMIDT,
(Lancaster.)
Schmidt—Christian, b. Feb. 10, 1742;
bap. May 2, 1742. Sponsors, Christian
Andereck and wife.
CHRISTIAN ANDERECK,
(Lancaster.)
Andereck—Catarina, b. Feb. 23, 1742;
bap. May 2, 1742. Sponsors, John
George Schmidt and wife.

GEORGE QUICKEL, JR. (Pequea.)
Quickel—Anna Catarina, b. March 23, 1742; bap. May 2, 1742. Sponsor, Anna Catarina Quickel.

PETER APFEL, (Monocacy.)
Apfel—Eva Rosina, b. May 9, 1742; bap. May 20, 1742. Sponsor, Eva Rosina Kauth.

CHRISTIAN GEIGER, (Hempfield.)
Geiger—Maria Margaretha, b. May 29, 1742; bap. July 4, 1742. Sponsors, Martin Hofman and his wife.

JOHN DIETRICH GAENER, (Lancaster.)
Gaener—Eva Catarina, b. May 6, 1742; bap. July 4, 1742. Sponsors, John George Snyder and wife Anna Catarina.

CHRISTOPH MEYER, (Lebanon.)
Meyer—John George, b. Dec. 4, 1735, bap. Apr. 18, 1736. Sponsors, John George Klein and his wife Anna.
——Maria Barbara, b. Aug. 12, 1738, bap. May 21, 1738. Sponsors, John Peter Kucher and wife Maria Barbara.
——Anna Maria, b. June 16, 1742, bap. July 18, 1742. Sponsors, Thomas Koppenhoefer and wife Anna Maria.

MICHAEL LAUER, (Swatara.)
Lauer—John Michael, b. June 29, 1742. b. July 18, 1742. Sponsors, Michael Spengel and his wife.
——Catharine Barbara, b. March 11, 1744, bap. April 15, 1744. Sponsors, Valentine Kuefer and wife Anna Barbara.

JAMES McNEESS, (Lebanon.)
McNeess—James, b. Sept. 4, 1741, bap. July 18, 1742. Sponsors, Anastasius Uhler and his wife Dorothea.

JOHN JOAKLES, (Swatara.)
Joakles—Anna Sara, b. Feb., 1742, bap. July 18, 1742. Sponsors, John Deeby and his wife.

JOHN WENDEL HEYL, (Swatara.)
Heyl—John Jacob, b. June 13, 1742, bap. July 18, 1742. Sponsors, John Jacob Dubs and Barbara Kappler.

CASPAR SCHMIDT, (Conewago.)
Schmidt—Maria Elisabetha, b. Nov. 8, 1742, bap. Nov. 23, 1742. Sponsors, Daniel Schlaegel and Maria Elisabetha Morgenstern.

JOHN REYNOLDS, (Swatara.)
Reynolds—Bridgitte, b. Nov. 20, 1742, bap. Dec. 21, 1742. Sponsors, Francis Reynolds, Patrick and Sarah McKue.
——Elisabetha, b. March 23, 1744, bap. April 15, 1744. Sponsors, Thomas and Elisabetha McKay, also Joseph Reynolds and Rebecca Reynolds.

——John, b. 1746, bap. 1746.
——Joseph, b. Nov. 10, 1747, bap. Nov. 24, 1747. Sponsors, Joseph Reynolds, Sarah McKue and Sarah Reynolds.

CHRISTOPH LABENGEIYER, (Swatara.)
Labengeiyer—Maria Catarina, b. May 18, 1730, bap. Sept. 29, 1730. Sponsor, Anna Maria Meyer.
——John Jacob, b. April 8, 1734, bap. April 21, 1734. Sponsors, John Jacob Beyer and his wife Margaretha.
——Anna Barbara, b. June 14, 1736, bap. July 18, 1736. Sponsors, Michael Ranek and his wife Anna Barbara.
——Christoph, with his second wife, b. in Oct., 1741, bap. April 15, 1742. Sponsors, Christoph Meyer and his wife.

JOHN BINDTNAGEL, (Swatara.)
Bindtnagel—Anna Sabina, b. Sept. 11, 1733, bap. Sept. 17, 1733. Sponsors, John Martin Meyle and his wife Anna Sabina.
——Johannes, b. Feb. 7, 1735, bap. March 23, 1735. Sponsor, Melchior Heuter.
——John Martin, b. Sept. 7, 1736, bap. Oct. 3, 1736. Sponsor, John Martin Meyle.

JOHN GEORGE ERGEBRECHT, (Lebanon.)
Ergebrecht—Catarina, b. March 26, 1733; bap. Sept. 17, 1733. Sponsor, Anna Catarina Mast.
——Anna Elisabetha, b. Feb. 20, 1735, bap. April 27, 1735. Sponsors, Jacob Mast and his wife.

FREDERICH HEINRICH GEELWICHS, (Conewago.)
Geelwichs—Catarina, b. Dec. 21, 1735, bap. Feb. 1, 1736. Sponsors, Jacob Verdriess and Catarina Euler.
——Catarina, b. Dec. 11, 1737, bap. May 23, 1738. Sponsors, Elias Daniel and Anna Eva Kuntz.
——George Karl, b. Sept. 16, 1739, bap. Nov. 13, 1739. Sponsor, George Karl Bernitz.

MICHAEL BAUER, (Swatara.)
Bauer—John Valentin, b. Sept. 17, 1739, bap. Oct. 21, 1739. Sponsors, John Valentin Stober and his wife Eva.
——John Martin, b. Dec. 27, 1741, bap. Jan. 1, 1742. Sponsors, Valentin Kuefer and Anna Maria Frederich.
——Anna Eva, b. July 28, 1746, bap. Aug. 17, 1746. Sponsors, Michael Spiegel and wife Anna Eva.
——Anna Maria, with second wife, b. Jan. 12, 1749, bap. March 19, 1749. Sponsors, Sigmund Haehnle and his wife.

HEINRICH KLEIN, (Lebanon.)
Klein—Anna, b. Feb. 26, 1737, bap. March 27, 1737. Sponsors, George Klein and his wife Anna.
——Sabina, b. Oct. 1, 1738, bap. Jan. 30, 1739. Sponsors, Philipp Schnatterle and his wife Sabina.
——Maria Barbara, b. April 6, 1740, bap. May 26, 1740. Sponsors, John Braechbil and his wife Maria Barbara.
——John George, b. March 2, 1742, bap. April 16, 1742. Sponsors, Philipp Schnatterle and his wife.

JOHN GEORGE KUENIG, (Tulpehocken.)
Kuenig—Anna Maria, b. Oct. 25, 1739; bap. Dec. 27, 1739. Sponsors, Sebastian Naess and Elizabeth Naess.
——George Jacob, b. Aug. 28, 1741, bap. Oct. 4, 1741. Sponsors, Sebastian Naess and Barbara Kuefer.

JOHN MARTIN MEYLE, (Lebanon.)
Meyle—Elisabetha, b. Nov. 7, 1733, bap. April 28, 1734. Sponsors, Michael Baettle and his wife.
——Johannes, b. Jan. 26, 1735, bap. May 25, 1735. Sponsors, John Bindtnagel and his wife.
——John Martin, b. July 25, 1737; bap. Dec. 25, 1737. Sponsors, Michael Baettle and his wife.
—— Heinrich, b. Jan. 16, 1742; bap. April 15, 1742. Sponsors, Heinrich Klein and his wife.

FREDERICK OHNSELT, (Opequon.)
Ohnselt—John, b. Oct. 22, 1741; bap. Nov. 22, 1741. Sponsors, John Herr and Maria Elisabetha Haussahn.

BERNHARDT FRIEDEL, (Swatara.)
Friedel—Susanna, b. May 16, 1743; bap. May 23, 1743. Sponsors, Martin Speck and his wife.
—— Jacob, b. Apr. 15, 1745; bap. Oct. 26, 1745. Sponsors, Jacob Preschinger and his wife.
—— John Martin, b. June 25, 1747; bap. Aug. 16, 1747. Sponsors, Martin Kappler and his wife.
—— John Bernhardt, b. Dec. 27, 1749; bap. March 18, 1750. Sponsors, Martin Kappler and his wife.
—— Elisabetha, b. Dec. 20, 1757; bap March 23, 1758. Sponsors, Adam Brecht and wife.

JOHN GEORGE HAEDDERICH, (Lebanon.)
Haedderich—Rosina, b. Jan. 15, 1743; bap. March 27, 1743. Sponsors, Christoph Meyer and his wife Rosina.

DAVID DREHER, (Lebanon.)
Dreher—John Heinrich, b. March 29, 1743; bap. May 23, 1743. Sponsors, John Heinrich Marcket and wife.

—— Daniel, b. March 11, 1752; bap. April 12, 1752. Sponsors, Daniel Born and Margaretha Speck.
—— Maria Barbara, b. Dec. 26, 1755; bap. Jan. 25, 1756. Sponsors, Leonhardt Kneuget and his wife.

MICHAEL UMBERGER, (Lebanon.)
Umberger—John Leonhardt, b. Aug. 28, 1743; bap. Sept. 25, 1743. Sponsors, Leonhardt Ramler and wife.

HEINRICH MERCK, (Swatara.)
Merck—Maria Barbara, b. Sept. 9, 1743; bap. Sept. 25, 1743. Sponsors, Michael Lauer and his wife.

THOMAS KREUEL, (Swatara.)
Kreuel—John Adam, b. Sept. 9, 1743; bapt. Sept. 26, 1743. Sponsors, John Adam Kreuel and his wife.
—— Johannes, b. May 14, 1747; bap. June 21, 1747. Sponsors, Johannes Schmeltzer and his wife.
—— Anna Catarina, b. May 5, 1750; bapt. June 20, 1750. Sponsor, Anna Catarina Zimmer.
—— Ana Maria, b. 1752; bapt. Jan. 1, 1753. Sponsors, Christoph Zimmer and Ana Maria Meyer.

JOHN MICHAEL ERNST HOERNER, (South Branch.)
Hoerner—Dorothea, b. 1741; bap. Oct. 9, 1743. Sponsors, Johannes Haag and his wife.

DANIEL LUCAS, (Tulpehocken.)
Lucas—Maria Magdalena, b. Oct. 1, 1743; bap. Oct. 20, 1743. Sponsors, Daniel Schneider and Maria Magdalena Eschberger.
—— Adelheit Elisabetha, b. March 26, 1747; bap. April 12, 1747. Sponsors, Sebastian Brosius and Adelheit Elisabetha Stofenberger.
—— Maria Catarina, b. Aug. 21, 1749; bap. Sept. 17, 1749. Sponsors, Jacob Koehrer and Maria Elisabetha Brosius.
—— Daniel—b. June 24, 1753; bap. July 1, 1753. Sponsors, Daniel Schneider and wife Magdalena.
—— Philipp Adam, b. Augst 11, 1755; bap. August 24, 1755. Sponsors, Philipp Gerhardt and his wife.

JACOB RUEGER, (Lebanon.)
Rueger—John Jacob, b. August 18, 1743; bap. Oct. 23, 1743. Sponsors, Heinrich Klein and his wife.

PETER HAEDDERICH, (Lebanon.)
Haedderich—John George, b. Sept. 12, 1743; bap. Oct. 23, 1743. Sponsors, John George Huber and his wife.

SEBASTIAN KOHLMANN, (Cacoosing.)
Kohlmann—Catarina Barbara, b. April 9, 1743; bap. Oct. 31, 1743. Sponsors,

Casper Maessner and wife, and Anna Maria Burckel.

HANS ADAM MUELLER, (Swatara.)
Mueller—John Heinrich, b. Sept. 23,1743; bap. Nov. 15, 1743. Sponsors, Heinrich Weschenbach and his wife Elisabetha.

JOHN ADAM KREUEL, (Lebanon.)
Kreuel—Maria Margaretha, b. Oct. 17, 1743; bap. Nov. 15, 1743. Sponsors, Thomas Kreuel and his wife.

CHRISTIAN SCHMIDT, (Swatara.)
Schmidt—Christian, b. Nov. 27, 1743; bap. Nov. 20, 1743. Sponsors, Christian Mueller and Margar. Creutzberger.
—— George Heinrich, b. Dec. 27, 1744; bap. Jan. 20, 1745. Sponsors, Heinrich Bruender and wife Ana Catarina.

JACOB SEIBERT, (Tulpehocken.)
Seibert—John Heinrich, b. Nov. 30, 1743; bap Dec. 28, 1743. Sponsors, Heinrich Lorentz and his wife Anna Johanna.

MICHAEL REISS, (Tulpehocken.)
Reiss—Maria Catarina, b. Oct. 28, 1743; bap. Dec. 28, 1743. Sponsors, George Mueller and wife Maria Catarina.
—— Magdalena, b. in 1745; bap. Dec. 22, 1745. Sponsors, John Peter Anspach and his wife.
—— Johannes, b. Oct. 26, 1747; bap. Nov. 22, 1747. Sponsors, John Wolfart and wife Catarina Agatha.
—— Anna Maria, b. Oct. 8, 1749; bap. Dec. 10, 1749. Sponsors, Michael Nef, jr., and wife Anna Maria.
—— John Ludwig, b. August 16, 1752; bap. Oct. 22. 1752. Sponsors, Johannes Schaefer and second wife.
—— Maria Elisabetha, b. Jan. 28, 1757; bap. Feb. 6, 1757. Sponsors, John Schaefer and second wife.

HEINRICH JOHN PETER SCHMIDT, (Tulpehocken.)
Schmidt—John, b. Dec. 9, 1743; bap. Dec. 28, 1743. Sponsors, John Heinrich Schmidt and wife Gertraudt.
—— Elisabetha, b. Feb. 25, 1748; bap. March 6, 1748. Sponsor, Elisabetha Schmidt.

HEINRICH BICKEL, (Tulpehocken.)
Bickel—Jacob, b. May 28, 1743; bap. Dec. 20, 1743. Sponsors, William Leitner and his wife.
—— Christian. b. May 11, 1745; bap. May 14, 1745. Sponsors, Christian Schmidt and his wife.

WENDEL HEYL, (Swatara.)
Heyl—Margaretha, b. Dec. 19, 1743; bap. Feb. 2, 1744. Sponsors, Frederich Haehnle and his wife Margaretha.

—— Anna Barbara, b. Oct. 27, 1745; bap. Nov. 30, 1745. Sponsors, the above.
—— Elizabetha, b. Nov. 24, 1747; bap. Jan. 6, 1748. Sponsors, the above.
——Christina, b. Nov. 23, 1751; bap. Dec. 2, 1751. Sponsors, the above.
——Anna, b. Feb. 19, 1754; bap. March 24, 1754. Sponsors. Andreas Murr and Catarina Roenninger.
—— Johannes, b. March 26, 1756; bap. April 15, 1756. Sponsors, Andreas Murr and his wife.
—— Jacob, b. June 6, 1742. Sponsor, Jacob Dubbs.

GEORGE ZEH (Swatara.)
Zeh—Anna Maria, b. Dec. 20, 1743; bap. Feb. 2, 1744. Sponsors, Heinrich Dubbs and his wife.

JOHN GEORGE MOHR (Swatara.)
Mohr—John Frederich, b. Jan. 22, 1744; bap. Feb. 2, 1744. Sponsors, John Friederich Rathfang and his wife Maria Elisabetha.

VINCENS KUEFER, (Lebanon.)
Kuefer—Valentin, b. March 5, 1745; bap. March 31, 1745. Sponsors, Valentin Kuefer and his wife Barbara.

JOHN KISTLER (Tulpehocken.)
Kistler—Maria Magdalena, b. Jan. 14, 1744; bap. Feb. 17, 1744. Sponsors, Johannes Immel, Elisabetha Lehmann and Anna Maria Kintzel.

CUNRADT MUELLER (Moselem.)
Mueller—Anna Catarina, b. Sept. 29, 1741; bap. Feb. 24, 1744. Sponsors, Anna Frantzina.
—— John Peter, b. Dec. 26, 1743; bap. Feb. 24, 1744. Sponsor, John Peter Merckel.

PETER LEPPO (Tulpehocken.)
Leppo — Maria Magdelena, b. Feb 20, 1744; bap. March 10, 1744. Sponsors, Philipp Adam Schirmann and Maria Magdelena Leppo, single.
—— Christina, b. Sept. 24, 1746; bap. Oct. 26, 1746. Sponsors, Seidel Neuman and Margaretha Gaensemer.
—— Maria Susanna, b. June 13, 1751; bap. July 21, 1751. Sponsors, John Meyer and wife Anna Maria.

JACOB FEHLER (Tulpehocken.)
Fehler—Anna Margaretha, b. Feb. 13, 1744; bap. March 17, 1744. Sponsors, Jacob Loewengut and wife Margaretha, also George Anspach and his wife Anna Catarina.
—— John Nicolus, b. Feb. 21, 1746; bap. March 17, 1745. Sponsors, John Nicolaus Loefner and wife, also Peter Riedtin and wife Anna Catarina Riedtin.

—— John Jacob b. April 13, 1746; bap. June 8, 1746. Sponsors, John Jacob Hofman and his wife.

—— Anna Barbara, b. May 1, 1749; bap. May 28, 1749. Sponsor, Anna Barbara Loewengut.

—— Maria Eva, b. Jan. 25, 1751; bap. Feb. 2, 1751. Sponsors, George Emmert and wife.

—— Leonhardt, b. Sept. 20, 1752; bap. Oct. 22, 1752. Sponsors, Leonhardt Reidt and Anna Catarina Riedt.

—— Anna Maria, b. Aug. 22, 1754; bap. Sept. 22, 1754. Sponsors, Jacob Loewengut and wife Catarina.

—— John Peter, b. Feb. 27, 1756; bap. May 30, 1756. Sponsors, Peter Schmidt and his wife.

JACOB VOELCKER, (Tulpehocken). Voelcker—Daniel, b. Feb. 4, 1744; bap. March 17, 1744. Sponsors, Daniel Geismer and his wife.

JACOB REUTER, (Cocalico.) Reuter—Elisabetha, b. March 2, 1744; bap. March 12, 1744. Sponsors, Nicolas Dehm and wife Elisabetha.

JAMES WILLIAMS, (Swatara.) Williams—Elizabeth, b. Nov. 1, 1743; bap. March 21, 1744. Sponsors, John Blum and wife Elizabeth.

TOBIAS BICKEL, (Tulpehocken.) Bickel—Christian,b. March 22, 1764; bap. March 31, 1764. Sponsors, Jacob Schnellbecker and his wife.

—— Johannes, b. March 16, 1744; bap. March 18, 1744. Sponsors, Heinrich Baseler.

—— Maria Margaretha, b. March 22, 1746; bap. July 5, 1746. Sponsors, The above and wife (2d wife.)

—— Simon, b. Feb. 1750; bap. March 5, 1750. Sponsors, Heinrich Baseler and wife.

—— Anna Maria, b. April, 1751; bap. May 28, 1751. Sponsors, Simon Baseler and Anna Maria Moseler.

—— Thomas, b. Oct. 20, 1752; bap. Jan. 5, 1753. Sponsor, Simon Carl.

—— Rosina, b. March 13, 1755; bap. May 4, 1755. Sponsors, Thomas Kuppenhoefer and wife Elisabetha.

—— John Jacob, b. April 24, 1757; bap. July 5, 1757. Sponsors, John Jacob Moser and wife Regina.

ANDREAS FRIEDERICH, (Conestoga.) Friederich—Johannes, b. Feb. 3, 1744; bap. March 23, 1744. Sponsors, Johannes Uhrich and his wife.

WILHELM HEDDERICH, (Northkill.) Hedderich—Anna Elisabetha, b. Dec. 27,

1743; bap. April 1, 1744. Sponsors, Heinrich Greber and his wife.

LUDWIG THOMAS, (Northkill.) Thomas—Anna Magdalena, b. Jan. 5, 1744. Sponsors, Jost Hedderich and his wife.

JOHANNES PONTIUS, (Swatara.) Pontius—John Heinrich, b. Feb. 24, 1744; bap. April 1, 1744. Sponsors, John Heinrich Zoeller and his wife.

—— John Peter, b. Oct. 22, 1747; bap. Oct. 25, 1747. Sponsors, Peter Hoffman and his wife.

—— Johannes, b. Aug. 16, 1751; bap. Aug. 18, 1751. Sponsors, Johannes Schnaebel and his wife.

JOHN WILHELM LEITNER, (Tulpehocken.) Leitner—Ana Maria, b. March 28, 1744, bap. April 2, 1744. Sponsors, John Riegel and wife Catarina Elisabetha.

—— Juliana, b. Jan. 24, 1746, bap. Feb. 16, 1746. Sponsors, Nicolaus Kintzor and wife Juliana.

—— George Daniel, b. Nov. 3, 1747; bap. Nov. 22, 1747. Sponsors, George Daniel Schneider and Esther Ferry.

—— John Jacob, b. Oct. 20, 1750, bap. Nov. 11, 1750. Sponsors, Jacob Etschberger and wife.

——Catarina, b. April 14, 1752, bap. April 26, 1752. Sponsors, Philipp Adam Schirman and wife.

—— Simon, b. Nov. 5, 1738, bap. Nov. 10, 1738. Sponsors, Simon Schirman and his wife.

JOHANNES RIEGEL, (Tulpehocken.) Riegel—Maria Catarina, b.March 6, 1744, bap. April 2, 1744. Sponsors, John George Schirman and wife Elisabetha Catarina.

—— Philipp Adam, b. Feb. 14, 1746, bap. Feb. 16, 1746. Sponsors, Philipp Adam Schirman and Maria Kanter.

—— Johannes, b. March 11, 1751, bap. March 31, 1751. Sponsors, John Klausser and his wife Barbara.

ABRAHAM WILLIAMS, (Swatara.) Williams—Margaretha, b. March 14, 1744, bap. April 15, 1744. Sponsors, John Tittle and wife Elisabetha.

——Abraham, b. March, 1748, bap. April 17, 1748. Sponsors, James Williams and wife.

NICOLAUS HAEFFNER, (Tulpehocken.) Haeffner—John Jacob, b. Aug. 7, 1744, bap. Aug. 19, 1744. Sponsors, John Jacob Seibert and wife.

—— Maria Johanna, b. May 29, 1747; bap. June 7, 1747. Sponsors, Heinrich Lorentz and his wife.

—— Maria Catarina, b. June 7, 1750; bap. June 24, 1750. Sponsors, Christian Lauer and wife.

GEORGE VEIT KAPP, (Swatara.)
Kapp—Margaretha, b. March 24, 1744; bap. April 15, 1744. Sponsors, George Frederich and his wife.

—— Anna Catarina, b. April 17, 1746; bap. April 27, 1746. Sponsors, Philipp Maurer and his wife.

—— Maria Magdalena, b. July 20, 1747; bap. Aug. 2, 1747. Sponsors, Frederich Haehnle and wife Margaretha.

—— Eva, b. April 18, 1749; bap. May 1, 1749. Sponsors, Peter Beettel and wife Eva.

—— Margaretha Elisabetha, b. July 16, 1751; bap. July 21, 1751. Sponsors, Frederich Haehnle and his wife.

—— Anna Barbara, b. Nov. 6. 1753; bap. Dec. 2, 1753. Sponsors, Peter Heckman and his wife.

MICHAEL KATZ, (Swatara.)
Katz—Ludwig Heinrich, b. April 4, 1744; bap. April 15, 1744. Sponsors, Ludwig Heinrich Schui and Cat. Elis. Goldman.

MARTIN SPECK, (Swatara.)
Speck—Anna Maria, b. Jan. 15, 1741; bap. April 16, 1742. Sponsors, Siegesmund Haehnle and his wife and Anna Maria Becker.

—— Martin, b. March 23, 1744; bap. April 15, 1744. Sponsors, Frederick Haehnle and his wife.

—— Speck, Eleanora, b. March 30, 1746; bap. April 27, 1746. Sponsors, Bernhardt Friedle and his wife.

—— John Michael, b. Dec. 29, 1750; bap. Jan. 21, 1751. Sponsors, Michael Kleber and wife Elizabetha.

—— John Jacob, b. April 29, 1753; bap. May 20, 1753. Sponsors, Michael Kleber and Elisabetha.

FREDERICH RATHFANG, (Swatara.)
Rathfang—Anna Margaretha, b. March 7. 1744; bap. April 15, 1744. Sponsors, Wilhelm Huber and wife.

CHRISTOPH UHRICH, (Tulpehocken.)
Uhrich—Maria Catarina, b. Jan. 29,1739; bap. Feb. 24, 1739. Sponsors, Valentin Unruh and wife.

—— Maria Appollonia, b. March 21, 1740; bap. March 30, 1740. Sponsors, Jacob Vollmer, sr. and wife.

GEORGE DANIEL GAENSEMER, (Tulpehocken.)
Gaensemer—Johannes, b. July 27, 1744; bap. Aug. 19, 1744. Sponsors, Johannes Knoll and his wife.

—— Catarina Barbara, b. Dec. 18,1746; Sponsors, John Heinrich Deck and Anna Barbara Teuber.

STEPHEN CUNRADT, (Swatara.)
Cunradt—John George, b. March 21, 1744; bap. April 29, 1744. Sponsors, Lorentz Hautz.

—— John Peter, b. July 27, 1745; bap. Sept. 1, 1745. Sponsors, George Peter Batdorf and Eva Elisabetha Ried.

—— Anna Elizabetha, b. Feb. 13, 1747; bap. March 15, 1747. Sponsors, Eva Elizabeth Ried.

—— John Stephen, b. Feb. 26, 1749; bap. March 5, 1749. Sponsors, John Jacob Loewengut.

—— Anna Margaretha, b. Feb. 2, 1751, b. March 3, 1751. Sponsors, George Lechner and wife.

—— George Philipp, b. Nov. 21, 1752, bap. Dec. 17, 1752. Sponsors, George Lechner and Anna Margar Lay.

—— John Nicolaus, b. Jan. 16, 1755, bap. Jan. 20, 1755. Sponsors, John Nicolaus Gebhardt and wife.

PHILIPP MAURER, (Swatara.)
Maurer—Catarina Margaretha, b. May 30, 1744, bap. June 10, 1744. Sponsors, Leonhardt Ramler and wife.

—— John Philipp, b. Nov. 15, 1746, bap. Nov. 23, 1746. Sponsors, John Veith Kapp and his wife.

—— John Jacob, b. June 9, 1748. bap. July 10, 1748. Sponsors, John Jacob Ramler and wife Margaretha.

—— Eva Margaretha, b. Oct. 30, 1749, bap. Nov. 20, 1749. Sponsors, Jacob Ramler and wife.

—— John George, b. April 23, 1751, bap. May 26, 1751. Sponsors, George Schaefer and wife.

—— Maria Elisabetha. b. July 25,1754; bap. Aug. 11, 1754. Sponsors, George Schumacher and wife Maria Eva.

—— George Michael. b. Jan. 13, 1756, bap. Jan. 25, 1756. Sponsors, the above.

JACOB SCHOPFF, (Northkill.)
Schopff—Maria Catarina, b. May 14, 1744, bap. June 24, 1744. Sponsors, Simon Schirmann and wife.

—— Anna Maria, b. May 30, 1748, bap. June 26, 1748. Sponsors, John Schopff and Anna Maria Hubele.

—— Frantz, b. July 7. 1750; bap. Aug. 19, 1750. Sponsors, John Frantz Leyenberger and wife.

JOHN ADOLPH HEINRICH, (Northkill.)
Heinrich—Anna Maria, b. Aug. 21, 1740; bap. Sept. 14, 1740. Sponsors, John Nicolaus Holder and wife.

—— Anna Elizabetha, b. July 24, 1740; bap. Aug. 19, 1744. Sponsors, Tobias Bickel and wife.

LEONHARDT ELLMECKER,
(Earltown.)
Ellmecker—Anna Margaretha, b. July 23, 1744; bap. Aug. 26, 1744. Sponsor, Hanna Boeszhaar.

BALTHASAR BOESZHAAR,
(Earltown.)
Boeszhaar—Elizabetha, b. July 22, 1744; bap. Aug. 26, 1744. Sponsors, Jacob Koppenhoefer and wife Elizabeth.

—— Juliana, b. 1746; bap. May 19, 1746. Sponsors, George Boeszhaar and wife.

JOHANNES HEDDERICH,
(Cacoosing.)
Hedderich—John Wirner, b. July 7, 1744; bap. Aug. 26, 1744. Sponsor, Wirner Weitzel.

GEORGE SCHIRMANN,
(Tulpehocken.)
Schirmann—Anna Maria, b. Oct. 3, 1744; bap. Oct. 14, 1744. Sponsors, Philip Adam Schirmann and Adelheit Pfaffenberger.

—— John Simon, b. Oct. 19, 1746; bap. Oct. 26, 1746. Sponsors, John Riegel and his wife.

JOHN JACOB VOLLMAR, Jr.,
(Tulpehocken.)
Vollmar—John Michael, b. Sept. 29, 1744; bap. Oct. 14, 1744. Sponsors, John Michael Vollmar and Barbara Karcher.

BERNHARDT RAUCH, (Northkill.)
Rauch—Elizabetha, b. Sept. 22, 1744; bap. Oct. 14, 1744. Sponsors, Abraham Huber and Elizabetha Albert.

—— Anna Margaretha, b. Oct. 7, 1746; bap. Oct. 26, 1746. Sponsors, Friederich Opp and wife.

—— Sabina, b. March, 1751; bap. April 15, 1751. Sponsors, Heinrich Sauter and wife Sabina.

JACOB DEGEN, (Swatara.)
Degen—Anna Regina, b. Sept. 22, 1744; bap. Oct. 12, 1744. Sponsors, Christian Battorf and Anna Regina Carstnitz.

JACOB HOFFMAN, (Tulpehocken.)
Hoffman—Eva Catarina, b. Nov.8, 1744; bap. Nov. 12, 1744. Sponsors, Christian Meyer and wife Catarina.

—— Anna Maria, b. Oct. 1, 1746; bap. Oct. 26, 1746. Sponsors, Hans Adam Heylmann and wife.

—— Juliana, b. Nov. 8, 1749; bap. Dec. 10, 1749. Sponsors, Christian Meyer and his wife.

—— Elizabetha, b. April 17, 1753; bap. April 20, 1753. Sponsors, Michael Wolfart and wife Elizabetha.

—— John Christian, b. March 6, 1755; bap. March 7, 1755. Sponsors, Christian Bechtel and wife Margaretha.

JOHN WOLFFERT, (Tulpehocken.)
Wolffert—John George Philip, b. Oct. 7, 1744; bap. Nov. 11, 1744. Sponsors, John George Brosius and wife Catarina.

VALENTINE KUEFFER,
(Tulpehocken.)
Kueffer—Ana Margaretha, b. Oct. 27, 1744; bap. Nov. 10, 1744. Sponsors, Vincens Kuefer and wife Ana Margaretha.

—— Elizabetha, b. March 17, 1747; bap. March 29, 1747. Sponsors, George Velty and wife.

—— Maria Barbara, b. Feb. 18, 1749; bap. March 3, 1749. Sponsors, Peter Heylmann and wife Sabine.

FRANTZ SEIBERT, (Swatara.)
Seibert—Margaretha, b. Oct. 12, 1744; bap. Nov. 25, 1744. Sponsors, Philip Schnatterle and wife.

OTTMAR SCHNAEBELE, (Swatara.)
Schnaebele—Maria Barbara, b. Oct. 17, 1744; bap. Nov. 25, 1744. Sponsors, Casper Schnaebele and wife Barbara.

PHILIP HOLINGER, (Lebanon.)
Holinger—Maria Barbara, b. Nov. 2, 1744; bap. Nov. 30, 1744. Sponsors, Leonardt Umberger and wife.

ADAM BACH, (Cacoosing.)
Bach—Anna Catarina, b. Nov. 12, 1744; bap. Dec. 3, 1744. Sponsors, George Jacob Schirmer and wife.

—— Anna Maria, b. Feb. 5, 1765; bap. April 14, 1765. Sponsors, George Ellinger and his wife.

MICHAEL GROSZMAN, (Warwick.)
Groszman—Maria Barbara, b. Sept. 11, 1742; bap. Oct. 16, 1742. Sponsors, Peter Tussing and wife Maria Barbara.

——Sophia, b. Nov. 18, 1744; bap. Dec. 4, 1744. Sponsors, Michael Baettly and Sophia Berin.

——Maria Barbara, b. Sept. 5, 1746; bap. Nov. 9, 1746. Sponsors, Casper Schnaebele and wife.

—— John Michael, b. Jan. 22, 1748; bap. Sept. 4, 1748. Sponsors, Casper Schnaebele and wife.

—— John Nicolaus, b. Feb. 5,1751; bap. March 4, 1751. Sponsors, John Nickel Jost and wife.

ABRAHAM HAASZ, (Northkill.)
Haasz—Maria Susanna, b. Sept. 28,

1744; bap. Nov. 9, 1744. Sponsors, Samuel Philbert and wife.

—— Maria Magdalena, b. March 7, 1753; bap. April 8, 1753. Sponsors, John Nicalaus Haag and Maria Mag. Aulenbach.

ADAM SCHAUER, (Northkill.)
Schauer—Catarina Elizabetha, b. Dec. 23, 1744; bap. Dec. 25, 1744. Sponsors, Michael Schauer and his wife.

PHILIP STRAUSS, (Northkill.)
Strauss—Anna Magdalena, b. Dec. 21, 1744; bap. Dec. 26, 1744. Sponsors, John Ebert and Ana Magdalena Reimer.

CASPER PHILIPPE.
Phillippe—John Heinrich, b. Oct. 16, 1746; bap. Oct. 26, 1746. Sponsors, John Heinrich Adolph and wife.

ANTONIUS HEMPERLE, (Lebanon.)
Hemperle—Anna Maria, b. Dec.15, 1744; bap. Jan. 6, 1745. Sponsors, John Bindnagle and wife.

—— Martin, b. 1747; bap. June 21, 1747. Sponsors, the above.

MICHAEL SPENGLER, (Tulpehocken.)
Spengler—John Michael, b. Sept. 15, 1744; bap. Oct. 28, 1744. Sponsors, John Nicholaus Lauer and Maria Catarina Moser.

GEORGE FRIEDERICH, (Swatara.)
Friederich—Margaretha, b. Dec. 21, 1744; bap. Jan. 15, 1745. Sponsors, Freiderich Haehnle and wife.

HEINRICH KICHLER,(Tulpehocken.)
Kichler—Juliana b. Jan. 3, 1745; bap. Jan. 20, 1745. Sponsors, Jacob Bortner and Juliana Audre.

PHILIPP GEBHARDT, (Tulpehocken.)
Gebhardt—John Heinrich, b. Jan. 8, 1745; bap. Jan. 20, 1745. Sponsors, Heinrich Beyer and wife Maria Elisabetha.

—— Peter, b. Dec. 22, 1746; bap. Jan. 19, 1747. Sponsors, Peter Gebhardt and wife Catarina.

—— Maria Eva, b. Nov. 3, 1748; bap. Nov. 13, 1748. Sponsor, Maria Eva Wolf.

—— John Philipp, b. Jan. 20, 1750; bap. Feb. 2, 1750. Sponsors, Johannes Ritscher and wife.

—— Valentine, b. Nov. 7, 1751; bap. Nov. 10, 1751. Sponsors, Johannes Meyer and wife.

MATTHEIS ALBRECHT, (Warwick.)
Albrecht—Eva Christina, b. Dec. 25, 1744; bap. Jan. 27, 1745. Sponsors, Martin Kapp and wife.

DANIEL RIEGEL.
Riegel—Johannes, b. Dec. 2, 1746; bap. Jan. 18, 1747. Sponsors, George Michael Wildfang and wife.

JOHN NICOLAUS ENSZMINGER, (Cocalico.)
Enszminger—John Heinrich, b. Jan. 29, 1745; bap. Jan. 30, 1745. Sponsors, John Heinrich Enszminger and wife Christina.

JACOB ZIEGER, (Lebanon.)
Zieger—Anna Maria, b. Dec. 3, 1744; bap. March 3, 1745. Sponsors, Jacob Schober and Anna Barbara Unler.

—— (Twins), b. Jan. 13, 1765. George Heinrich and Anna Maria Elisabeth; bap. Jan. 25, 1765. Sponsors, George Heinrich Reinoehl and wife, Christoph Meyer and wife Catarina.

JACOB HOLTZINGER, (Cocalico.)
Holtzinger—John, b. Feb. 12, 1745; bap. March 10, 1745. Sponsors, John Ulrich and wife Margaretha.

ALBRECHT STRAUSS, (Northkill.)
Strauss—Maria Barbara, b. Nov. 16, 1735; bap. Jan. 11, 1736. Sponsors, George Graf, Jr. and Maria Barbara Zerv.

—— John Jacob, b. May 5, 1737; bap. May 19, 1737. Sponsors, John Jacob Zerbe and wife.

—— Maria Elisabeth, b. May 5, 1737; bap. May 19, 1737. Sponsor, Heinrich Beyer.

—— Anna Elisabetha, b. March 25, 1739; bap. April 22, 1739. Sponsors, Martin Zerbe and wife.

—— Maria Eva Rosina, b. Nov. 6, 1742; bap. Nov. 28, 1742. Sponsors, Heinrich Gruber and wife.

—— Maria Catarina, b. March 6, 1745; bap. March 17, 1745. Sponsors, Andreas Kraft and his wife.

—— John Philipp, b. Jan. 4, 1748; bap. Feb. 7, 1748. Sponsors, Philipp Meeth and wife.

—— Maria Christina, b. July 26, 1751; bap. August 18, 1751. Sponsors, Peter Muench and wife.

—— Maria Susanna, b. Oct. 5, 1753; bap. Oct. 21, 1753. Sponsors, Andreas Shade and Maria Susanna Haag.

—— John Samuel, b. May 13, 1756; bap. May 30, 1756. Sponsors, Samuel Philbert and wife.

DAVID RIEHL, (Heidelberg.)
Riehl—John Adam, b. August 12, 1751; bap. August 18, 1751. Sponsors, Jacob Sensebach and wife.

GEORGE BRENDEL, (Moden Creek.)
Brendel—Eva Catarina, b. Feb. 25, 1745;

bap. March 24, 1745. Sponsors, George Hoeger and his wife.

JOHN JACOB ZERWE,(Tulpehocken.)
Zerwe—Anna Christina, b.Dec. 25, 1736; bap. Jan. 2, 1737. Sponsors, George Peter Zerwe and wife.
—— John Michael, b. April 20, 1738; bap. April 30, 1738. Sponsors, John Michael Busch and wife.
—— John Valentin, b. June 24, 17±1; ban. July 6, 1741. Sponsor, Engelhard Flory.

JOHN HEINRICH ZELLER, JR.,
Tailor,
(Tulpehocken.)
Zeller—John Heinrich, b. March 5, 1745; bap. March 26, 1745. Sponsors, John Heinrich Zeller, Sr. and wife.

SEBASTIAN HUBER, (Tulpehocken.)
Huber—John Wilhelm, b. Jan. 26, 1745; bap. July 7, 1745. Sponsors, John Wilhelm Kayser and Juliana Andre.

JOHN KITZMUELLER.
Kitzmueller—John Leonhardt, b. Feb. 13, 1745; bap. March 26, 1745. Sponsors, Leonhardt Ramler and wife Margaretha.

JOHANNES LANG, (Northkill.)
Lang—Johannes, b. Aug. 21, 1737; bap. Feb. 5, 1737. Sponsors, Johannes Schaefer and wife Susanna.
—— Anna Margaretha, b.Feb. 21, 1740; bap. March 30, 1740. Sponsors, Ludwig Wagner and wife.
—— Jacob, b. Jan. 12, 1742; bap. Jan. 24, 1742. Sponsors, Jacob Schopf and wife.
—— John George Thomas, b. July 1, 1746; bap. July 6, 146. Sponsors, Thomas Kern and wife Margaretha.

PETER TUSZING, (Cocalico.)
Tuszing—John Philip, b.March 16, 1745; bap. April 7, 1745. Sponsors, Philipp Schaefer and wife Christina.

CHRISTIAN ZWEYSICH, (Northkill.)
Zweysich—John Cunradt, b. March 29, 1747; bap. April 12, 1747. Sponsors, Cunradt Long and wife.
—— Maria Christina, b. March 23, 1749; bap. April 2, 1749. Sponsors, Nicolaus Long and Maria Christina Mueller.
—— John George, b. 1751; bap. March 29, 1752. Sponsors, George Christ and wife.

GEORGE FAUST, (Northkill.)
Faust—A daughter b. April 12, 1747, bap. May 10, 1747. Sponsors, Philipp Faust and wife.
——Magdalena Elizabetha, b. in Sep.,

1749, bap. Oct. 15, 1749. Sponsors, Caspar Hedderich's wife.
——John George, b. Nov. 22, 1757, bap. Dec. 8, 1757. Sponsors, John George Haag and Catarina Muench.

TOBIAS DITTES, (Tulpehocken.)
Dittes—Jacobina, b. April 13, 1745, bap. April 13, 1745. Sponsors, Christian Meyer and wife Catarina.

MATTHEIS DORNBACH,
(Northkill.)
Dornbach—Anna Margaretha, b. Dec.22, 1747, bap. March 6. 1748. Sponsors, Herman Rorber and Anna Margaretha Schneider.
——Maria Elizabetha, b. May 16, 1750, bap. June 24, 1750. Sponsors, Michael Roomer and wife.
——John Wilhelm, b. Sep. 18, 1752, bap. Oct. 22, 1752. Sponsors, John Wilhelm Neumeister and wife.

PETER GEBHARDT,
(Tulpehocken.)
Gebhardt—John George, b. April 14, 1745, bap. April 14, 1745. Sponsors, Philipp Gebhardt. also John George Schirman and wife.
——Anna Maria, b. Oct. 25, 1747, bap. Nov. 22, 1747. Sponsors, John Heinrich Deck and Catarina Elizabetha Fischer.
——Juliana, b. Nov. 4, 1748, bap. Nov. 13, 1748. Sponsors, Nicolaus Kintzer and wife Juliana.
—— John Nicolaus, b. May 30, 1751, bap. June 23, 1751. Sponsors, John Nickel Kintzer and wife Juliana.
—— Elizabetha, b. Jan. 20, 1755, bap Jan. 26, 1755. Sponsors, Johannes Gebhardt and Elizabetha Terrin.

JOHN ZERWE AND WIFE
CATARINA, (Tulpehocken.)
Zerwe—Maria Catarina, b. April 8, 1745, bap. April 14. 1745. Sponsors, Jacob Zerwe and wife.
—— Johannes, b. March 23, 1748, bap. April 3, 1748. Sponsors, John Oberle and Catarina Heck.
—— Christian. b. Dec. 25, 1750. bap. Feb. 3, 1751. Sponsors, Christian Gruber and wife.
—— Anna Elizabetha, b. Oct., 1753; bap. Oct. 21, 1753. Sponsors, (?).
—— Anna Christina, b. Feb. 10, 1756; bap. March 7, 1756. Sponsors, Martin Stuep and wife Christina.
—— Catarina Elizabetha, b. Jan. 6, 1759; bap. Feb. 4, 1759. Sponsors, John George Ried and wife.
—— Maria Margaretha, b. May 6,1761; bap. May 24, 1761. Sponsors, Albrecht Strauss and wife.

GEORGE CASPER RASCH,
(Lebanon.)
Rasch—Elizabetha b. Jan. 29, 1745; bap. May 1, 1745. Sponsor, Catarina Ort.
—— Anna Magdalena, b. Jan. 4, 1747; bap. March 29, 1747. Sponsor, Anna Maria Ergebrecht.
—— Johannes, b. July 27, 1757; bap. Sept. 25, 1757. Sponsors, John Eberhard Kress and Barbara Stuck.
—— Anna Barbara, b. May 23, 1760; bap. June 15, 1760. Sponsors, Peter Shaaf and wife.

PHILIPP HEILIGER, (Northkill.)
Heiliger—Christina Barbara, b. Feb. 8, 1748; bap. March 6, 1748. Sponsors, Peter Muench and Christina Barbara.

JOHANNES MUELLER,
(Tulpehocken.)
Mueller—John Melchior, b. 1745; bap. May 12, 1745. Sponsors, Melchior Taefer and Margaretha Bleystein.
—— Maria Agatha, b. June 2, 1748; bap. June 26, 1748. Sponsors, John Roolfert and wife Maria Agatha.

PHILIPP PETRY, (Northkill.)
Petry—Anna Catarina, b. April 27, 1745; bap. May 12, 1745. Sponsors, Heinrich Adolph and wife.

JACOB REUTER, (Moden Creek.)
Reuter—Magdalena, b. May 22, 1745; bap. June 3, 1745. Sponsors, Balthasar Rathgeber and wife.

CASPER ECKERT, (Moden Creek.)
Eckert—Eva Maria, b. April 25, 1745; bap. June 3, 1745. Sponsors, George Ruhlmann and Eva Maria Scheidt.

JACOB SCHUPP, (Tulpehocken.)
Schupp—John Martin, b. March 31, 1745; bap. June 9, 1745. Sponsors, Martin Stuep and wife Susanna.

JOHN GEORGE PFAFFENBERGER
(Tulpehocken.)
Pfaffenberger—John George, b. May 29, 1745; bap. June 9, 1745. Sponsors, John George Schirman and wife.

WILLIAM GALLY, (Tulpehocken.)
Gally—Catarina Barbara, b. May 26, 1745; bap. June 9, 1745. Sponsors, Melchior Taefeler and Catarina Barbara Dollmar.

HEINRICH BEYER, (Tulpehocken.)
Beyer—Anna Catarina, b. July 25, 1745; bap. Aug. 4, 1745. Sponsors, George Gaertner and his wife.
—— Anna Magdalena, b. July 16, 1747; bap. Aug. 2, 1747. Sponsors, Leonhardt Ramler and wife Anna Margaretha.
—— Johannes, b. Feb. 4, 1749; bap.

Feb. 6, 1749. Sponsors, Johannes Meyer and wife.
—— Maria Salome, b. Nov. 2, 1754; bap. Nov. 10, 1754. Sponsors, John Meyer and wife Anna Maria.
—— John Jacob, b. Dec. 12, 1756; bap. Jan. 8, 1757. Sponsors, George Gaertner and his wife.

MARTIN BRAUN, (Conestoga.)
Braun—Catarina Barbara, b. Aug. 1, 1745; bap. Aug. 11, 1745. Sponsors, Thomas Lauer and wife.

GEORGE HATZ, (Lebanon.)
Hatz—Elizabetha Barbara, b. July 2, 1745; bap. Aug. 18, 1745. Sponsors, John Adam Hambrecht and wife.

NICOLAUS ELI, (Tulpehocken.)
Eli—Maria Catarina, b. Aug. 14, 1745; bap. Sept. 1, 1745. Sponsors, John Meyer and wife.
—— Christian, b. March 2, 1748; bap. March 6, 1748. Sponsors, Christian Meyer and wife.

JOHN ADAM SONNTAG,
(Tulpehocken.)
Sonntag—Maria Catarina, b. Aug. 11, 1745; bap. Sept. 1, 1745. Sponsors, Nicolaus Mueller and wife.

MICHAEL SPIEGEL, (Swatara.)
Spiegel—Gottfried, b. Oct. 16, 1745; bap. Oct. 26, 1745. Sponsors, Michael Bauer and wife.
—— Eva Christina, b. Sept. 19, 1747; bap. Oct. 11, 1747. Sponsors, Michael Bauer and Joseph Heller's wife.

ADAM FABER, (Swatara.)
Faber—Barbara, b. Sept. 29, 1745; bap. Oct. 26, 1745. Sponsors, Philip Schnatterle and his wife.
—— Philipp, b. Feb. 18, 1747; bap. March 29, 1747. Sponsors, the above.
—— Johannes, b. Feb. 7, 1750; bap. March 18, 1750. Sponsors, Bernhardt Faber and his wife.

JOHN GEORGE SPAREN,
(Earl Town.)
Sparen—Philipp Adam, b. Oct. 6, 1745; b. Nov. 3, 1745. Sponsors, Philipp Adam Diller and wife.

MARTIN KAPPLER, (Swatara.)
Kappler—Susanna, b. Oct. 22, 1745; bap. Nov. 30, 1745. Sponsors, Bernhardt Friedle and wife Dorothea.
—— Christina Magdalena, b. April 5, 1735; bap. June 17, 1753. Sponsors, Philipp Jacob and Magdalena Roof.

PETER EISENHAUER, (Swatara.)
Eisenhauer—Petrus, b. Sept. 6, 1745; bap. Oct. 13, 1745. Sponsors, Valentine Kuefer and wife.

—— Maria Barbara, b. Aug. 22, 1747; bap. Jan. 6, 1748. Sponsors, Michael Bauer and Maria Barbara Graefin.

—— John Nicolaus, b. May 6, 1749; bap. May 14, 1749. Sponsors, John Nicolaus Eisenhauer and wife.

—— George Michael, b. Aug. 4, 1751; bap. Sept. 1, 1751. Sponsors, Michael Graf and Magdalena Eisenhauer.

—— John Frederich, b. Oct. 6, 1753; bap. Oct. 7, 1753. Sponsors, John Nicolaus Eisenhauer and wife.

—— Maria Magdalena, b. March 7, 1756; bap. March 21, 1756. Sponsors. John Lohmueller and Maria Magdal. Eisenhauer.

—— Anna Maria Elisabetha, b. April 25, 1759; bap. June 10, 1759. Sponsors, ——

—— Samuel, b. Nov. 25, 1763; bap. Sept. 6, 1764? Sponsors, Michael Graf and his wife.

—— John Jacob, b. April 13, 1777; bap. Aug. 24, 1777. Sponsors, John Jacob Neff and wife.

GEORGE SCHIFLER, (Tulpehocken.)
Schifler—John George, b. Nov. 30, 1745; bap. June 8, 1746. Sponsors, John George Unruh and wife.

HANS GEORGE ZIEGLER.
(Tulpehocken.)
Ziegler—Anna Barbara, b. Nov. 24, 1745; bap. June 8, 1746. Sponsors, Hans George Unruh and his wife.

GEORGE ANDREAS ZIEGLER,
(Lebanon.)
Ziegler—John Thomas, b. Dec. 15, 1745; bap. Feb. 2, 1746. Sponsors, John Thomas Madern and his wife.

JOHANN CASPER STOEVER,
(Lebanon.)
Stoever—Maria Catarina, . May 6, 1734; bap. May 12, 1734. Sponsors, John Jacob Kitzmueller and wife Anna Maria, also Ludwig Stein and wife Maria Catarina.

—— John Caspar, b. March 10, 1736; bap. March 14, 1736. Sponsors. Michael Beyerle and wife, also Peter Ensminger and wife.

—— Anna Margaretha, b. Aug. 21, 1738; bap. Sept. 10, 1738. Sponsors, George Klein and wife Anna, Martin Weidtmann and wife Margaretha.

—— Anna Christina, b. Nov. 24, 1740; bap. Dec. 2, 1740. Sponsors, Michael Oberle and wife Christina Barbara and Anna Frantzina Merckling.

—— Sophia Magdalena, b. April 26, 1743; bap. May 12, 1743. Sponsors, Adam Lesch and wife Sophia, also Peter Anspach and wife Magdalena.

—— Anna Maria, b. Jan. 27, 1746; bap. Feb. 2, 1746. Sponsors, John Jacob Kitzmueller and wife Anna Maria, also Friederich Kraemer and wife Anna Maria.

—— John Adam, b. June 18, 1748; bap. July 19, 1748. Sponsors, Johannes Bischoff and wife and Adam Simon Kuhn and wife.

—— Tobias, b. Feb. 11, 1751; bap. Feb. 17, 1751. Sponsors, Tobias Werner Ev. Luth. minister and his wife, also Elisabetha Templemann.

—— Johannes, b. July 5, 1753; ap. July 15, 1753. Sponsors, Johannes Schwab and wife Eva Margaretha.

—— John Frederich, b. Dec. 16, 1755; bap. Dec. 18, 1755. Sponsors, Johann George Sprecher and wife Eva Margaretha, also Freiderich Kraemer and wife (absent).

—— John Frederich, b. Sept. 20, 1759; bap. Sept. 30, 1759. Sponsors, Christoph Freiderich Wegman and wife Anna Maria.

JOHN GEORGE WEBER,
(Tulpehocken.)
Weber—John Adam, b. Jan. 14, 1746; bap. Feb. 16, 1746. Sponsors, John Adam Weber and Barbara Jaeger.

BALTHASAR RIEM, (Tulpehocken.)
Riem—Johannes, b. Feb. 10, 1746; bap. Feb. 16, 1746. Sponsors, Johannes Riem and Maria Canter.

—— Maria Appollonia, b. May 28, 1748; bap. Nov. 11, 1748. Sponsor, Appollonia Mueller.

JACOB KINTZEL, (Tulpehocken.)
Kintzel—Elizabetha, b. Dec. 8, 1745; bap. Feb. 17, 1746. Sponsors, Anna Elisabetha Lehman and Sara Heckerdorn.

—— Johannes, b. June 24, 1748; bap. June 26, 1748. Sponsors, John Philipp Schneider and wife.

JOHN PHILIPP SCHNEIDER
(Tulpehocken.)
Schneider—John Abraham, b. Feb. 17, 1746; bap. Feb. 17, 1746. Sponsors, Jacob Fischer and wife Maria Elisabetha, also Heinrich Beyer and wife.

—— Johannes, b. June 12, 1748; bap. June 26, 1748. Sponsors, Johannes Ramler and Maria Elisab. Brenner.

JOHN NICOLAUS GEBHARDT,
(Swatara.)
Gebhardt—John Jacob, b. Dec. 25, 1745; bap. Feb. 26, 1746. Sponsors, John Jacob Kitzmueller and wife Anna Maria   .

—— John Phillip, b. June 27, 1748; bap.

July 10, 1748. Sponsors, Philipp Hautz and his wife.
—— Anna Catarina, b. Dec. 16, 1750; bap. Jan. 6, 1751. Sponsors, Sebastian Stein and wife Anna Catarina.
—— Anna Barbara ,b. July 12, 1753; bap. July 29, 1753. Sponsors, Philipp Gerhart and his wife.
—— Johannes, b. Jan. 6, 1756, bap. Jan. 11, 1756. Sponsors,Johannes Gebhart and —— Korr.

JACOB WUEST, (Moden Creek.)
Wuest—Barbara, b. Jan. 19, 1746, bap. March 9, 1746. Sponsors, Christian Krebs and Eva Franckhauser.
—— Eva Margaretha, b. Sept. 1, 1749, bap. Oct. 8, 1749. Sponsors Peter Franckhauser and wife Eva.

JOHANNES CLAUSSER, (Tulpehocken.)
Clausser—Simon. b. Feb. 24, 1746, bap. March 16, 1746. Sponsors, Simon Schirman and his wife.
—— Philipp Adam. b. March 10, 1748, bap. March 29, 1748. Sponsors, Philipp Adam Schirman and wife.

JACOB DONNTHEUER, (Tulpehocken.)
Donntheuer—John Christian, b. Feb. 15, 1746, bap. March 16, 1746. Sponsors, Christian Ohrendorf and Maria Margaret Schaeffer.
—— Susanna, b. June 25, 1747, bap. Aug. 2, 1747. Sponsors, Martin Stuep and wife Susanna.

PHILIPP SCHAEFER, (Cocalico.)
Schaeffer—John Philipp, b. Feb. 8, 1746, bap. March 23, 1746. Sponsors, Stephen Boeringer and wife.

STEPHEN BOERINGER, (Warwick.)
Boeringer—John Philipp, b. Feb. 22, 1746, bap. March 23, 1746. Sponsors, John Philipp Schaefer and wife.

ANDREW KOCHDORFER, (Swatara.)
Kochdorfer—Geo. Philipp, b. April 8, 1746, bap. May 8, 1746. Sponsors, Geo. Philip Ruhl and Anna Margaret Roth.
—— John Christoph, b. Aug. 11, 1750; bap. Sept. 16, 1750. Sponsor, Christoph Kaysser.

NICOLAUS COERPER, (Moden Creek.)
Coerper—John Andreas, b. April 27, 1746, bap. May 4,1746. Sponsors, John Andreas Gansert and wife, and also Andreas Coerper and Catarina Kuenig.

MICHAEL KISSINGER, (Moden Creek.)
Kissinger—Anna Maria, b. Feb. 3, 1746,

bap. May 4, 1746. Sponsors, Jacob Worst and Ana Maria Ulrich.

HEINRICH ENSMINGER, (Cocalico.)
Ensminger—Anna Catarina. Sponsors, George Wirnss and Ana Catarina Ensminger.

PHILIPP ADAM DILLER, (Earl Town.)
Diller—Philipp Adam, b. May 16, 1746; bap. May 19, 1746. Sponsors, John George Sparen and wife.
—— Eva Barbara, b. March 3, 1748; bap. March 14, 1748. Sponsors, Michael Diebentorffer and wife.

ABRAHAM KERN, (Moden Creek.)
Kern—Anna Catarina, b. April 14, 1746; bap. May 19, 1746. Sponsors, Andreas Gansert and wife Margaretha.

JOHN MEETH, (Bern Township.)
Meeth—Johanna Maria, b. Dec. 13, 1743; bap. Dec. 25, 1745. Sponsors, Philipp Meeth and wife.

JOHN JACOB SOERER, (Atolhoe.)
Soerer—Johannes, b. March 7, 1746; bap. June 8, 1746. Sponsors, John Thonteur and wife.
—— Anna Magdalena, b. Jan. 21, 1749; bap. April 2, 1749. Sponsors, Andreas Scheidt and wife.
—— Maria, b. June 8, 1751; bap. June 23, 1751. Sponsors, George Dollager and wife Maria.
—— John Jacob, b. Nov. 5, 1753; bap. Nov. 16, 1753. Sponsors, Jacob Hoffman and wife.
—— John Cunradt, b. Feb. 1756; bap. Feb. 8, 1756. Sponsors, Cunradt Lang and wife Barbara.

JOHN GEORGE WEBER.
Weber—John Adam, b. Feb. 14, 1746; bap. Feb., 1746. Sponsors, John Adam Weaver and Barbara Jeager.

PHILIPP SCHWEICKERT, (Conestoga.)
Schweickert—Susanna, b. May, 1746; bap. June 15, 1746. Sponsors, Johannes Uhrich and his wife.

JOSEPH RITTER, (Earl Town.)
Ritter—Catarina, b. March 10, 1748; bap. March 14, 1748. Sponsors, Antonius Fllenecker (Ellmecker?) and Catarina Ringer.

JOHN GEORGE SCHADE, (Tulpehocken.)
Schade—Catarina Barbara. b. Feb. 2, 1746; bap. March 16, 1746. Sponsors, John George Meyer and Catarina Gotteskind.

MARTIN FREY, (Cocalico.)
Frey—Maria Catarina, b. June 1, 1746;

bap. July 12, 1746. Sponsors, Abraham Kern and his wife.

ABRAHAM BOLLENBACHER,
(Northkill.)

Bollenbacher—Abraham, b. May 16, 1746; bap. Sept. 28, 1746. Sponsors, Abraham Haass and wife.

LEONHARDT CUNRADT,
(Tulpehocken.)

Cunradt—John Joseph, b. March 19, 1740; bap. July 6, 1746. Sponsors, Jacob Hoffman and wife.

—— Leonhardt, b. Aug. 18, 1742; bap. July 6, 1746. Sponsor, Nicolaus Gauger.

—— Christian, b. Jan. 19, 1745; bap. July 6, 1746. Sponsors, Christian Meyer and wife.

—— Maria Magdalena, b. March 27, 1747; bap. Aug. 30, 1747. Sponsors, Gottfried Roehrer and wife Maria Magdalena.

JOHN WOHLLEBEN, (Tulpehocken.)

Wohlleben—Anna Maria Elisabetha, b. July 2. 1746; bap. July 6, 1746. Sponsors, Jacob Loewengut and Maria Elisabetha Ehrhardt.

—— John Peter, b. Dec. 16. 1747; bap. Dec. 21, 1747. Sponsors, Peter Leppo and wife Susanna, and also Peter Windelblech and wife Catarina.

—— Philipp Jacob, b. Nov. 28, 1748; bap. Dec. 11, 1748. Sponsors, John Philipp Schneider, Philipp Noll, Jacob Goldtman, Maria Sara Becker and Maria Catarina Schultz.

FRIEDERICH TROESTER,
(Tulpehocken.)

Troester—Maria Dorothea, b. June 24, 1746; bap. July 6, 1746. Sponsors, Ulrich Spiess and wife Maria Dorothea.

CHRISTOPH HEDDERICH,
(Tulpehocken.)

Hedderich—Anna Margaretha, b. June 3, 1746; bap. July 6, 1746. Sponsors, Michael Reiss and wife Anna Margaretha.

—— Maria Barbara, b. March 31, 1753; bap. June 17, 1753. Sponsors, Michael Axer and wife Barbara.

TOBIAS BICKEL, (Tulpehocken.)

Bickel—Maria Margaretha, b. June 22, 1746; bap. July 7, 1746. Sponsors, Heinrich Baseler and wife.

JAMES WILLIAMS, (Swatara.)

Williams—Benjamin, b. Feb., 1746; bap. Aug. 17, 1746. Sponsors, Benjamin Clark and wife.

—— Christina, b. Jan. 1749; bap. May 14, 1749. Sponsors, Philipp Kolb and Christina Kolb.

—— Johannes, b. July 4, 1762; bap. Sep. 5, 1762. Sponsors, Johannes Dietz and wife Eva Elisabetha.

JOHN PETER WISSENANDT,
(Moden Creek.)

Wissenandt—John Peter, b. June 22, 1746; bap. June 29, 1746. Sponsors, John Nicolaus Zeller and wife Margaretha.

JACOB KOPPENHOEFER,
(Earl Town.)

Koppenhoefer—John George, b. June 25, 1746; bap. July 13, 1746. Sponsors, Balthasar Boesshaar and wife Anna.

PHILIPP BEYER, (Lebanon.)

Beyer—Catarina, b. July 15, 1744; bap. Aug. 12, 1744. Sponsors, Adam Ulrich and Catarina Buerger.

—— Eva, b. July 18, 1746; bap. July 20, 1746. Sponsors, Jacob Dietz and Eva Buerger.

JOHN THONTHEUR, (Atolhoe.)

Thontheur—Christian, b. June 10, 1747; bap. Aug. 30, 1747. Sponsors, Christian Meyer and wife Catarina and also Joseph Roth.

GEORGE VELTEY, (Swatara.)

Veltey—Johannes, b. July 1, 1746; bap. Aug. 17, 1746. Sponsors, Valentin Kuefer and his wife.

—— John Cunradt, b. April 8, 1749; bap. May 1, 1749. Sponsors. Cunradt Goer and his wife.

—— Maria Barbara, b. June 15, 1750; bap. Aug. 5, 1750. Sponsors, Michael Boltz and wife.

—— John Heinrich, b. Jan., 1755; bap. Feb. 22, 1755. Sponsors, Ulrich Jeckel and wife.

—— Juliana, b. Feb. 28, 1757; bap. March 19, 1757. Sponsors, Adam Ulrich and wife.

—— John Ulrich, b. Nov. 3, 1759; bap. Dec. 23, 1759. Sponsors, Ulrich Jeckel and wife.

—— Sebastian, b. Sept., 1762; bap. Oct. 17. 1762. Sponsors, Ulrich Jeckel and wife.

—— Anna Barbara. b. Sept., 1766; bap. Oct. 26. 1766. Sponsors. George Obermeyer and wife Anna Barbara.

PHILIPP FIRNSZLER, (Lebanon.)

Firnszler—John George, b. March 27, 1746; bap. July 20, 1746. Sponsors, Michael Boltz and his wife.

MARTIN STUEP, (Tulpehocken.)

Stuep—John Heinrich, b. July 7, 1746; bap. Aug. 3, 1746. Sponsors, Heinrich Beyer and his wife.

JACOB HUBELER, (Tulpehocken.)

Hubeler—Anna Margaretha, b. July 27,

1746; bap. Aug. 3, 1746. Sponsors, Frederich and wife Anna Margaretha.

MARTIN NOECKER, (Tulpehocken.) Noecker—Maria Magdalena, b. July 12, 1746; bap. Aug. 3, 1746. Sponsors, Nicolaus Mueller, jr., and Maria Mag. Battorff.

PETER BUCHER, (Swatara.) Bucher—Martinus, b. Aug. 1, 1746; bap. Aug. 17, 1746. Sponsors, George Meyer and wife.

PETER SCHLOSSER, (Lebanon.) Schlosser—George Ernst, b. Aug. 8, 1746; bap. Sept. 4, 1746. Sponsors, George Steitz and his sister-in-law Margaretha.

JOHANNES SCHAEFFER, (Cocalico.) Schaeffer—John Heinrich, b. Aug. 15, 1746; bap. Sept. 7, 1746. Sponsors, John Heinrich Sauer and wife Dorothea.

JOSEPH KELLER, (Atolhoe.) Keller—Anna Margaretha, b. July 22, 1746; bap. Aug. 31, 1746. Sponsors, Anna Margaretha Bleystein.

MATTHEIS BRICKLER, (Atolhoe.) Brickler—John Peter, b. Aug. 12, 1746; bap. Aug. 31, 1746. Sponsors, Peter Brosius and Maria Catarina Crist.

—— John Gottfried, b. Sept. 9, 1747; bap. Sept. 27, 1747. Sponsors, John Gottfried Roehrer and wife Magdalena.

—— John Jacob, b. Nov. 16, 1752; bap. Nov. 19, 1752. Sponsors, John Jacob Bickel and Anna Barbara Gebhardt.

—— Eva Margaretha, b. Feb. 13, 1755; bap. June 1, 1755. Sponsors, Johannes Gebhardt and Margaretha Ritzman.

JOHN JONES, (Atolhoe.) Jones—Phillipina Christina, b. May, 1746; bap. Aug. 31, 1746. Sponsors, Florina Burringer and wife Phillipina Christina.

LEONHARDT BILLMEYER, (Manheim.) Billmeyer—John Martin, b. July, 1746; bap. Sept. 9, 1746. Sponsors, Martin Schreiner and wife Margaretha.

ADAM ULRICH, (Lebanon.) Ulrich—Christoph, b. Aug. 22, 1746; bap. Sept. 4, 1746. Sponsors, Christoph Widder and his wife Christina.

CHRISTOPH WIDDER, (Lebanon.) Widder—John Michael, b. Aug. 1, 1746; bap. Sept. 14, 1746. Sponsors, Adani Ulrich and wife Juliana.

PETER CREUTZER, (Atolhoe.) Creutzer—John Michael, b. Sept. 22, 1746; bap. Sept. 28, 1746. Sponsors,

John Michael Reiss and wife Anna Margaretha.

—— Andreas, b. Oct. 30, 1755; bap. Nov. 16, 1755. Sponsors, Andreas Graff and his wife.

VALENTIN MEYER, (Atolhoe.) Meyer—John Ludwig, b. Sept. 27, 1746; bap. Sept. 28, 1746. Sponsors, John Ludwig Kornmann and wife.

JOHANNES WOLLENWEBER, (Swatara.) Wollenweber—Margaretha, b. Sept. 17, 1746; bap. Oct. 12, 1746. Sponsors, Frederich Haehnly and wife.

JOHN NICOLAUS SIMON, (Atolhoe.) Simon—John Peter, b. Sept. 24, 1746; bap. Oct. 26, 1746. Sponsors, John Peter Hoffman and wife.

FRIEDERICH KRAEMER, (Moselem.) Kraemer—John George, b. Oct. 4, 1746; bap. Oct. 28, 1746. Sponsors, John George Merckling and Anna Hill.

—— Maria Catarina, b. Jan. 31, 1748; bap. March 7, 1748. Sponsor, Maria Catarina Stoever.

JACOB KUTZ, (Moselem.) Kutz—Johannes, b. Sept. 18, 1746 bap. Oct. 28, 1746. Sponsors, Johannes Reuss and Rosina Hofmann or Lehman.

JACOB KINTZER, (Lebanon.) Kintzer—Walther, b. Sept. 21, 1746; bap. Nov. 9, 1746. Sponsors, Seideler Newman and Sabina Bindtnagel.

MATTHEIS TAEFFELER, (Tulpehocken.) Taeffeler—Anna Elizabetha, b. Oct. 26, 1746; bap. Nov. 23, 1746. Sponsors, Nicolaus Deck and wife.

—— Anna Catarina, b. Nov. 1748; bap. Nov. 1748. Sponsors, Jacob Katterman and wife Anna Catarina.

—— Christian, b. Dec. 23, 1753; bap. Dec. 25, 1753. Sponsors, Christian Lutz and wife.

—— Maria Barbara, b. Dec. 23, 1753; bap. Dec. 25, 1753. Sponsors, Wilhelm Penssinger and Maria Barbara Fischer.

MARTIN TROESTER, (Altolhoe.) Troester—John Michael, b. Nov. 18, 1746 bap. Dec. 21, 1746. Sponsors, John Michael Axer and his spouse.

—— Anna Elizabetha, b. June 18, 1753; bap. July 1, 1753. Sponsors, Nicolaus Haeffner and his wife.

EGIDIUS MEYER, (Atolhoe.) Meyer—Maria Eva, b. Nov. 23, 1746; bap. Dec. 21, 1746. Sponsors, Bernhardt Motz and wife Eva Maria.

CASPER ELIAS DILLER, (Earltown.)
Diller—Charlotte Barbara, b. Dec. 27,
1746; bap. June 26, 1747. Sponsors,
Peter Oberkehr and wife Charlotte.
MICHAEL KLEBER, (Swatara.)
Kleber—George Ludwig, b. July 4, 1736;
bap. Sept. 12, 1736. Sponsors, George
Ludwig Friedel and wife.
—— Anna Maria, b. Sept. 9, 1738; bap.
Jan. 30, 1739. Sponsors, Heinrich
Kline and wife Anna Maria.
——Michael, b. March 1, 1740; bap.
March 26, 1741. Sponsors, Heinrich
Klein and wife Anna Maria.
—— Barbara, b. Feb. 28, 17444; bap.
March 18, 1744. Sponsors, Ottmar
Schnaebele and wife Barbara.
—— John Bernhardt, b. Jan. 17, 1747;
bap. Feb. 1, 1747. Sponsors, Bern-
hardt Friedel and wife.
—— Susanna, b. Feb. 19, 1749; bap.
March 19, 1749. Sponsors, Martin
Speck and wife Susanna.
—— John Martin, b. Aug. 15, 1751;
bap. Sept. 1, 1751. Sponsors, the
above.
—— Heinrich, b. April 18, 1754; bap.
May 19, 1754. Sponsors, Heinrich
Sauter and wife Sabina.
ABRAHAM HUBELER,
(Tulpehocken.)
Hubeler—Maria Barbara, b. Feb. 23,
1747; bap. March 15, 1747. Sponsors,
John Melchior Detzler and Maria Bar-
bara Hubeler.
PETER HOFFMAN, (Tulpehocken.)
Hoffman—Johannes, b. March 11, 1747;
bap. March 15, 1747. Sponsors, Jo-
hannes Pontius and wife.
ALBRECHT SIECHLE, (Lebanon.)
Siechle—Anna Catarina, b. March 1,
1747; bap. March 29, 1747. Sponsors,
Anna Catarina Baseler and Maria Cat-
arina Stoever.
GEORGE SCHIRMAN.
Schirman—Simon, b. Jan. 22, 1743; bap.
Jan. 23, 1743. Sponsors, Simon Schir-
man and wife.
—— Anna Maria, b. Oct. 3, 1744; bap.
Oct. 14, 1744. Sponsors, Philipp Adam
Schirman and Adelheit Pfostberger.
—— Joh. Simon, b. Oct. 19, 1746; bap.
Oct. 26, 1746. Sponsors, Johannes
Riegel and wife.
PETER HEYDT, (Lebanon.)
Heydt—Abraham, b. March 15, 1747;
bap. April 4, 1747. Sponsors, Abraham
Heydt and his wife Magdalena, Cas-
per Low and his wife Anna Margare-
tha.
CHARLES KONNOWAY. (Lebanon.)
Konnoway—Catarina, b. Feb. 19, 1747;

bap. April 4, 1747. Sponsors, Jacob
and Barbara Schilling.
—— Arthur, b. Nov. 3, 1745; bap. Feb.
11, 1746. Sponsors, Abraham Heydt
and his wife.
WILLIAM KALLY, (Tulpehocken.)
Kally—John Heinrich, b. March 17,
1747; bap. April 12, 1747. Sponsors,
John Heinrich Deck and Catarina Do-
rum.
—— John George, b. Sept. 11, 1747;
bap. Sept. 14, 1749. Sponsors, Mel-
chior Taefeler and wife.
JACOB THANI, (Atolhoe.)
Thani—John George, b. Feb. 28, 1747;
bap. April 12, 1747. Sponsors, John
George Emmert and his wife.
NICOLAUS KINTZER, (Tulpehocken.)
Kintzer—Juliana, b. April 30, 1747; bap.
May 10, 1747. Sponsors, Daniel
Schneider and Juliana Andre.
—— John Jacob, b. July 8, 1750 bap.
July 22, 1750. Sponsors, Jacob Seibert
and wife.
—— Anna Elizabetha, b. July 19, 1752;
bap. Aug. 16, 1752. Sponsors, John
Nicolaus Kuntz and wife Anna Eliza-
beth.
—— Maria Margaretha, b. July 19,
1755; bap. Jan. 26, 1755. Sponsors,
Sebastian Brosius and wife Maria Mar-
garetha.
FLORIAN BUWINGER,
(Tulpehocken.)
Buwinger—Johann Leonhardt, b. April
20, 1747; bap. June 7, 1747. Sponsors,
Leonhardt Ramler and wife.
MICHAEL SCHAURER, (Heidelberg.)
Schauer—Anna Maria, b. Nov. 19, 1730;
bap. Dec. 13, 1730. Sponsors, Hein-
rich Zeller and wife.
JOHN GEORGE HAAK, (Northkill.)
Haak—Maria Susanna, b. Nov. 14, 1734;
bap. Jan. 8, 1735. Sponsor, Maria Su-
sanna Dieter.
ROBERT JONES,(deceased),(Swatara.)
Jones—John, b. June 27, 1744; bap. Oct.
11, 1747. Sponsors, Wendel Heyl and
wife Anna.
—— Margaretha, b. May 12, 1746; bap.
Oct. 11, 1747. Sponsors, James Clark
and wife Margaretha.
FREDERICH TROESTER, (Swatara.)
Troester—John Heinrich,b. Nov. 2, 1747;
bap. Nov. 22, 1747. Sponsors, John
Heinrich Roetelstein and wife.
—— John Jacob, b. Feb. 3, 1751; bap.
March 13, 1751. Sponsors, John Jacob
Spiess and Elisab. Catarina Simon.
WILHELM VIEL, (servant at Merian.)
Viel—Johannes, b. Oct. 27, 1747; bap.

Nov. 22, 1747. Sponsors, Johannes Wildfang and wife.

JOHANN GEORGE KASTNITZ, (Swatara.)
Kastnitz—George Noah, b. Dec. 13, 1747; bap. Jan. 24, 1748. Sponsors, Noah Friederich and Elisabetha Kastnitz.
—— Christina Johannetta, b. April 26, 1749; bap. May 14, 1749. Sponsors, Noah Friederich and Johannetta Mueller.
—— Catarina Elisabetha, b. 1752; bap. July 5, 1752. Sponsors, Wendel Ronning and wife.

MICHAEL SCHWARTZ, (deceased), (Swatara.)
Schwartz—Margaretha, b. Jan. 16, 1748; bap. Jan. 29, 1748. Sponsors, Frederich Haehnle and wife Margaretha.

JACOB RAMMLER and wife Eva Margaretha.
Rammler—Eva Margaretha, b. Jan. 13, 1748; bap. Feb. 6, 1748. Sponsors, Michael Koppenhoefer and wife Eva Margar.
—— John Michael, b. Dec. 4, 1750; bap. Dec. 23, 1750. Sponsors, the above.
—— Martin, b. June 23, 1753; bap. July 2, 1753. Sponsors, Martin Kappler and wife.

PETER ZERWE, (Tulpehocken.)
Zerwe—Anna Elizabetha, b. Dec. 20, 1747; bap. March 16, 1748. Sponsors, Magar. Elisabetha Emmerich.

GEORGE REED, (Dorum's son-in-law), (Swatara.)
Reed—John George, b. Feb. 20, 1748; bap. Feb. 6, 1749. Sponsors, Peter Brosius and Catarina Dor.

JACOB REESS, (Swatara.)
Reess—John George, b. Jan. 23, 1748; bap. April 3, 1748. Sponsors, John George Emmert and wife.
—— John Nicolaus David, b. May, 1746; bap. May 1, 1748. Sponsors, John Nicolaus Deck and wife. *Illegitimate Son of Mrs. Reess before marriage.

JOHANNES CLAUSSER, (Tulpehocken.)
Clausser—Philipp Adam, b. March 10, 1748; bap. March 29, 1748. Sponsor, Philipp Adam Schirmann.

GEORGE MICHAEL WILDTFANG, (Tulpehocken.)
Wildtfang—Elizabetha Catarina, b. March 6, 1748; bap. April 3, 1748. Sponsors, George Schirmann and wife.
—— Maria Margaretha, b. Oct. 15, 1751; bap. Oct. 27, 1751. Sponsors, Leonhardt Fischer and Margaretha Speck.

JACOB KITZMUELLER, (Swatara.)
Kitzmueller—John Caspar, b. March 25, 1746; bap. April 1, 1746. Sponsors, John Caspar Stoever and wife Maria Catarina.
—— Maria Catarina, b. March 26, 1748; bap. April 5, 1748. Sponsors, John Caspar Stoever and wife Maria Catarina.
—— Andreas, b. Nov. 14, 1733. Sponsors, Andreas Kraft and wife.
—— Anna Maria, b. May 28, 1735. Sponsor, Anna Maria Meivel.
—— John Jacob, b. Aug. 22, 1736. Sponsor, John Kitzmueller, sr.
—— Anna Margaretha, b. May 7, 1738. Sponsors, John Keller and wife.
—— Maria Catarina, b. May 9, 1740. (Died.)
—— Johannes, b. May 14, 1742. Sponsors, Jacob Kintzer and wife.
—— George Adam, b. Jan. 22, 1744. Sponsors, Geo. Thomas Suter and wife.

DAVID FISCHER, (Swatara.)
Fischer—John Jacob, b. April 8, 1748; bap. April 17, 1748. Sponsors, John Jacob Weyman and Margaretha Kober.

JACOB ENGELMANN, (Earltown.)
Engelmann—John George, b. Jan. 24, 1748; bap. May 8, 1748. Sponsors, John George Sparen and his wife.

JOHANNES HOLLENBACH, (Lebanon.)
Hollenbach—Maria, b. Feb. 9, 1748; bap. June 12, 1748. Sponsors, Bernhardt Friedel and wife Dorothea.
—— Jinny Maria, b. 1751; bap. May 12, 1751. Sponsors, Adam Ulrich and wife.
—— John Mattheis, b. 1753; bap. April 23, 1753. Sponsors, John Adam Herbert.
—— Anna Maria, b. 1761; bap. Aug. 2, 1761. Sponsors, John Kissner and wife Sabina.

MICHAEL AVER, (Atolhoe.)
Aver—Anna Elisabetha, b. June 15, 1748; bap. June 26, 1748. Sponsors, Jacob Roehrer and Anna Elisabetha Spiess.
—— Anna Catarina, b. June 17, 1749; bap. June 25, 1749. Sponsors, Heinrich Schuhen and wife.
—— Eva Margaretha, b. Jan. 19, 1751; bap. Feb. 2, 1751. Sponsors, Nicolaus Leyenberger and Maria Eva Spiess.
—— Maria Magdalena, b. March 8, 1752; bap. April 9, 1752. Sponsors, Christoph Hedderich and wife.

ANDREAS KRAFFT, (Northkill.)
Krafft—John, b. Sept. 30, 1731; bap. Nov. 14, 1731. Sponsors, John Jacob

Kitzmueller and his stepmother Margaretha.
—— Anna Maria, b.April 16, 1733; bap. Sept. 16, 1733. Sponsors, John Jacob Kitzmuellerand wife Ann Maria.
—— Anna Margaretha, b. Dec. 27,1734; bap. Dec. 28, 1734. Sponsor, Anna Margaretha Tegin.
—— Maria Catarina, b. March 15, 1736; bap. July 25, 1736. Sponsor, Maria Elisabetha Beyer.
—— Maria Elisabetha, b. April 17,1737; bap. July 17, 1737. Sponsors, Heinrich Beyer and wife.
—— Justina Catarina, b. March 4,1739; bap. April 22, 1739. Sponsors, Justina Catarina Kayser.
—— Andreas, b. Feb. 1, 1741; bap. April 12, 1741. Sponsors, Andreas Kochenderfer and wife.
—— Maria Magdalena, b. Sept. 7, 1742; bap. Oct. 18, 1742. Sponsors, John Michael Krafft and wife.
—— Susanna, b. April 9, 1744; bap. April 29, 1744. Sponsors, Samuel Philbert and wife Susanna.

SAMUEL PHILBERT, (Northkill.)
Philbert—Maria Catarina, b. Oct. 25, 1739; bap. Dec. 30, 1739. Sponsors, Andreas Krafft and wife.
—— Anna Elisabetha, b. Dec. 6, 1741; bap. Dec. 7, 1741. Sponsor, Anna Elisabetha Krafft.
—— John Philipp, b. Dec. 7, 1743; bap. Dec. 27, 1743. Sponsors, Philipp Meeth and wife.
—— John Peter, b. Aug. 22, 1746; bap. Aug. 31, 1746. Sponsors, Peter Muench and wife.
—— Maria Christina, b. May 25, 1749; bap. May 28, 1749. Sponsors, Peter Muench and wife Christina.

LUDWIG WAGNER, (Northkill.)
Wagner—Maria Elisabetha, b. Feb. 17, 1741; bap. April 12, 1741. Sponsors, Maria Elisabetha Fischer and Eva Maria Rosina Gruber.
—— Maria Eva Rosina, b. Aug. 19, 1743; bap. Sept. 11, 1743. Sponsors, the above.
—— Ludwig Adam, b. April 18, 1746; bap. May 11, 1746. Sponsors, Heinrich Gruber and Hieronymus Fischer.
—— Maria Margaretha, b. Feb. 16, 1750; bap. March 4, 1750. Sponsors, Heinrich Gruber and Maria Elisabetha Fischer.

WILHELM ALBERT, (Northkill.)
Albert—John Adam, b. Feb. 27, 1741; bap. April 12, 1741. Sponsors, John Adam Bollman and wife, also Elisabetha Krafft.

JOHN GOTTFRIED FIEDLER, (Northkill.)
Fiedler—Catarina, b. Dec. 18, 1740; bap. July 5, 1741. Sponsors, Michael Schauer and wife.
—— Andreas, b. Nov. 6, 1742; bap. Nov. 28, 1742. Sponsors, Andreas Krafft and wife.
—— Maria, b. Aug. 5, 1745; bap. Sept. 1, 1745. Sponsors, Heinrich Frey and wife Catarina.
—— Margaretha, b. Dec. 10, 1747; bap. Dec. 20, 1747. Sponsors, Albrecht Strauss and wife.
—— John Peter, b. Feb. 23, 1750; bap. April 1, 1750. Sponsors, Heinrich Fiedler and wife.

JACOB FUCHS, (Northkill.)
Fuchs—Anna Elisabetha, b. Oct. 19, 1741; bap. Dec. 7, 1741. Sponsors, John Jacob Rehm and Anna Elisabetha Ermentrout.
—— Anna Maria, b. Jan. 1, 1743; bap. Jan. 15, 1743. Sponsors, John Nicolaus Holder and wife.
—— Anna Margaretha, b. Oct. 18, 1747; bap. Oct. 25, 1747. Sponsors, Johannes Eckert and wife Engel.

CHRISTIAN GRUBER, (Northkill.)
Gruber—John George, b. Feb. 16, 1743; bap. Feb. 20, 1743. Sponsors, Heinrich Gruber and wife.
—— Susanna, b. Aug. 12, 1746; bap. Aug. 31, 1746. Sponsors, Martin Stuep and wife Susanna.
—— Maria Catarina, b. Dec. 10, 1748; bap. Jan. 8, 1749. Sponsors, John Zerwe and wife.
—— John Adam, b. March 30, 1752; bap. April 26, 1752. Sponsors, John Adam Gruber and Eva Rosina Schauer.
—— John Albrecht, b. May 9, 1754 (?); bap. June 2, 1754. Sponsors, Albrecht Strauss and wife.
—— Anna Margaretha, b. April 2, 1759; bap. April 16, 1759. Sponsors, Johannes Kaufman and wife.

PHILIP PETRY, (Northkill.)
Petry—John George, bap. Nov. 6, 1743. Sponsors, John George Bechtel and Margaretha Retnel.
—— Anna Catarina, b. April 27, 1745; bap. May 12, 1745. Sponsors, Heinrich Adolph and wife.
—— Catharina Elisabetha, b. Aug. 10, 1746; bap. Aug. 31, 1746. Sponsors, John Nicolaus Bechtel and Catarina Krauel.
—— John Jacob, b. Jan. 21, 1748; bap. Feb. 7, 1748. Sponsors, John Jacob Heck and Maria Elisabetha Gossler.
—— John Nicolaus, b. Feb. 27, 1750;

bap. Aug. 19, 1750. Sponsors, Nicolaus Holder and wife.

THOMAS MUELLER, (Northkill.)
Mueller—John Michael, b. July 3, 1746; bap. July 6, 1746. Sponsors, John Michael Kayser and Christian Mueller.
—— Maria Margaretha, b. Dec. 11, 1748; bap. Jan. 11, 1748 (9?). Sponsors, Nicolaus Lang, Johannes Lang, Anna Maria Lang and Anna Margaretha Hoegel.

JOHN PHILIPP STRAUSS, (Northkill.)
Strauss—Anna Magdalena, b. Dec. 21, 1744; bap. Dec. 26, 1744. Sponsors, John Ebert and Anna Magdalena Reimer.
—— Anna Elisabetha, b. Sept. 18, 1746; bap. Sept. 28, 1746. Sponsors, Dinnes Kirschner and wife.
—— Maria Christina, b. Feb. 20, 1749; bap. March 5, 1749. Sponsor, Maria Christina Meeth.
—— Caspar, b. Jan. 27, 1751; bap. Feb. 3, 1751. Sponsors, Caspar Mengel and wife Maria Christina.
—— Maria Catharina, b. Dec. 22, 1752; bap. Jan. 14, 1753. Sponsors, Johannes Zerwe and wife Catarina.
—— John Philipp, b. Nov. 9, 1754; bap. Nov. 17, 1754. Sponsors, John Philipp Meeth and wife Anna Maria.
—— John Jacob, b. May 5, 1757; bap. May 29, 1757. Sponsors, John Jacob Strauss and Barbara Haag.
—— Christian, b. June 16, 1760; bap. June 29, 1760. Sponsors, Christian Gruber and wife Anna Kunigunda.
—— John Matthias, b. April 19, 1762; bap. May 9, 1762. Sponsors, Mattheis Kaempf and wife Magdalena.

GOTTFRIED ROEHRER, (Atolhoe.)
Roehrer—Anna Catarina, b.Sept.24,1748; bap. Oct. 16, 1748. Sponsors, Jacob Roehrer and Anna Catarina Etsschberger.
—— Juliana, b. Jan. 14, 1751; bap. Feb. 2, 1751. Sponsors, Nicolaus Kintzer and wife Juliana.
—— John Jacob, b. April 10, 1753; bap. April 20, 1753. Sponsors, Jacob Roehrer and wife Anna Elizabetha.
—— Anna Maria, b. Sept. 24, 1755; bap. Oct. 14, 1755. Sponsors, Leonhardt Anspach and wife.
—— Maria Magdalena, b. Dec. 7, 1757; bap. Dec. 11, 1757. Sponsor, Dorothea Roehrer.
—— Gottfried, b. Jan., 1763; bap. Feb. 24, 1753. Sponsors, Friederich Hofman and wife.

JOHN MARTIN DILLER, (Earltown.)
Diller—Johannes, b. Nov. 26, 1748; bap. Dec. 5, 1748. Sponsors, Isaac Brubacher and wife Anna Maria.

JOSEPH GRUENEWALD, (Conestoga.)
Gruenewald—Christina Barbara, b. Nov. 6, 1748; bap. Dec. 6, 1748. Sponsors, Michael Oberlin and wife Christina Barbara.

JOHN ANDREAS CAMMERER, (Warwick.)
Cammerer—Maria Barbara, b. Oct. 16, 1748; bap. Nov. 19, 1748. Sponsors, Martin Hoffman and wife Maria Margaretha.

MATTHEIS BOESSHAAR, (Swatara.)
Boesshaar—John Peter, b. Nov. 29, 1748; bap. Dec. 25, 1748. Sponsors, Melchior Huengerer and wife Elizabetha.
—— John George, b. July 3, 1751; bap. Aug. 4, 1751. Sponsors, John George Huengerer and Sabina Schnatterle.

JOHANN PHILIPP SCHREINER, (Manheim.)
Schreiner—John Michael, b. Jan. 7, 1749; bap. Jan. 16, 1749. Sponsors, John Michael Beyerle and wife Anna Maria.

MATTHEIS KAEMPFFER, (Northkill.)
Kaempffer—Maria Appollonia, b. Nov. 22, 1748 bap. Feb. 6, 1749. Sponsors, Johannes Meeth and wife.
—— Anna Barbara, b. Dec. 17, 1749; bap. Feb. 3, 1750. Sponsors, Johannes Lang and wife.
—— John Philipp, b. Oct. 24, 1751; bap. Nov. 11, 1751. Sponsors, John Philipp Strauss and wife.

JOHANNIS WALTHER, (Northkill).
Walther—Johannes, b. Jan. 6, 1749; bap. March 5, 1749. Sponsors, John Meeth and wife.

GOTTFRIED RATTENAUER, (Tulpehocken).
Rattenauer—John George, b. March 1, 1749; bap. March 24, 1749. Sponsors, George Sauter and wife, also, Johannes Wohlleben and his wife.

NICOLAUS MARRETH, (Warwick).
Marreth—Michael, b. March 8, 1749; bap. March 28, 1749. Sponsors, Michael Klein and wife.
—— John Nicolaus, b. Nov. 5, 1752; bap. Dec. 25, 1752. Sponsors, Martin Spickler and wife.

DANIEL HOFFMANN, (Donegal.)
Hoffman—Maria Margaretha, b. March 2, 1749; bap. March 28, 1749. Sponsors, Martin Hoffman and wife.

JOHN HEINRICH DECK, (Altolhoe.)
Deck—Johannes, b. April 1, 1749; bap.
April 2, 1749. Sponsors, Johannes
Deck and Anna Barbara Hubeler.
—— Hieronymus, b. March 9, 1751;
bap. March 31, 1752. Sponsors, Hier-
onymus Deck and Barbara Deckin.

JOHANNES SCHMELTZER.
(Swatara.)
Schmeltzer—Jacobina, b. April 13, 1749;
bap. May 1, 1749. Sponsors, Jacob
Haeckert and wife.
—— John Jacob, b. 1752; bap. July 5,
1752. Sponsors, Jacob Haeckert and
wife.

ADAM KLEIN, (Swatara.)
Klein—Anna Barbara, b. April, 1749;
bap. May 1, 1749. Sponsors, Casper
Korr and wife.

PHILIP KOLB, (Swatara.)
Kolb—John Christoph, b. Dec. 1, 1748;
bap. May 1, 1749. Sponsors, Carl Veit
and wife.

JACOB MOSER, (Swatara.)
Moser—Christina, b. March 20, 1749;
bap. May 14, 1749. Sponsors, Heinrich
Bachman and wife.

CASPER JOST, (Swatara.)
Jost—Anna Maria, b. April 13, 1749; bap.
May 14, 1749. Sponsors, Peter Hed-
derich and his wife.

GEORGE RIEDT, (Summer Mountain.)
Riedt—Eva Margaretha, b. July 13, 1749;
bap. Aug. 20, 1749. Sponsors, Marga-
retha Dorothea Boeckel.
—— Christina Barbara, b. Oct. 6, 1751;
bap. Nov. 10, 1751. Sponsors, Jacob
Bich and wife.
—— John Jacob, b. Aug. 8, 1754; bap.
Sept. 22, 1754. Sponsors, Jacob Riedt
and wife Eva Maria.

DANIEL SCHNEIDER, (Atolhoe.)
Schneider—John Nicolaus, b. Sept. 10,
1749 bap. Sept. 17, 1749. Sponsors,
John Nicolaus Kintzer and wife.
—— Maria Elizabetha, b. April 9, 1751;
bap. April 28, 1751. Sponsors, Nicolaus Brosius and Maria Elizabetha
Stuep.
—— Maria Catarina, b. Feb. 19, 1753;
bap. March 11, 1753. Sponsors, Johannes Zerwe and wife.
—— John Abraham, b. Feb. 11, 1755;
bap. March 9, 1755. Sponsors, Abraham Schneidter and wife.

CUNRADT FOERSTER, (Altolhoe.)
Foerster—John Peter, b. Sept. 25, 1749;
bap. Oct. 15, 1749. Sponsors, Peter
Stein and —— Fisher.
—— Anna Elizabetha, b. Jan. 29, 1754;
bap. Feb. 10, 1754. Sponsors, Johannes Apfel and his wife.

—— Christina, b. June 30, 1756; bap.
July 25, 1756. Sponsors, Christian
Fisher and Cartarina Hofman.

GEORGE SCHUETZ, (Swatara.)
Schuetz—John Leonhardt, b. Oct. 16,
1749; bap. Jan. 3, 1750. Sponsor,
Leonhardt Mueller.

JOSEPH ROTH, (Atolhoe.)
Roth—John Heinrich, b. 1750; bapt. Feb.
4, 1750. Sponsors, ——

JOHN JACOB GASSERT, (Atolhoe.)
Gassert—Johannes, b. March 10, 1750;
bap. April 1, 1750. Sponsors, John
Suter and Eva Ziegeler.
—— Jacob John, b. Dec. 1, 1752; bap.
Dec. 17, 1752. Sponsors, Jacob Gas-
sert and Elizabetha Wolf.
—— John Balthaser, b. May 1, 1755;
bap. May 4, 1755. Sponsors, Balthaser
Stammgas and wife Elizabetha.
—— Maria Margaretha, b. May 18,
1757; bap. June 26, 1757. Sponsors,
Jacob Soerer and his wife.

FRIEDERICH STUEP,
(Blue Mountain.
Stuep—Johannes, b. March 3, 1750; bap.
April 1, 1750. Sponsors, John Lang
and Maria Margar. Hoegel.

PETER GOETTEL, (Swatara.)
Goettel—Maria Eva, b. May 11, 1750;
bap. June 10, 1750. Sponsors, Veit Kapp
and wife Gertraud.

PHILIPP KREBER, (Atolhoe.)
Kreber—John Philipp, b. July 8, 1750;
bap. July 22, 1750. Sponsors, John
Meyer and wife Anna Maria.

JACOB RIESS, (Swatara.)
Riess—Jacob, b. Aug. 9, 1750; bap. Aug.
19, 1750. Sponsors, Thomas Bauer and
wife.

SEBASTIAN BROSIUS, (Atolhoe.)
Brosius—Maria Catarina, b. Sept. 11,
1750; bap. Sept. 16, 1750. Sponsors,
Daniel Lucas and wife.
—— Maria Magdalena, b. Feb. 3, 1752;
bap March 1, 1752. Sponsors, Abra-
ham Schneider and wife Magdalena.
—— Maria Elisabetha, b. July 30, 1753;
bap. Aug. 26, 1753. Sponsors, Jacob
Roeher and wife.
—— Juliana, b. Aug. 23, 1755; bap.
Aug. 24, 1755. Sponsors, Nicolaus
Kintzer and wife Juliana.
—— John Nicolaus, b. Sept. 12, 1757;
bap. Sept. 18, 1757. Sponsors, Nicolaus
Brosius and wife.

JOHANNES RITSCHER,
(Summer Mountain.)
Ritscher—Anna Margaretha, b. Aug.,
1750; bap. Sept. 16, 1750. Sponsors,
Philipp Gebhardt and wife Anna Mar-
garetha.

THOMAS BAUER, (Bethel.)
Bauer—John Jacob, b. Oct. 3, 1750; bap. Oct. 28, 1750. Sponsors, Michael Spiegel and wife.
—— Eva, b. Feb. 22, 1753; bap. March 11, 1753. Sponsors, Michael Mooser and wife.

MICHAEL MOOSER, (Atolhoe.)
Mooser—Erdtmann, b. Oct. 25, 1750, bap. Nov. 11, 1750. Sponsors, Erdtmann Kappy and —— Riedt.
—— Michael, b. March 13, 1752; bap. March 29, 1752. Sponsors, Thomas Bauer and wife Barbara.
—— Christina Catarina, b. Sept. 3, 1752; bap. Sept. 22, 1754. Sponsors, Christoph Lutz and wife Elisabetha.
—— Anna Barbara, b. May 27, 1756; bap. June 7, 1756. Sponsors, John Gebhardt and Anna Barbara Korr.

GEORGE SCHAETTERLE, (Tulpehocken.)
Schaetterle—Christina, b. Aug. 19, 1750; bap. Dec. 9, 1750. Sponsors, Peter Muench and wife Christina.

JOHN HEINRICH STEIN, (Atolhoe.)
Stein—John and Christian, b. Dec. 3, 1750; bap. Dec. 9, 1750. Sponsors, Christian Meyer and wife.
—— John Sebastian, b. March 28, 1752; bap. March 29, 1752. Sponsors, John Sebastian Stein and wife Anna Catarina.
—— Anna Maria, b. March 12, 1754; bap. April 7, 1759. Sponsors, Jacob Vollmar and wife Maria Appollonia.

HEINRICH KITTNER, (Northkill.)
Kittner—Johanna Catarina, b. Oct. 25, 1750; bap. Dec. 9, 1750. Sponsors, Balthasar Umbehag and Justina Prossmann.
—— John Jacob, b. March 29, 1752; bap. April 26, 1752. Sponsors, Jacob Reusser, jr., and wife.
—— John Nicolaus, b. April 24, 1754; bap. May 5, 1754. Sponsors, John Nicolaus Bechtel and wife.
—— Christina Catarina, b. May 2, 1756; bap. May 30, 1756. Sponsors, George Adam Geiss and Justina Prossmann.
—— George Adam, b. Oct. 12, 1758; bap. Nov. 8, 1758. Sponsors, George Adam Geiss and wife Anna Barbara.

JACOB ROEHER, (Atolhoe.)
Roeher—Maria Catarina, b. Dec. 31, 1750; bap. Jan. 6, 1751. Sponsors, Nicolaus Brosius and Maria Elisab. Stuep.
—— Anna Margaretha, b. Nov. 18, 1752; bap. Nov. 19, 1752. Sponsors, Sebastian Brosius and wife.
—— John Jacob, b. Dec. 8, 1754; bap.

Dec. 16, 1754. Sponsors, Gottfried Roehrer and wife Magdalena.

CLEMENS GILLIGHAN, (Swatara.)
Gillighan—John, b. Oct. 21, 1750; bap. Jan. 21, 1751. Sponsors, John Eisenhauer and sister.

ABRAHAM STEIN, (Atolhoe.)
Stein—Anna Magdalena, b. Jan. 29,1751; bap. Feb. 2, 1751. Sponsors, Tobias Dittes and wife.
—— Johannes, b. June 15, 1752; bap. July 19, 1752. Sponsors, John Stein and Anna Elisabetha Friederich.
—— Maria Catarina, b. March 31, 1754; bap. April 7, 1754. Sponsors, Gottfried Roehrer and wife Magdalena.
—— Abraham, b. Jan. 6, 1756; bap. Jan. 11, 1756. Sponsors, John George Ludwig and wife Maria Christina.
—— John Jacob, b. Oct. 20, 1757; bap. Nov. 6, 1757. Sponsors, Jacob Stein and Dorothea Roehrer.

HEINRICH ADAM SCHNEIDER, (Atolhoe.)
Schneider—John George, b. Jan. 1751; bap. Feb. 2, 1751. Sponsors, John George Brosius and wife.
—— John Heinrich, b. Jan., 1751; bap. Feb. 2, 1751. Sponsors, John Heinrich Schuhehn and wife.
—— John Abraham, b. Oct. 11, 1754; bap. Oct. 20, 1754. Sponsors, John Abraham Schneider and wife.

HEINRICH HINNEN, (Northkill.)
Hinnen—Anna Catarina,b. Feb. 18, 1751; bap. March 3, 1751. Sponsors, Wilhelm Giesemann and wife.

WENDEL BRECHT, (Bern.)
Brecht—John Heinrich, b. Feb. 1, 1751; bap. March 3, 1751. Sponsors, John Heinrich Martin.

MARTIN SPECHT, (Bern.)
Specht—Maria Philippenia, b.March 12, 1751; bap. June 23, 1751. Sponsors, Ludwig Wagner and daughter Magdalena, also Christina Glassbrenner.
—— John George Martin, b. in 1753; bap. Aug. 26, 1753. Sponsors, George Ludwig Wagner and wife.

CHIRURGUS and MEDICUS JOHN GEORGE TRIPPNER and wife ANNA ELIZABETH, (Tulpehocken.)
Trippner—John Peter Leonhardt, b. Feb. 20, 1751; bap. March 3, 1751. Sponsors, John Peter Muench and wife Christina Barbara.

GEORGE KANTNER, (Tulpehocken.)
Kantner—John Jacob, b. March 2, 1751; bap. March 31, 1751. Sponsors, Jacob Bortner and wife.

ABRAHAM SCHNEIDER, (Atolhoe.)
Schneider—John Abraham, b. March 7,
1751; bap. March 31, 1751. Sponsors,
Abraham Stein and wife Anna Maria.
—— George Martin, b. Aug. 16, 1753;
bap. Aug. 26, 1753. Sponsors, George
Thomas Bauer and wife.

GEORGE SCHAEFFER,
("Across the Large Swatara.")
Schaeffer—John Philipp, b. Nov. 27,
1750; bap. April 14, 1751. Sponsors,
Philipp Maurer and wife.

GEORGE RIEDT, (Swatara.)
Riedt—Andreas, b. April 6, 1751; bap.
April 28, 1751. Sponsors, Andreas
Schmidt and wife.
—— Anna Susanna, b. Jan. 28, 1753;
bap. Feb. 11, 1753. Sponsors, Michael
Hartman and Susanna Thorum.

JACOB GREIM, (Bern.)
Greim—John Sebastian, b. Nov. 23, 1750;
bap. April 28, 1751. Sponsor, Sebastian Rutt.
—— Maria Salome, b. Jan. 27, 1753;
bap. March 11, 1753. Sponsors, Sebastian Greim and wife.

PETER HECKMAN, (Swatara.)
Heckman—Ana Maria, b. 1751; bap.
April 28, 1751. Sponsors, George
Friederich and wife.
—— Elizabetha Margaretha, b. April
1, 1753; bap. April 22, 1753. Sponsors.
George Friederich and wife.
—— John Peter, b. Sept., 1754; bap.
Oct. 20, 1754. Sponsors, Veit Kapp
and wife Gertraudt.

JOHN ZOELLER, JR., (Tulpehocken.)
Zoeller—Frantz Paul, b. April 8, 1751;
bap. May 26, 1751. Sponsors, Frantz
Wendrich and wife Elisabetha.

DANIEL RAUSCH, (Hanover.)
Rausch—Anna Eva, b. April 11, 1751;
bap. May 27, 1751. Sponsors, John
Brown and wife Ana Eva.
—— John Daniel, b. 1753; bap. July 15,
1753. Sponsors, Mattheis Pflantz and
wife Elisabetha.

PETER SUMI, (Swatara.)
Sumi—Anna Margaretha, b. April 9,
1751; bap. June 23, 1751. Sponsors,
John Adam Stein and wife.

MICHAEL SUMI. (Swatara.)
Sumi—Anna Margaretha, b. March 29,
1751; bap. June 23, 1751. Sponsors,
Ana Margaretha Guschwa.

HERMAN LATTUR AND WIFE
BARBARA,
(Warwick.)
Lattur—Susanna Margaretha, b. July 7,
1751; bap. August 11, 1751. Sponsors,
Martin Spickler and wife.

JACOB ETSCHBERGER, (Atolhoe.)
Etschberger—John Philipp, b. June 21,
1751; bap. Aug. 18, 1751. Sponsors,
George Philipp Dollinger and wife
Maria.

BERNHARDT FABER, (Swatara.)
Faber—Maria Barbara, b. Aug. 7, 1751;
bap. Aug. 17, 1751. Sponsors, Adam
Faber and wife.
—— Margaretha, b. May 20, 1755; bap.
June 8, 1755. Sponsors, Adam Faber
and wife Anna Maria.

MICHAEL BURGER, (Heidelberg.)
Burger—Sebastian, b. May 11, 1751; bap.
Aug. 18, 1751. Sponsors, Sebastian
Obold and his wife.

JOHN NICOLAUS FRINGER,
(Tulpehocken,)
Fringer—John Nicholas, b. Sept. 10,
1751; bap. Sept. 15, 1751. Sponsors,
John Nicolaus Leyenberger and Mag-
dalena Aulenbach.

NICOLAUS WOLF, (Bethel.)
Wolf—Carolus b. Oct. 20, 1751; bap. Oct.
27, 1753. Sponsors, Carl Scheidt and
wife.
—— Maria Margaretha b. Sept. 22,
1753; bap. Oct. 7, 1753. Sponsors, Cunradt Rounner and sister Margaretha.

PETER FISCHER, (Northkill.)
Fischer—John Philip, b. Oct. 14, 1751;
bap. Nov. 10, 1751. Sponsor, John
Philip Meeth and wife.

FREIDERICH GLASSBRENNER,
(Northkill.)
Glassbrenner—John Friederich, b. Oct.
30, 1751; bap. Nov. 10, 1751. Sponsors,
Ludwig Wagner and wife.

BALTHASAR UNBEHAGEN AND
WIFE APPOLONIA,
(Northkill.)
Unbehagen—Elisabetha, b. Oct. 23, 1751;
bap. Nov. 10, 1751. Sponsors, Frantz
Prossman and Elisab. Strauss.
—— Samuel, b. Feb. 3, 1754; bap. Feb.
10, 1754. Sponsors, Samuel Philbert
and wife Susanna.
—— Justina Catarina, b. Dec. 7, 1755;
bap. Dec. 14, 1755. Sponsors, Jacob
Strauss and Just. Catar. Prossman.
—— Catarina, b. March 10, 1758; bap.
April 2, 1758. Sponsors, Catar. Elisab.
Haag and Thomas Philbert.
—— John Thomas, b. April 12, 1762;
bap. May 9, 1762. Sponsors, Thomas
Filbert and Susanna Knopf.
——Jonas, b. Sept. 19, 1763; bap. Oct.
2, 1763. Sponsors, Jonathan Eckert
and wife Maria Catarina.

HEINRICH HOLTZMAN, (Atolhoe.)
Holtzman—Heinrich Friederich, b. Oct. 15, 1751; bap. Nov. 10, 1751. Sponsors, Gottfried Roehrer and wife.

ADAM FIX, (Atolhoe.)
Fix—Eva Margaretha, b. Oct. 17, 1751; bap. Nov. 10, 1751. Sponsors, Wilhelm Kayser and wife.

LUDWIG POTTS, (Atolhoe.)
Potts—Anna Barbara, b. Oct. 14, 1751; bap. Nov. 10, 1751. Sponsors, Jacob Hubele and wife.

ADAM SIMON, (Codorus.)
Simon—Andreas, b. Nov. 16, 1751; bap. Nov. 25, 1751. Sponsors, Andreas Kuertzel and wife Dorothea.

MICHAEL ALBERT, JR.,
(Blue Mountain.)
Albert—John Wilhelm, b. Feb., 1752; bap. March 1, 1752. Sponsors, John Wilhelm Albert and wife.

JOHN ADAM LUCAS, (Codorus.)
Lucas—Maria Elisabetha, b. Nov. 9, 1751; bap. Nov. 25, 1751. Sponsors, Daniel Dieb and wife.

JOHANNES MERTZ, (Northkill.)
Mertz—Maria Barbara, b. Nov. 25, 1751; bap. Dec. 8, 1751. Sponsors, John Nickel Haag and Maria Barbara Strauss.

GOTTFRIED BAUMGAERTNER,
(Bethel.)
Baumgaertner—John Jacob, b. Dec. 7, 1751; bap. Dec. 22, 1751. Sponsors, Wendel Heyl and wife Anna.

ADAM KLEIN, (Bethel.)
Klein—John Gottlieb, b. Dec. 9, 1751; bap. Dec. 22, 1751. Sponsors, John Gottlieb Thurm and Jacob Vornwalt and wife.

VALENTINE BENDER, (Atolhoe.)
Bender—George Valentine, b. Feb. 2, 1752; bap. March 1, 1752. Sponsors, Valentin Meyer and Elisabetha Stein.

CASPER WEBER, (Swatara.)
Weber—John Adam, b. Jan. 2, 1752; bap. Jan. 7, 1752. Sponsors, Wendel Heyl and wife Anna.
—— Maria Catarina, b. Nov. 25, 1759; bap. Dec. 23, 1759. Sponsors, Peter Felten and wife.

WENDEL ROENNINGER, (Swatara.)
Roenninger—Maria Margar. Barbara, b. Dec. 24, 1751; bap. Jan. 7, 1752. Sponsors, Martin Eisenhauer and wife Barbara.
—— Maria Salome, b. May 27, 1756; bap. June 13, 1756. Sponsors, Friederich Haehnle and wife.

JOHANNES BECKER, (Atolhoe.)
Becher—Catarina Barbara, b. Jan. 5, 1752; bap. Feb. 2, 1752. Sponsors, Jacob Wolf and wife.

GEORGE WOLF, (Atolhoe.)
Wolf—Anna Margaretha, b. Jan. 19, 1752; bap. Feb. 2, 1752. Sponsors, Jacob Wolf and wife.

ANDREAS WINTER,(Bern Township.)
Winter—Justina Margaretha, b. Nov. 30, 1751; bap. Feb. 2, 1752. Sponsors, Simon Muench and Justina Margaretha Specht.

CUNRANDT WIRTH,
(Blue Mountain.)
Wirth—George Wilhelm, b. Dec. 29, 1751; bap. Feb. 3, 1752. Sponsors, George Wilhelm Berger and Gertraudt Wagner.

JOHANNES HAEFFELE, (Swatara.)
Haeffele—Margaretha, b. Feb. 1, 1752; bap. Feb. 17, 1752. Sponsors, Cunradt Roenninger and Margaretha Speck.

ANDREAS KASTNITZ, (Swatara.)
Kastnitz—John Frantz, b. Jan. 28, 1752; bap. May 30, 1752. Sponsors, John Frantz Fuchs and wife.

PETER BECKER, (Swatara.)
Becker—Maria Elizabetha, b. Feb. 2, 1752; bap. March 30, 1752. Sponsors, Dorst Brechbiel and wife.

JOHN PETER SPAT, (Swatara.)
Spat—Maria Salome, b. March 27, 1752; bap. March 30, 1752. Sponsors, John Michael Huber and wife.

MARTIN EISENHAUR, (Swatara.)
Eisenhauer—Johannes, b. June, 1752; bap. July 5, 1752. Sponsors, not given.
—— George Martin, b. March, 1754; bap. April 7, 1754. Sponsors, George Graff and wife.
—— John Peter, b. March 17, 1756; bap. March 21, 1756. Sponsors, Peter Schuy and Anna Margaretha Eisenhauer.
—— John Valentin, b. 1759; bap. 1759. Sponsor, Valentine Keller.

ADAM GREIM, (Bern.)
Greim—John George, b. Oct. 11, 1752; bap. Oct. 22, 1752. Sponsors, John George Haag and Catarina Muench.

ANDREAS KISSINGER.
No entry excepting under b. Oct. 10, 1752.

GEORGE GORDON, (Bethel.)
Gordon—Maria Margaretha, b. Sept. 6, 1752; bap. Nov. 6, 1752. Sponsors, Wendel Heyl and Elizabetha Grayu.

JOHANNES SCHAEFER, (Atolhoe.)
Schaefer—John Adam, b. Nov. 12, 1752; bap. Nov. 19, 1752. Sponsors, John Adam Koller and wife.

JOHN LEHN, (Bethel.)
Lehn—Johannes Jacob, b. Sept. 24, 1752; bap. Nov. 19, 1752. Sponsors, John Jacob Thani and his wife.

PETER RADEBACH, (Northkill.
Radebach—John Nicolaus, b. Dec. 4, 1752; bap. Dec. 17, 1752. Sponsors, John Nicolaus Haag.
—— Anna Catarina, b. 1754; bap. May 5, 1754. Sponsors, Heinrich Radebach and wife.
—— Anna Elizabetha, b. Oct. 23, 1755; bap. Dec. 14, 1755. Sponsors, George Radebach and Anna Elizabetha Philbert.
—— Maria Margaretha, b. March 9, 1757; bap. April 3, 1757. Sponsors, George Zimmerman and MariaMargaretha Radebach.

MARTIN SPICKLER, (Warwick.)
Spickler—John Martin, b. Dec. 12, 1752; bap. Dec. 25, 1752. Sponsors, John Nicolaus Marreth and wife.

JOHN EISENHAUER, (Bethel.)
Eisenhauer—Anna Margaretha, b. Feb. 14, 1753; bap. March 26, 1753. Sponsors, John Nicolaus Eisenhauer and wife.

SIMON ESCHBACH, (Atolhoe.)
Eschbach—Anna Elizabetha, b. Feb. 2, 1753; bap. Feb. 11, 1753. Sponsors, George Berger and Anna Elizabetha Spiess.

MATTHEIS REICH, (Atolhoe.)
Reich—Eva Kunigunda, b. Feb. 10, 1753; bap. Feb. 11, 1753. Sponsors, George Jacob Schirman and wife.

STEPHEN LAUMANN, (Warwick.)
Laumann—Catarina Sophia, b. Feb. 14, 1753 bap. Feb. 18, 1753. Sponsors, Daniel Huber and wife Sophia.

CARL SCHMIDT, (Bethel.)
Schmidt—Eva, b. Dec. 17, 1752; bap. Feb. 25, 1753. Sponsors, Lorentz Hautz and wife.
—— Susanna, b. Oct. 27, 1754; bap. Nov. 3, 1754. Sponsors, Peter Klein and Susanna Grossmann.

ANDREAS EUB, (Warwick.)
Eub—Christina Barbara, b. Feb. 14, 1753; bap. March 18, 1753. Sponsors, Jacob Wentz and wife.

SERENIUS SCHAEFER, (Bethel.)
Schaefer—Elizabetha, b. Feb. 10, 1753; bap. March 26, 1753. Sponsors, John Schmetter and wife.

JOHN ADAM HERBERT, (Hanover.)
Herbert—John Adam, b. March 16, 1753;

bap. March 26, 1753. Sponsor, George Scheidt.
—— Catarina Margaretha, b. Sept. 5, 1757; bap. Feb. 19, 1758. Sponsors, Peter Walmer and wife.
—— John, b. Jan. 8, 1760; bap. Feb. 24, 1760. Sponsor Johannes Brechbiel, Jr.
—— Susanna, b. June, 1762; bap. July 25, 1762. Sponsors, Thomas Koppenhoefer and wife.

ADAM MADERN ,(Bern.)
Madern—John Nicolaus, b. March 25, 1753; bap. April 8, 1753. Sponsors, John Nicolaus Bahler and wife.

JACOB LORESCH, (Bethel.)
Loresch—Margaretha, b. April 8, 1753; bap. April 22, 1753. Sponsors, Frederich Haehnle and wife.
—— Maria Barbara, b. March 21, 1755; bap. April 13, 1755. Sponsors, N. N.

ANTONIUS NAGEL, (Bethel.)
Nagel—Maria Barbara, b. April 9, 1753; bap. April 22, 1753. Sponsors, Balthaser Nolld and Barbara Nagle.
—— Maria Dorothea, b. Dec. 20, 1754; bap. Jan. 19, 1755. Sponsors, John Elder and wife Dorothea.
—— Eva Catarina, b. March 9, 1756; bap. March 21, 1756. Sponsors, Martin Oberlin and wife.

GEORGE MUENCH, (Bern.)
Muench—Simon, b. March 20, 1753; bap. May 6, 1753. Sponsors, Simon Muench and wife.
—— Catarina Margaretha, b. June 5, 1754; bap. Aug. 25, 1754. Sponsors, Peter Muench and wife Christina.
—— Anna Margaretha, b. May 24, 1756; bap. June 7, 1756. Sponsors, George Gutman and wife.

ISAACK SCHERFF, (Hanover.)
Scherff—John Heinrich, b. May 4, 1753; bap. May 31, 1753. Sponsors, Heinrich Webber and wife.

CHRISTIAN PFAFFENBERGER, (Atolhoe.)
Pfaffenberger—Johannes, b. May 20, bap. June 3, 1753. Sponsors, John Pfaffenberger and Dorothea Stuep.

GEORGE TITTEL, (Hanover.)
Tittle—John Adam, b. July 24, 1752; bap. June 17, 1753. Sponsors, Heinrich Wegner and wife Barbara.
—— Johannes, b. Nov., 1755; bap. Dec. 18, 1755. Sponsors, Anastasius Uhler and wife.
—— John Peter, b. 1759; bap. April 15, 1759. Sponsor, Christoph Uhler.
—— John George, b. Oct., 1761; bap. Nov. 22, 1761. Sponsors, John Diel and Elizabetha Clarck.

JACOB FRIEDERICH KUEMMER-
LIN, (Across the Mountain.)
Kuemmerlin—John Michael, b. March 5,
1753; bap. July 1, 1753. Sponsors,John
Michael Folmer and wife Magdalena
Regina.

SEBASTIAN GREIM, (Bern.)
Greim—Christina Cordula, b. June 17,
1753; bap. July 1, 1753. Sponsors,
Jacob Greim and wife Christina Cordula.

JACOB LEININGER, (Atolhoe.)
Leininger—Johannes, b. June 24, 1753;
bap. July 1, 1753. Sponsors, Andreas
Schafer and wife Catarina.

CUNRADT SCHARFF, (Atolhoe.)
Scharff—Catarina Margaretha, b. Sept.
23, 1752; bap. Oct. 22, 1752. Sponsors,
Jacob Loewengut and wife, both
senior and junior.

ADAM BRECHT, (Bethel.)
Brecht—Maria Elisabetha, b. June 15,
1753; bap. Aug. 12, 1753. Sponsors,
Jacob Eprecht and wife.

GEORGE MAESS, (Bethel.)
Maess—Anna Margaretha, b. June 10,
1753; bap. Aug. 12, 1753. Sponsors,
Herman Eckel and wife.

SEBASTIAN WILDFANG, (Atolhoe.)
Wildfang—Peter, b. Aug. 18, 1753; bap.
Aug. 26, 1753. Sponsors, Peter Geb-
hart and wife.

NICOLAUS BROSIUS, (Atolhoe.)
Brosius—Anna Catarina, b. Sept. 15,
1753; bap. Sept. 24, 1753. Sponsors,
Johannes Steingrau and Anna
Schaefer, both single.
——— John Nicolaus, b. Dec. 25, 1754;
bap. Jan. 1, 1755. Sponsors, John
Nickel Kintzer and wife Juliana.
——— Maria Margaretha, b. Feb. 1757;
bap. March 6, 1757. Sponsors, N. N.

THOMAS DOWNSEN,(Atolhoe.)
Downsen—Anna Margaretha, b .Sept. 9,
1753; bap. Oct. 21, 1753. Sponsors,
John Wohlleben and wife.

ADAM JACOBI, (Northkill.)
Jacobi—John Nicolaus, b. Jan. 28, 1757;
bap. Feb. 6, 1757. Sponsors, John
Nicolaus Haag and wife.

GOTTLIEB THUERNER, (Bethel.)
Thuerner—Agnes Magdalenea, b. Oct.
1753; bap. Nov. 5, 1753. Sponsors,
Jacob Haecker and wife.
——— John Wilhelm. b. Feb., 1757; bap.
March 13, 1757. Sponsors, John Popp
and also Barbara Haecker.

NICOLAUS KLESTMANN, (Atolhoe.)
Klestmann—Catarina Barbara, b. Dec.
21, 1753; bap. Dec. 25, 1753. Sponsors,
Andreas Schaefer and wife.

GEORGE FREY, (Derry.)
Frey—George Michael, b. 1753; bap. Jan.
2, 1754. Sponsors, Michael Huber and
wife.

JACOB FISCHER, (Bern.)
Fischer—Mattheis Samuel, b. Dec., 1753;
bap. Jan. 13, 1754. Sponsors, Mattheis
Philbert and wife.

GEORGE DIELMANN, (Bethel.)
Dielmann—Andreas, b. Dec. 27, 1753;
bap. Jan. 27, 1754. Sponsors, Michael
Weber and Eva Goettel.
——— Anna Margaretha, b. Sept. 13,
1758; bap. Sept. 24, 1758. Sponsors,
Michael Braun and wife Anna Juliana.
——— Susanna Rosina, b. Aug. 1763; bap.
Aug. 31, 1763. Sponsors, Heinrich
Mueller and Susanna Rosina Heinrich.
——— Cunradt, b. Oct. 25, 1765; bap.
Nov. 1, 1765. Sponsor,Cunradt Weber.

CHRISTIAN BECHTEL, (Atolhoe.)
Bechtel—Eva Catarina, b. Feb. 9, 1754;
bap. Feb. 10, 1754. Sponsors, Jacob
Hofman and wife.

ADAM HAUSSHALTER, (Gummery.)
Hausshalter—Elisabetha, b. Jan. 19,
1754; bap. Feb. 12, 1754. Sponsors,
Johannes Lehn and wife.

CHRISTOPH SCHUPP, (Derry.)
Schupp—Johannes, b. Jan. 7, 1754; bap.
Feb. 25, 1754. Sponsors, George Bals-
pach, jr., and Margaretha Chagoin.

JACOB SCHUETZ, (Paxton.)
Schuetz—Johannes, b. Dec. 1, 1753; bap.
Feb. 25, 1754. Sponsors, Jacob Lentz
and wife Maria Elisabetha.

JACOB LENTZ, (Paxton.)
Lentz—Philipp Jacob, b. Dec. 1, 1753;
bap. Feb. 25, 1754. Sponsors, Philipp
Fischer and Elizabeth, N. N.

GEORGE HUBER, (Derry.)
Huber—Rosina Margaretha, b. Feb. 3,
1754; bap. Feb. 25, 1754. Sponsors,
Mattheis Wiehmar and wife Margar,
also Rosina Hummel.

ADAM RITTER, (Derry.)
Ritter—Philipp Adam, b. Jan. 9, 1754;
bap. Feb. 25, 1754. Sponsors, Philipp
Adam Balmer and Juliana Nagel.

JOHANNES WUERTZ, (Bern.)
Wuertz—Johannes, b. March 21, 1754;
bap. April 7, 1754. Sponsors, Johannes
Kloss and Barbara Strauss.

NICHOLAUS BECHTEL, (Bern.)
Bechtel—John Nicholaus, b. April 28,
1754; bap. May 5, 1754.

JOHANNES HAFFNER(Bethel.)
Haffner—Catarina Elisabetha, b. April
18, 1754; bap. May 19, 1754. Sponsors, Gottfried Stempel and wife.

WILHELM STEIN, (Atolhoe.)
Stein—John Abraham, b. Sept. 13, 1754; bap. Sept. 22, 1754. Sponsor,Abraham Schneider.

JOHANNES APPEL, (Atolhoe.)
Appel—Catarina, b. June 25, 1752; bap. July, 1752. Sponsors, Cunradt Foerster and wife.
—— Barbara, b. Nov. 5, 1754; bap. Nov. 17, 1754. Sponsors,Thomas Bauer and wife Barbara.

SEBASTIAN WILDFANG, (Atolhoe.)
Wildfang—Elisabetha, b. Dec. 13, 1754; bap. Dec. 15, 1754. Sponsors, Michael Wolfert and wife.

JOHANNES EISENHAUER, (Bethel.)
Eisenhauer—George Philipp, b. Dec. 19, 1754; bap. Jan. 13, 1755. Sponsor, George Philipp Schnatterle.

NICOLAUS WAMSSER, (Atolhoe.)
Wamsser—Maria Magdalena, b. Oct. 14, 1754; bap. Feb. 9, 1755. Sponsors, Jacob Foerster and wife.

ANDREAS SCHMIDT,
(Summer Mountain.)
Schmidt—John George, b. Jan. 24, 1755; bap. Feb. 9, 1755. Sponsor, Anna Barbara Gebhardt.

CUNRADT ROENNINGER, (Bethel.)
Roenninger—Susanna Margar., b. Jan. 26, 1755; bap. Feb. 23, 1755. Sponsors, Michael Haehnle and wife.

FRIEDERICH WIELANDT,
(Atolhoe.)
Wielandt—Maria Catarina,b. Feb., 1755; bap. March 9, 1755. Sponsors, Jacob Soerer and wife.

JACOB BREHM, (Bethel.)
Brehm—Margaretha Elisabetha, b. Feb. 9, 1755; bap. Feb. 16, 1755. Sponsors, Robert Grain and wife.

JOHN JACOB METZ, (Atolhoe.)
Metz—Gearge Jacob, b. March 1755; bap. April 6, 1755. Sponsors, George Flohr and wife.

ANDREAS SCHADT, (Tulpehocken.)
Schadt—John Jacob, b. May, 1755; bap. June 1, 1755. Sponsors, Jacob Gicker and wife Maria Catarina.
—— Maria Catarina, b. June 11, 1756; bap. July 27, 1756. Sponsors, Maria Catarina Philbert and Jacob Strauss.
—— Samuel, b. March 22, 1758; bap. April 2, 1758. Sponsors, Samuel Philbert and wife Susanna.
—— Anna Elisabetha, b. Sept. 16, 1759; bap. Sept. 23, 1759. Sponsors, John Albert and Anna Elisabetha Philbert.
—— John Michael, b. May 10, 1761; bap. May 24, 1761. Sponsors, John Michael Kehl and wife Catarina.

—— Maria Susanna, b. Nov. 29, 1762; bap. Dec. 19, 1762. Sponsors, Sauel Filbert and wife Susanna.
—— Andreas, b. Nov. 8, 1764; bap. Dec. 2, 1764. Sponsors, Balthasar Unbehagen and wife.

JOHN NICOLAUS SCHAEFER,
(Atolhoe.)
Schaefer—Johannes, b. June 21, 1752; bap. June 29, 1755. Sponsors, John Haag and Catarina Schaefer.

CASPAR SPRING, (Atolhoe.)
Spring—John Frederick, b. June 2, 1755; bap. July 27, 1755. Sponsors, John Frederick Wieland and wife Anna Eva.

PHILIPP METZGER, (Bethel.)
Metzger—Anna Maria, b. Aug. 13, 1755; bap Sept. 7, 1755. Sponsors, Herman Degreif and wife.

JOHN GEORGE HAAG, Jr., and wife
ANNA MARGAR., (Northkill.)
Haag—Maria Barbara, b. Sept. 15, 1755; bap. Sept. 21, 1755. Sponsors, Cunradt Crist and Maria Barbara Haag.
—— Anna Catarina, b. Nov. 21, 1757; bap. Dec. 11, 1757. Sponsors, John Nicolaus Holder, jr., and wife.
—— George Michael, b. May 12, 1762; bap. June 5, 1762. Sponsors, John Nicolaus Bechthold and wife Margaretha.

ADAM BRECHT, (Bethel.)
Brecht—Christian, b. Sept. 8, 1755; bap. Oct. 5, 1755. Sponsors, Christian Kaufman and wife Magdalena.
—— Maria Margaretha, b. Jan. 8, 1758; bap. March 11, 1758. Sponsors, Bernhardt Friedel and wife Margaretha.

BERNHARDT MANN, (Bethel.)
Mann—Catarina Elisabetha, b. Aug. 18, 1755; bap. Oct. 5, 1755. Sponsors, Phillip Schnatterle and Catarina Elisabetha Eissenhauer.

CHRISTIAN KAUFMAN, (Bethel.)
Kaufman—Anna Maria, b. Oct. 22, 1755; bap. Nov. 30, 1755. Sponsors, Adam Mosser and Anna Maria Dub.
—— Veronica, b. May 7, 1762; bap. May 30, 1762. Sponsors, John Eisenhauer and wife Veronica.

JACOB SCHUETZ (Paxtang.)
Schuetz—Maria Elisabetha, b. Oct. 29, 1755; bap. Dec. 30, 1755. Sponsors, Moritz Diehle and Maria Elisabetha Scheetz.

ADAM WIRTH, (Derry.)
Wirth—John Adam, b. Dec. 18,1755; bap. Dec. 25, 1755. Sponsors, John Wolf Kissner and wife Sabina.
—— Johannes, b. 1758; bap. Feb. 24,

1758. Sponsors, John Kissner Schnock and sister.
—— John Christian, b. 1759; bap. Dec. 26, 1759. Sponsors, Christian Schnock and wife.
—— John Jacob, b. Feb. 1763; bap. March 25, 1763. Sponsors, John Jacob Wolf, jr., and —— Schnug.

WILHELM LITZ, (Derry.)
Litz—Eva Catarina, b. Jan. 1756; bap. Jan. 26, 1756. Sponsors, Michael Bohr and Eva Barbara Deininger.

DAVID MUELLER, (Northkill.)
Mueller—John Thomas, b. Jan. 21, 1756; bap. Feb. 8, 1756. Sponsors, John Thomas Philbert and Elisabetha Strauss.

ANDREAS MORR and wife CATARINA, (Bethel.)
Morr—Anna Catarina, b. Feb. 3, 1756; bap. Feb. 23, 1756. Sponsors, Wendell Heyl and wife Anna.
—— Christina, b. Aug. 4, 1757; bap. Aug. 28, 1757. Sponsors, Michael Weber and wife.

CASPAR SCHNAEBELE (Anabaptist) and wife LUTHERAN, (Bethel.)
Schnaebele—Sophia Sabina, b. Jan. 21, 1756; bap. Feb. 23, 1756. Sponsors, Sabina Sauter.
—— John Jacob, b. Nov. 27, 1758; bap. April 15, 1759. Sponsors, Anastasius Uhler and wife Dorothea.

PETER NIESZ, (Bethel.)
Niesz—Maria Barbara, b. March 17, 1756; bap. March 21, 1756. Sponsors, John Caspar Stoever, jr., and Maria Barabara Nagel.

MATTHEIS WAGNER, (Northkill.)
Wagner—Johannes, b. April 22, 1756; bap. May 30, 1756. Sponsors, John Kaufman and wife Barbara.
—— Anna Catarina, b. Sept. 15, 1758; bap. Sept. 17, 1758. Sponsors, John Zerwe and wife Catarina.

JACOB WENTZ, Lebanon, (Kruppen.)
Wentz—Maria Catarina, b. May 27, 1756; bap. June 6, 1756. Sponsors, David Herbster and wife.
—— John Jacob, b. Jan. 1758; bap. Feb. 12, 1758. Sponsors, the above.

JOHN GAMBIL, (Lebanon.)
Gambil—Susanna, b. June 5, 1756; bap. June 14, 1756. Sponsors, Ralph Whiteside and wife Sarah Wilson.

JOHN GEORGE STAUCH, Atolhoe.)
Stauch—John Nicolaus, b. June 7, 1756; bap. June 27, 1756. Sponsors, John Nicolaus Deck, jr., and Anna Maria Pressler.

GEORGE PRESSLER, (Atolhoe.)
Pressler—Anna Margaretha, b. May 30,

1756; bap. June 27, 1756. Sponsors, Abraham Reiber and wife.

CHRISTOPH SCHAUM, (Atolhoe.)
Schaum—Christian, b. July 13, 1756; bap. July 25, 1756. Sponsors, Christian Meyer and wife Catarina.

JOHANNES STEIN and wife,(Atolhoe.)
Stein—Johannes, b. July 5, 1756; bap. July 25, 1756. Sponsors, Wilhelm Stein and Anna Margaretha Gebhardt.

JACOB KAUFMAN, (Northkill.)
Kaufman—Maria Appollonia, b. Nov. 25, 1756; bap. Dec. 12, 1756. Sponsors, Balthasar Unbehagen and wife.

MICHAEL GRAFF, (Bethel,Berks Co.)
Graff—Maria Elisabetha, b. Dec. 8, 1756; bap. Dec. 26, 1756. Sponsors, Jacob Stein and Maria Elizabetha Meyer.

JOHANNES SCHUY, (Bethel, Lancaster Co.)
Schuy—Johannes, b. Jan. 9, 1757; bap. March 13, 1757. Sponsors, John Lohmueller and Barbara Hautz.

JOHN NICOLAUS HAAG, (Bern.)
Haag—John Nicolaus, b. March 27, 1757; bap. April 3, 1757. Sponsor, John Nicolaus Schaefer.
—— John George, b. July 9, 1758; bap. July 23, 1758. Sponsors, George Radebach and Elizabetha Haag.
—— Maria Catarina, b. Sept. 13, 1763; bap. Oct. 7, 1763. Sponsors, Jonathan Eckert and wife Catarina.

JACOB SOERER, Jr., (Atolhoe.)
Soerer—Eva Catarina, b. March 22, 1757; bap. April 3, 1757. Sponsors, John Deck and Eva Catarina Weiland.

NICOLAUS SCHLESSMANN, (Atolhoe.)
Schlessmann—Maria Eva, b. March 6, 1757; bap. April 3, 1757. Sponsors, Hans George Diemer and Maria Eva Hofman.

SIMON ESPERT, (Lebanon.)
Espert—John George, b. Aug. 20, 1767; bap. Sept. 25, 1757. Sponsors, George Schumacker and wife.
—— Anna Elizabetha, b. April, 1765; bap. May 12, 1765. Sponsors, Arnold Scherertz and wife.

FRIEDERICH KRAMER, (Bethel.)
Kramer—John Jacob, b. April 10, 1757; bap. May 8, 1757. Sponsors, Jacob Eprecht and wife.

NOAH FRIEDERICH, (Bethel.)
Friederich—John George, b. March 27, 1757; bap. May 8, 1757. Sponsors, George Friederich and wife.

JOHANNES KUEMMERLING. (Deceased.)
Kuemmerling—Johannes, b. Dec., 1756;

bap. May 8, 1757. Sponsors, Johannes Dieb, jr., and wife.

MICHAEL MALFAIR, (Derry.)
Malfair—Michael, b. June 17, 1757; bap. July 10, 1757. Sponsors, Adam New and wife.

—— Anna Maria, b. Jan. 1766; bap. Feb. 9, 1766. Sponsors, John Christoph Friederich and wife Anna Maria.

JACOB BONNET, (Krupp Church.)
Bonnet—Rosina, b. Sept. 17, 1757; bap. Sept. 24, 1757. Sponsors, Christoph Meyer and wife Rosina.

JACOB WAGNER, (Bethel.)
Wagner—Cunradt, b. Sept. 15, 1757; bap. Sept. 26, 1757. Sponsors, Wilhelm Hardt and wife.

CHRISTIAN PHILIPPY, (Cocalico.)
Philippy—Anna Maria, b. Aug., 1757; bap. Oct. 8, 1757. Sponsors, John Nicolaus Ensminger, jr., and Anna Maria Nef.

JOHN ADAM LANG, (Moden Creek.)
Lang—Christina Catarina, b. Oct. 8, 1757; bap. Oct. 9, 1757. Sponsors, John George Martin and wife.

JOHN CASPER STOEVER, Jr., (Bethel.)
Stoever—Anna Margaretha, b. Jan. 24, 1758; bap. Feb. 12, 1758. Sponsors, Heinrich Bickel and Anna Margaretha Stoever, both single.

—— Maria Catarina, b. Aug. 4, 1759; bap. Aug. 25, 1759. Sponsor, Maria Catarina Stoever, sr.

—— Anna Christina, b. Aug. 2, 1761; bap. Aug. 9, 1761. Sponsor, Anna Christina Stoever.

—— Anna Maria, b. Nov. 3, 1763; bap. Dec. 11, 1763. Sponsor, Anna Maria Stoever.

—— John Casper, b. Feb. 27, 1765; bap. March 24, 1765. Sponsors, John Casper Stoever sr., and his wife Maria Catarina.

—— John Adam, b. May 29, 1767; bap. May 31, 1767. Sponsor, John Adam Stoever.

—— Anna Christina, b. Aug. 15, 1769; bap. Aug. 20, 1769. Sponsors, Johannes Fehler and wife Catarina.

—— Tobias. Sponsor, Tobias Stoever.

—— Anna Eva. Sponsors, Philipp Firnssler and wife Anna Christina.

—— John Frederick, b. Aug. 1, 1776; bap. Aug. 25, 1776. Sponsors, John Casper Stoever and wife Catarina.

JOHANNES SCHNEIDER and wife EVA, (Derry.)
Schneider—Eva Margaretha, b. Feb. 10, 1758; bap. Feb. 24, 1758. Sponsors, Philipp Schneider and Eva Margaretha Oberlin.

CHRISTOPH MUENCH and wife ANNA MARIA. (Bern.)
Muench—John George Michael, b. Feb. 6, 1758; bap. March 5, 1758. Sponsors. John George Michael Muench and —— Strauss.

—— John Philipp, b. Nov. 1, 1759; bap. Nov. 18, 1759. Sponsors, John Nicolaus Holder, jr., and wife Catarina.

JOHN MARTIN KUEFER and wife ELISABETHA. (Bethel.)
Kuefer—Anna Maria, b. Feb. 26, 1758; bap. March 11, 1758. Sponsors, Heinrich Dupp and wife.

—— John Frederich, b. Nov. 17, 1762; bap. Dec. 5, 1762. Sponsors, Casper Heussler and wife.

—— Elizabetha, b. Jan. 5, 1765; bap. March 10, 1765. Sponsors, Cunradt Gerhardt and Maria Elizabetha Kuefer.

—— Maria Elizabetha, b. Dec. 3, 1766; bap. March 15, 1767. Sponsors, Nicolaus Biel and wife Maria Elizabetha.

JACOB SCHNAEBELE, (Bethel.)
Schnaebele—Maria Barbara, b. Jan. 29, 1758; bap. March 11, 1758. Sponsors, Ottmar Schnaebele and wife.

PHILIPP BRUECKER and wife CATARINA, (Bern.)
Bruecker—John Michael, b. June 12, 1758; bap. June 25, 1758. Sponsors, John Michael Albert and wife Maria Margaretha.

VALENTIN GERHARDT, (Bethel.)
Gerhardt—Maria Catarina, b. Sept. 11, 1758; bap. Sept. 24, 1758. Sponsors, Heinrich Schnatterle and Anna Catarina Uhler.

JACOB WALTHER and wife ANNA MARIA, (Northkill.)
Walther—John David, b. Oct. 2, 1758; bap. Oct. 15, 1758. Sponsors, John David Fiess and wife Anna Maria.

—— David, b. July 15 (?), 1761; bap. July 19 (?), 1761. Sponsors, John Jacob Fiess and wife Anna Maria.

—— John Jacob, b. Dec. 19, 1762; bap. Feb. 24, 1763. Sponsors, George Haag sr., and wife Appolonia.

MARTIN SCHMIDT, (Swatara.)
Schmidt—John George, b. Oct. 4, 1758; bap. Oct. 22, 1758. Sponsors, George Glassbrenner and wife.

GEORGE ADAM GEISZ and wife ANNA BARBARA, (Northkill.)
Geisz—George Adam, b. April 11, 1759; bap. April 16, 1759. Sponsors, John George Haag, jr., and wife Margaretha.

—— Catarina Elizabeth, b. June 19, 1760; bap. June 29, 1760. Sponsors, Michael Beyer and Catarina Elizabetha Haag, on the day of marriage.

—— John Michael, b. Jan. 12, 1762; bap. Feb. 14, 1762. Sponsors, Michael Beyer and wife.

—— Philipp Jacob, b. Sept. 6, 1763; bap. Oct. 2, 1763. Sponsors, Philipp Jacob Geiss and wife.

JOHANNES LEYDIG and wife, (Hanover.)

Leydig—John Jacob, b. March 4, 1759; bap. April 15, 1759. Sponsors, John Jacob Cantz and Anna Catarina Uhler.

—— Maria Catarina, b. Dec., 1761; bap. Dec. 13, 1761. Sponsors, Dorst Brechbiel and wife.

HANS GEORGE DUMM, (Lebanon.)

Dumm—Anna Sabina, March, 1759; bap. April 15, 1759. Sponsors, John Wolf Kissner and wife Anna Sabina.

JACOB DREISCH and wife SUSANNA (Heidelberg.)

DREISCH—George Leonhardt, b. Feb., 1757; bap. April 23, 1759. Sponsors, John Leonhardt Dreisch.

—— John Reichardt, b. Dec. 25, 1758; bap. April 23, 1759. Sponsors, John Leonhardt Dreisch.

—— Rosina, b. Dec. 25, 1760; bap. March 19, 1761. Sponsors, Jacob Wentz and wife.

GOTTFRIED STEUPEL, (Lebanon.)

Steupel—Rosina, b. June 1, 1759; bap. June 24, 1759. Sponsors, David Herbster and wife Rosina.

—— John David, b. Feb., 1763; bap. Feb. 20, 1763. Sponsors, David Herbster and second wife Anna Maria.

—— Eva Catarina, b. Jan., 1760; bap. Feb. 26, 1766. Sponsors, George Mueller and wife.

MICHAEL SAUSZER, (Northkill.)

Sauszer—Catarina Elizabetha, b. Oct. 4, 1759; bap. Oct. 21, 1759. Sponsors, Mattheis Wagner and wife.

PETER FISCHER, (Lebanon.)

Fischer—Johannes, b. Oct. 14, 1759; bap. Nov. 11, 1759. Sponsors, John Dups and Margaretha Boecklin.

—— Barbara, b. July 13, 1765; bap. July 14, 1765. Sponsors, Heinrich Boeckle and wife Anna Maria.

—— John Jacob, b. Nov. 5, 1765; bap. Nov. 16, 1766. Sponsors, Jacob Engel and wife Margaretha.

ANDREAS BARTRUFF, (Lebanon.)

Bartruff—Anna Margaretha, b. Feb. 11, 1759; bap. March 11, 1759. Sponsors, John Wilhelm Klein and Anna Margar. Schuetz.

MARTIN MEYLY, JR., (Lebanon.)

Meyly—Anna Sabina, b. April 17, 1760; bap. May 25, 1760. Sponsors, Jacob Weber and Anna Sabina Meyly.

JACOB STRAUSS and wife ELISABETHA, (Bern.)

Strauss—Albrecht, b. June 22, 1760; bap. June 29, 1760. Sponsors, Albrecht Strauss and wife Anna Margaretha.

—— Johannes, b. June 27, 1762; bap. July 3, 1762. Sponsors, John Lang and Catarina Strauss.

—— David, b. July 9, 1764; bap. July 15, 1764. Sponsors, David Brecht and wife.

CASPER HEUSZLER and wife MARIA EVA, (Bern.)

Heuszler—Maria Magdalena, b. Sept, 24, 1760; bap. Sept. 21, 1760. Sponsors, Christian Maessner and wife.

CASPER HISZLER and wife ROSINA, (Bethel.)

Hinszler—Maria Magdalena, b. Sept. 24, 1760; bap. Oct. 5, 1760. Sponsors, George Sydebueger and wife.

SEBASTIAN NAGEL and wife MARIA MAGDALENA, (Bethel.)

Nagel—John Christian, b. Oct. 24, 1760; bap. Nov. 30, 1760. Sponsors, John Christian Koch and wife.

—— Anna Maria Barbara, b. Feb. 17, 1762; bap. Feb. 21, 1762. Sponsors, John Caspar Stoever and wife.

—— Johannes, b. Sept. 2, 1763; bap. Sept. 18, 1763. Sponsors, Johann Christian Lauer.

GEORGE SEDELMEYER and wife MAGDAL., (Bethel.)

Seidelmeyer—Anna Rosina, b. March 3, 1761; bap. March 19, 1761. Sponsors, Casper Heussler and wife Rosina.

—— John Caspar, b. March 17, 1762; bap April 4, 1762. Sponsors, Caspar Roeder and Regina Gerhard.

—— Maria Elisabetha, b. June, 1767; bap. July 12, 1767. Sponsors, Ulrich Joeckel and wife.

—— Heinrich, b. Oct. 9, 1774; bap. Oct. 18, 1774. Sponsors, Heinrich Schnatterle and wife Barbara.

JOHN DANIEL MADERN and wife ELISABETHA, (Bethel.)

Madern—Maria Eva Rosina, b. April 19, 1761; bap. May 17, 1761. Sponsors, Maria Eva Strauss.

—— John Thomas, b. 1762, bap. Oct. 31, 1762. Sponsors, John Thomas Madern and wife Veronica.

—— Michael, b. Oct., 1766; bap. Oct. 26, 1766. Sponsors, John Thomas Madern and wife Vernica.

JACOB WAGNER and wife MARIA APPOLLONIA, (Northkill.)

Wagner—Susanna Catarina, b. May 17, 1761; bap. May 24, 1761. Sponsors, Mattheis Muench and wife.

CHRISTIAN LUTZ.
Lutz—Christian, b. June 24, 1761; bap. July 12, 1761. Sponsors, George Glassbrenner and wife Elisabetha.

PETER HEDDERICH, JR., and wife MARGARETHA, (Hanover.)
Hedderich—John Peter, b. June 12, 1761; bap. July 26, 1761. Sponsors, John Peter Hedderich, Sr., and wife Philippina.

GEORGE BALZ OR BATZ and wife BARBARA.
Balz or Batz—John George, b. Aug. 17, 1761; bap. Sept. 22, 1761. Sponsors, John Weidelblech and wife Elisabetha.

THOMAS WAR.
War—Maria Margaretha, b. July 14, 1761; bap. Oct. 4, 1761. Sponsors, Nicolaus Ensminger and wife Maria Margar.

PHILIPP SCHNATTERLE, (Bethel.)
Schnatterle—Sabina Elisabetha, b. June 25, 1761; bap. Oct. 18, 1761. Sponsor, Sabina Schnatterle.

HEINRICH MUELLER and wife JACOBINA, (Bethel.)
Mueller—John Bernhardt, b. Sept., 1761; bap. Oct. 18, 1761. Sponsors, John Boesshaar and wife.

CHRISTOPH WITTMYER, (Bethel.)
Wittmyer—Maria Barbara, b. Nov. 2, 1761; bapt. Nov. 16, 1761. Sponsors, Ottmar Schnaebele and wife Barbara.
—— Anna Maria—b. Dec. 19, 1763; bap. Jan. 6, 1764. Sponsors, John Adam Kern and wife Anna Maria and Widow Anna Maria Fischer.

WENDEL KELLER, (Lebanon.)
Keller—Jacobina Rosina, b. Nov. 14, 1761; bap. Nov. 29, 1761. Sponsors, Michael Laurie and wife.
—— George Wendel, b. July, 1764; bap. July 24, 1764. Sponsors, Michael Balmer and wife.

JOHN MARTIN GROSZ and wife CATARINA, (Paxtang.)
Grosz—Elisabetha, b. Nov. 15, 1761; bap. Dec. 21, 1761. Sponsors, Jacob Kuenig and Elisabetha Schuetz.

MATTHIAS HEESZE and wife EVA CATARINA, (Swatara.)
Heesze—Johannes, b. Dec., 1761; bap. Dec. 20, 1761. Sponsors, Michael Zimmerman and wife Eva.
—— John Michael, b. Feb., 1765; bap. March 3, 1765. Sponsors, the above.
—— Eva Catarina, b. Oct., 1767; bap. Nov. 8, 1767. Sponsors, —— Weber and Catarina Zimmerman.

MARX SCHWENCK, (Northkill.)
Schwenck—Adam, b. Dec. 26, 1761; bap. April 11. 1762. Sponsors, John Adam Madern and wife Magdalena.

JOHANNES ACHE, (Bern.)
Ache—Maria Susanna, b. April 18, 1762; bap. June 2, 1762. Sponsors, Samuel Philbert and wife Susanna.

NICOLAUS SALADIN and wife ELISABETHA, (Bern.)
Saladin—Anna Catarina, b. March 28, 1762; bap. June 6, 1762. Sponsors, Andreas Reindzel and Catarina Kaufman.

JOHN CHRISTIAN UHRICH and wife, (Tulpehocken.)
Uhrich—Johannes, b. Oct., 1762; bap. Oct. 31, 1762. Sponsors, Jacob Eprecht and wife.

GEORGE MEYER and wife ANNA BARBARA, (Bethel.)
Meyer—Maria Elisabetha, b. Oct. 22, 1762; bap. Nov. 14, 1762. Sponsors, Philipp Jacob Bortner and wife Elisabetha.
—— Anna Maria, b. Dec., 1766; bap. Jan. 18, 1767. Sponsors, George Felty and wife Anna Maria.

PHILIPP JACOB BORTNER, and wife MARIA ELISABETHA, (Bethel.)
Bortner—Heinrich, b. April 24, 1761; bap. May, 1761. Sponsors, Heinrich Mueller and wife Jacobina.
—— John George, b. Feb. 1, 1763; bap. April 1, 1763. Sponsors, George Velten and wife Anna Maria.
—— Johannes, b. June 3, 1765; bap. June 16, 1765. Sponsors, Johannes Felten and wife.

DAVID JONES.
Jones—Jonathan, b. March 27, 1761; bap. Aug. 31, 1763. Sponsors, Henry Sowder and wife Sabina.

JOHANNES LANG and wife MARIA CATARINA, (Bern.)
Lang—Johannes Jacob, b. July 10, 1763; bap. Aug. 7, 1763. Sponsors, Jacob Lang and wife.

MICHAEL KREHL, (Bethel.)
Krehl—John Michael, b. Oct. 20, 1763; bap. Nov. 20, 1763. Sponsors, Nicolaus Wolf and wife.
—— Carolus, b. July, 1766; bap. Aug. 3, 1766. Sponsors, Carl Schedt and wife.

PAULUS BRICKLE and wife CATARINA, (Atolhoe.)
—— Born 1763, Nov. 26; bap. Nov. 27, 1763.

LEONHARDT HERGER, (Bethel.)
Herger—Anna Margaretha, b. Oct. 30, 1763; bap. Jan. 6, 1764. Sponsors, Cunradt Schmidt and wife Anna Margaretha.

DANIEL WUNDERLICH and wife EVA BARBARA, (Paxtang.)
Wunderlich—Eva Barbara, b. Feb. 27, 1764; bap. March 4, 1764. Sponsors, Christoph Shupp, jr., and Catarina Siechlin.

PETER ALBERT, (Bethel.)
Albert—John Peter, b. March 30, 1764; bap. May. 13. 1764. Sponsors, Martin Hess and wife.

THOMAS FILBERT and wife CATARINA, (Bern.)
Filbert—Samuel, b. May 16, 1764; bap. May 20, 1764. Sponsors, Samuel Filbert and wife Susanna.

NICOLAS DOYLE and wife ELIZABETH, (Derry.)
Doyel—John, b. June 2, 1764; bap. June 24, 1764. Sponsors, John Oehrle and wife Regina.

HEINRICH WEBERT and wife ELIZABETHA, (Bern.)
Webert—John Heinrich, b. July 19, 1764; bap. Aug. 12, 1764. Sponsors, John Heinrich Ache and wife Maria Catarina.

GEORGE GEISSEMANN.
Geissemann—Anna Maria, b. Jan. 25, 1765; bap. April 14, 1765. Sponsors, Adam Bach and wife Barbara.

JACOB SCHAACK and wife BARBARA.
Schaack—Anna Elizabetha, b. April, 1765; bap. May 12, 1765. Sponsors, —— Schaack and wife Elizabetha.

JOHN ADAM HERBERT and wife CATARINA, (Hanover.)
Herbert—John Thomas, b. Nov., 1764; bap. April 21, 1765. Sponsors Thomas Baseler and wife.
—— Eva Margaretha, b. July, 1774; bap. July 30, 1764. Sponsors, Thomas Koppenhoeffer and wife.

BURCKHARDT BOHR and wife LUCIA HENRIETTA, (Hanover.)
Bohr—John Mattheis, b. May, 1765; bap. June 16, 1765. Sponsors Mattheis Bohr and Elizabetha Catarina Neu.

PHILIP GRUENENWALDT, (Lebanon.)
Gruenenwaldt—Maria Margaretha, b. July 18, 1765; bap. July 18, 1765. Sponsors, Christoph Embisch and wife.

GEORGE FEDERHOFF and wife ANNA ELIZABETHA, (Lebanon Township.)
Federhoff—John Friederich, b. Aug. 6,

1765; bap. Aug.11, 1765. Sponsors, Friederich Jensel and wife Maria Agnes.

CHRISTOPH EMBISCH and wife (Lebanon.)
Embisch—Johannes, b. Sept. 5, 1765; bap. Sept. 8, 1765. Sponsors, Phillip Gruenenwalt and wife.
——John Friederich, b. Feb. 22, 1767; bap. March 8, 1767. Sponsors, Philipp Marstaller and wife.

TOBIAS BICKEL and wife (Tulpehocken.)
Bickel—Maria Catarina, b. Sept. 9, 1765; bap. Spet. 10, 1765. Sponsors, Jacob Schmidt and wife Juliana.
—— Eliabetha, b. Sept. 9, 1765; bap. Sept. 10, 1765. Sponsors, Jacob Schmidt and wife Elizabetha.
—— John Tobias, b. Sept., 1766; bap. Sept. 21, 1766. Sponsors, John Jacob Schmidt and wife Margaretha.

ANDREAS HOERAUF and wife, (Swatara.)
Hoerauf—John Heinrich, b. Sept., 1765; bap. Sept. 15, 1765. Sponsors, Johannes Oehrle and wife Regina.

ADAM SCHNEIDER and wife, (Bethel.)
Schneider—Maria Magdalena, b. Oct. 26, 1764; bap. Sept. 29, 1765. Sponsors, Heinrich Naess and Maria Magdalena Haehnle.

GEORGE SCHILL and wife, (Bethel.)
Schill—John Peter, b. Oct. 11, 1765; bap. Oct. 27, 1765. Sponsors, Nicolaus Biel and Barbara Kuefer.

CARL SCHEDT and wife, (Williams Borough.)
Schedt—Margaretha, b. Dec., 1765; bap. Jan. 19, 1766. Sponsors, Michael Grehl and wife Margaretha.

JOHANNES SCHWARTZ and wife Esther, (Lebanon Town.)
Schwartz—Johannes. Sponsors, George Sprecher and wife Margaretha.

JACOB SPRECHER and wife Dorothea, (Krupp Church.)
Sprecher—John Christoph, b. Sept. 10, 1766; bap. Sept. 20, 1766. Sponsors, George Sprecher and wife Eva Margaretha.

JACOB WEBER and wife Anna Maria, (Lebanon.)
Weber—Maria Catarina, b. Dec. 26, 1766; bap. Jan. 11, 1767. Sponsors, Heinrich Boeckle and wife.

JAMES WILLIAMS and wife, now dead, (Bethel.)
Williams—Johannes, b. Jan. 10, 1767;

bap. Jan. 18, 1767. Sponsors,Johannes Diebin and Margar. Haehnlin.

JOHN NICOLAUS BIEL and wife Maria Elisab., (Bethel.)
Biel—John Freiderich, b. Feb. 8, 1767; bap. March 15, 1767. Sponsors,Martin Kuefer and wife Maria Elisabetha.

PETER ELSZER and wife Anna Margaretha, (Warwick.)
Elszer—Peter, b. Feb. 14, 1767; bap. March 23, 1767. Sponsors, George Michael Eichelberger and wife.

JOHN ROESZLE,
(Krupp Church, of Lancaster.)
Roeszle—Susanna, b. June 13, 1767; bap. Aug. 2, 1767. Sponsors, George Eberle and wife Susanna.

JOHANNES HUBER and wife ELISAB., (Lebanon.)
Huber—John Jacob, b. July 27, 1767; bap. Aug. 2, 1767. Sponsors, Jacob Stieb and wife.

JACOB ZIEGLER, Jr., and wife JUDITH, (Lebanon.)
Ziegler—Philip Jacob, b. July, 1767; bap. Aug. 2, 1767. Sponsors, Philipp Brenner and wife.

MARTIN KUEMMERLING and wife ANNA MAGAR., (Bethel.)
Kuemmerling—Christoph Freiderich, b. Aug. 22; bap. Sept. 6, 1767. Sponsors, Christoph Frederich Weyman and wife Eva Maria.

GEORGE GLASS and wife EVA ELIZABETH.
Glass—Christian, b. Dec. 25, 1768; bap. Jan. 29, 1769. Sponsors, Jost Schwertzel and wife Susanna.

PETER KRAEMER and wife MARGARETHA, (Lebanon.)
Kraemer—John Adam, b. Feb. 19, 1767; bap. March 22, 1767. Sponsors, John Adam Waible and wife Anna.

CHRISTOPH ZIEBOLD and wife BARBARA, (Lebanon.)
Ziebold—Catarina, b. July 19, 1769; bap. July 24, 1769. Sponsors, Conradt Braun, Sr., and wife Agnes.
—— Anna Maria, b. July 19, 1769; bap. July 24, 1769. Sponsors, Michael Rieder and wife Anna Maria.

ANDREAS VOGEL and wife ANNA MARIA, (Hanover.)
Vogel—Andreas, b. (posthumous.), Jan. 1770; bap. Jan. 14, 1770. Sponsors, John Martin Lang and Hannah Zimmerman.

FRANCIS GUARD and REBECCA MARTIN.
Guard—Joseph, b. Feb. 4, 1770; bap. Feb.

5, 1771. Sponsors, John Martin and his wife Sarah.

LORENTZ STRICKER and wife, BARBARA, (Hanover.)
Stricker—Johannes Wilhelm, b. Feb. 26, 1771; bap. April 1, 1771. Sponsors, Jacob Wolf and wife Elisabetha.

PHILIPP JACOB GEISS and wife APPOLLONIA.
Geiss—Catarina, b. Sept. 17, 1753; bap. Sept., 1753. Sponsors, George Adam Geiss and Catarina Muench.

HEINRICH MEYER.
Meyer—John George, b. March, 1775; bap. May 14, 1775. Sponsors, John Roessle and wife.

JOHN NICOLAUS BOPP and wife CATAR. MARGAR., (Swatara.)
Bopp—Catarina, b. Jan. 28, 1776; bap. Feb. 11, 1776. Sponsors, Peter Felt and wife Catarina.

CHRISTIAN STUCKY and wife ANNA MARIA, (Hanover.)
Stucky—Anna Maria, b. Jan., 1776; bap. May 5, 1776. Sponsors, Wilhelm Hedderich and wife Margaretha ——.

JOHANNES GASSERT and wife ANNA MARIA, (Bethel.)
Gassert—Johannes, b. June 28, 1776; bap. Aug. 25, 1776. Sponsors, Martin Kuefer and wife Elisabetha.

JACOB NEFF and his wife, (Williamsborough.)
Neff—John Heinrich, b. Feb. 20, 1778; bap. April 5, 1778. Sponsors, Carl Schedt and wife Eva.

GEORGE WALMER and wife, (Hanover.)
Walmer—Johannes, b. June 15, 1778; bap. Oct. 17, 1778. Sponsors, Johannes Walmer and wife Christina.

MATTHEIS BRAUNWELL and wife, (Kruppen Land.)
Braunwell—John Heinrich, b. Oct. 11, 1778; bap. Dec. 6, 1778. Sponsors, Martin Weitz and wife.

————

(These entries were made after the death of John Casper Stoever in 1779.)

FREDERICK STOEVER.
Johann Frederick Stoever and wife Margaretha nee Daenscherlz.
Stoever—Maria Catarina b. Jan. 9, 1781; bap. Jan. 18, 1781. Sponsors, Catarina Stoever, widow.
—— Maria Catarina, b. 1782; bap. Oct. 9, 1782. Sponsor, Catarina Stoever, widow.

—— John Frederich, b. April 15, 1785; bap. May, 1785. Sponsors, Samuel Mery and wife Catarina.
—— John Jacob, b. June 10, 1787; bap. July, 1787. Sponsors, John Caspar Stoever and wife Barbara.
—— Johannes, b. Nov. 29, 1789; bap. July. Sponsors, John Stoever and his wife.
—— William, b. Aug. 21, 1792; bap.

Nov. 28, 1792. Sponsors, Johannes Stoever (son of Adam) and Catarina Franck, both single.
——John Philipp, b. April 8, 1795; bap. April, 1795. Sponsors, John Philipp Fernsler.
—— Cattarina, b. Oct. 13, 1798; bap. Nov. 4, 1798. Sponsors, Johann Gloninger and wife Catarina.

MARRIAGES.

Record of persons united in Matrimony by me, John Casper Stoever, Evangelical Lutheran Minister in Pennsylvania, Anno 1730:

1730.

March 18. Daniel Rausch and Elisabetha Optograef, Providence.
April 27. Andreas Sebastian and Albertina Krauss, Hanover.
May 30. Wilhelm Tscheill and Regina Leiter, Leacock.
May 31. Heinrich Bayer and Elisabertha Maria Zerwe, Tulpehocken.
October 6. Peter Schell and Maria Catarina Walborn, Tulpehocken.
Oct. 20. Johann Caspar Bergheimer and Elisabetha Catar. Kaeufer (or Kraeuser?), Providence.
Oct. 21. John Heinrich Krebs and Maria Barbara Krim, Hanover.
Oct. 27. John Kitzmueller, sr., and Margaretha Mack, Earl Town.
Oct. 28. Leonhardt Grau and Susanna Simons, Cocalico.
Nov. 9. John George Schumacher and Catarina Drechsler, Macungie.

1731.

Feb. 9. Jno. Jacob Mueller and Anna Maria Apollonia Hartman, Providence.
Feb. 18. John Jacob Schwartz and Anna Catarina Rul, Maxatawny.
Feb. 25. Francis Reynolds and Catarina Steitz, Quittapahila.
April 18. Robert Shmidt and Sarah Grand, Oley.
April 26. John Philipp Firnszler and Maria Barbara George, Lancaster.
May 5. John Urban Lang and Catarina Blum, Tulpehocken.
Jne 5. John Kitzmueller, jr., and Philippina Christian Mack, Earl Town.
Sept. 23. Charles Fulk and Catarina Harry, Manatawney.

Oct. 19. Roger Evans and Margaretha German, Nantmeal.
Dec. 21. John Morgan and Anne Flannery, Colebrook Dale.

1732.

Jan. 25. John Shmidt and Margaretha Pickets, Manatawny.
Feb. 19. William Evans and Catharine Weaker, Oley.
Feb. 20. Water Field and Anna Tomson, Colebrook Dale.
April 25. John Jacob Kitzmiller and Anna Maria Somner, Earl Town.
May 2. Peter Jacob Fehler and Maria Otilia Weiler, Oley.

1733.

April 10. Friederich Heinrich Geelbwicks and Maria Dorothea Euler, Providence.
June 12. John Martin Koeblinger and Catarina Schneider, Hanover.
June 18. Matheis Ochs and Anna Maria Steitz, Hanover.
June 19. John Adam Romich and Maria Ursala Kraemerin, Skippach.
June 22. Carl Valentin Michael Schuetz and Juliana Lips, Chestnut Hill.
July 1. Andreas Beyer and Susanna Catarina Berghmer, Providence.
August 25. John Bartolomeus Hornberger and Anna Elisabetha Reiffen, Chestnut Hill.
August 28. John Michael Fischer and Anna Margaretha Kemp, Schuylkill.
Sept. 27. John Jung and Elisabetha Catarina Rul, Moselem.
Oct. 15. Hieronymus Glantz and Erna Barbara Mack, Philadelphia.
Oct. 28. John Adam Schuler and Anna Elisabetha Kling, Chestnut Hill.
Nov. 9. Andreas Stautzenberger and Johanna Francis, Lampert.
Nov. 20. John George Kuntz and Catarina Ochs, Hanover.

Nov. 28. Mattheis Naesz and Maria Barbara Hoerdter, Skippach.

Dec. 11. Sebastian Zimmerman and Anna Elisabetha Levandt, Maxataney.

Dec. 18. Johannes Kepner and Elisabetha Kaerchner, Chestnut Hill.

Dec. 18. Johannes Boehm and Anna Maria Burger, Providence.

Dec. 25. Johann Michael Probst and Anna Maria Keller, Cocalico.

Dec. 26. John Leonhardt Immel and Maria Burckert, Lancaster.

Dec. 30. John Adam Stoll ad Margaretha Saber, Earl Town.

1734.

Jan. 6. Balthasar Schneider and Anna Catarina Schmidt, Chestnut Hill.

Jan. 7. Geo. Peter Bisswanger and Justina Elis. Riess, Geramntown.

Jan. 8. John George Kohl and Barbara Beer, Skippach.

Jan. 29. Tobias Moser and Ursula Margar. Meyer, Hanover.

Feb. 11. Johannes Huber and Elisabetha Hoerdter, Oley Mountain.

March 8. Michael Nold and Maria Barbara Pfleuger, Maselein.

March 11. Johann Frederich Hartman and Mar. Lindemann, Philadelphia.

March 25. John Jacob Kuhn and Lucia Roht, New Goschenhoppen.

April 15. Jacob Gerber and Agnes Baseler, Philadelphia.

April 28. Nicolaus Brintzler and Anna Margaretha Ort, Lancaster.

April 28. Ottmar Schnaebele and Anna Margaretha Baetlin, Lancaster.

May 21. Christoph Amborn and Susanna Klauer, Coventry.

June 6. John Michael Mooser and Ursula Dumb, New Goschenhoppen.

June 25. Jacob Heller and Anna Barbara Pfautz, Leacock.

July 22. Antonius Kneussel and Anna Barbara Doerr, Lancaster.

August 13. Johann Adam Tiffenbach and Maria Sybilla Koebel, Tulpehocken.

Sept. 3. Adolf Mohr and Margaretha Schuetz, Leacock.

Oct. 1. John Jacob Weynamdt ad Anna Stephan, Leacock.

Oct. 21. Jacob Mueller and Margaretha Walther, Frankford, at Delaware River.

Oct. 27. Philipp Rudiesile and Susanna Beyer, Conestoga.

Nov. 12. Philipp Diebo and Magdalena Biber, Coventry.

Nov. 14. John Adam Schillich and Rosina Widder, Cocalico.

Dec. 3. Nicolaus Coerper and Margaretha Marstaller, Skippach.

Dec. 18. Christoph Meyer and Anna Rosina Kopfenhoefer, Lebanon.

Dec. 29. Jacob Wuertz and Anna Barbara Hoof, Coventry.

1735.

Jan 7. John George Petry and Sabina Roth Cumru.

Jan. 10. David Bier and Elisabetha Trabern, Coventry.

March 9. John Philipp Hoffman and Maria Anna Dieter, Tulpehocken.

April 1. Martin Frey and Maria Magdalena Willheut, Codorus.

April 22. Paulus Bung and Maria Barbara Catermaenn, Cocalico.

April 29. John Mattheis Wagner and Elisabetha Stuep, Tulpehocken.

May 4. George Adam Heyl and Anna Elisabetha Madinger, Lancaster.

May 25. George Adam Stiess and Susanna Fechter, Lancaster.

June 2. Michael Will and Christina Puder, Leacock.

June 17. Johannes Mueller and Anna Martin Spatz, Cocalico.

June 17. John Casper Dorst and Anna Elisabetha Ferrar, Cocalico.

July 1. John George Heyl and Margaretha Dill, Leacock.

August 10. John George Bohrman and Catharina Motz, Warwick.

August 15. Nicolaus Koger and Maria Elisabetha Willheut, Codorus.

August 16. Two English couples at Susquehanna River, in Creesop's house.

Oct. 6. John Peter Kucher and Anna Bar. Koephenhoefer Lebanon.

Oct. 14. John Wilhelm Albert and Maria Eva Allgeyer, Leacock.

Oct. 16. Valentin Schultz and Maria Eva Stocker, Conestoga.

Oct. 17. Friederich Linnenburger and Anna Catarin Hildebrandt, Conestoga.

Nov. 2. John George Hauck and Anna Maria Zint, Conestoga.

Nov. 18. Peter Becker and Susanna Holtzbaum, Conestoga.

Nov. 25. Michael Raup and Anna Maria Meihel, Earl Town.

Nov. 30. Martin Schoeffle and Elisabetha Sieber, Conestoga.

Dec. 26. Laurentz Weber and Anna Maria Kirchhoefer, Leacock.

Dec. 30. John Caspar Schaffner and Anna Maria Knobel, Lancaster.

Dec. 30. Christian Andereck and Anna Catarina Jung, Lancaster.

1736.

Jan. 12. John Geo. Riegel and Anna Maria Plattner, Tulpehocken.

Jan. 13. Valentin Schneider and Anna Kiebing, Cocalico.

Jan. 20. Michael Kopf and Maria Margaretha Frey, Moden Creek.

Jan. 20. George Hoegie and Anna Eva Frey, Moden Creek.

Feb. 10. Jacob Schreyak and Barbara Wolff, Hempfield.

March 9. Jacob Verdriess and Catarina Euler, Warwick.

March 21. George Michael Koch and Anna Catarina Ergebrecht, Warwick.

March 29. Solomon Kremlich and Anna Christina Lapp, Perkiomen.

May 3. Two English couples at Opecken, in the presence of Lord Fairfax, in the county of Orange and in the colony of Virginia.

May 25. Heinrich Klein and Anna Maria Bettlin, Warwick.

May 30. Nicolaus Mueller and Catarina Lechner, Warwick.

June 12. Valentin Groh and Elisabetha Schaeffer, Helm Town.

June 14. Wilhelm Ellbrodt and Anna Beschel, Warwick.

June 14. Heinrich Bischoff and Elisabetha Ellrodt, Warwick.

June 22. Jacob Heyl and Catarina Riehl, Lancaster.

Aug. 29. Johannes Schreyack and Susanna Kirn, Lancaster.

Aug. 31. John Carl Hornberger and Ana Eva Saur, Leacock.

Nov. 9. John Leonhardt Billmeyer and Anna Bart, Leacock.

Dec. 14. Heinrich Geiger and Anna Barbara Becher, Earl Town.

1737.

Feb. 1. Thomas Willson and Anna Catharina Henckel, Lancaster.

Feb. 1. Joseph Mayhuw and Elisabetha Swinehardt, Lancaster.

Feb. 3. Johannes Sawer and Anna Currey, Leacock.

Feb. 7. John Peter Wissenandt and Maria Magdalena Suni, Cocalico.

Feb. 13. Jacob Spannseiler and Elis. Magdalena Schmidt, Lancaster.

Feb. 22. George Stephan Baumann and Maria Catar. Ergebrecht, Warwick.

April 19. Martin Koeller and Magdalena Leitner, Leacock.

April 25. Philipp Knopff and Maria Elisabetha Hoffman, Earl Town.

May 3. Anastasius Uhler and Dorothea Terg, Lancaster.

May 10. Michael Bintz and Anna Elisabetha Huber, Earl Town.

June 8. John Hodge and Elisabeth Windseeth, Jacob Thigh and Mary White, Daniel Hoolman and Elizabeth Cartlay, North River, Shenandoah, vulgo. Cockel Town in Orange county, in the Colony of Virginia.

June 20. Christian Loeffel and Maria Barbara Wittner, Catores.

June 21. Johannes Cledy and Esther Tusser, Beaver Creek.

June 21. Andreas Grass and Barbara Cledy, Beaver Creek.

July 3. John George Schmidt and Catarina Jung, Lancaster.

Aug. 15. Patrick Block and Mary Black, Lancaster.

Sept. 7. Valentin Mueller and Elizabetha Dorothea Lochmann, Earl Town.

Sept. 13. Johannes Uhrich and Margaretha Brenneis, Cocalio.

Sept. 14. Christoph Neumeister and Anna Louis, Earl Town.

Oct. 10. Leonhard Hof and Elizabehta Stout, Swatara.

Oct. 23. John Jacob Frank and Anna Catarina Boller, Lancaster.

Oct. 24. Michael Wittmer and Veronica Huber, Hampfield.

Nov. 21. Philipp Ziegeler and Margaretha Schmidt, Cadorus.

Nov. 21. George Meyer and Christina Ziegeler, Codorus.

Dec. 4. William Lightel and Nolly Owens, Lancaster.

Dec. 15. Antonius Rosenbaum and Barbara Baumaenn, Earl Town.

Dec. 20. Jonas Donner and Anna Schreyack, Cocalico.

1738.

Jan. 9. Johannes Riegel and Catarina Elizabetha Schirmann, Tulpehocken.

Jan. 15. Jacob Forsett and Eva Margaretha Weyer, Tulpehocken.

Jan. 15. Michael Becker and Anna Margaretha Diel, Lancaster.

Jan. 17. John George Ziegeler and Margaretha Hamspacher, Codorus.

Jan. 23. Edward Thurnbury and Elizabeth Burney, Warwick.

Jan. 23. ...chard Rampton and Elizabetha Grandy, Warwick.

Jan. 24. Adam Vollmar and Anna Margaretha Eichelberger, Conestoga.

Feb. 6. John Welsh and Elizabeth Whitside, Quittapahila.

Feb. 7. Johannes George Glassbrenner and Elizabetha Fischer, Tulpehocken.

Feb. 8. Johannes George Laub and Anna Winger, Tulpehocken.

Feb. 8. Johannes Kittner and Barbara Heinrich, Tulpehocken.

Feb 12. John George Loewenstein and Catarina Ruscher, Lancaster.

Feb. 14. Erasmus Holtzapfel and Christina Ruscher, Earl Town.

Feb. 21. Johannes Volckman and Elizabeth Ferrir, Leacock.

March 21. Johannes Jacob Dambach and Maria Elizabetha Seyboldt, Lancaster.

March 26. Jonas Wolf and Anna Catherine Becker, Lancaster.

April 4. John Frederich Eichelberger and Maria Magdalena Beber, Conestoga.

April 4. Johann Peter Anspach and Magdalena Bockenmeyer, Tulpehocken.

April 4. George Meyer and Barbara Zerve, Tulpehocken.

April 21. Johann Jacob Weller and Anna Barbara Vieruhr, Hellam.

April 22. John Hannthorn and Frances Low, Codorus.

April 23. Johan George Gemeinhardt (or Schweinhardt) and Elizabetha Scholl, Lancaster.

April 25. Johannes Ernst and Susanna Leitner, Leacock.

May 22. John Jacob Scherer and Philippia Hauck, Codorus.

May 22. John George Wolf and Anna Maria Schmidt, Codorus.

June 5. John Jacob Neuschwanger and Maria Gertraudt Brumbach, Opaken.

June 14. Patrick Kue and Martha Markley, Earl Town.

June 25. Johannes Kuntz and Anna Elizabetha Catherine Stoever, Earl Town.

June 27. Johann Friederich Stein and Catherine Traber, Conestoga.

June 27. John Heinrich Schultz and Anna Margaretha Rothrock, Conestoga.

June 27. Mattheis Marcker and Catharina Schreier, Mannheim.

July 2. John Mountgomery and Esther Hueston, Earl Town.

Aug. 2. Mattheis Schierisser and Catarina Koppenhoefer, Lebanon.

Aug. 8. James McCall and Jane Harris, Earl Town.

Aug. 8. Justus Simon Wagner and Maria Elizabetha Klein, Moden Creek.

Aug. 13. John Sharp and Margaretha McCnely, Lancaster.

Aug. 13. Johannes Moll and Susanna Heintzmaenn, Lancaster.

Aug. 14. Thomas Schmidt and Esther Diren, Earl Town.

Sept. 10. Peter Cornelius and Anna Catharina Vogel, Earl Town.

Oct. 2. Robert Chreesty and Isabel Teep, Lancaster.

Oct. 5. George Anderson and Elizabeth McDowel, Earl Town.

Oct. 8 . Alexander Makintyer and Margaretha Mt. Gommery, Earl Town.

Oct. 15. Andreas Kraemer and Magdalena Birckel, Lancaster.

Nov. 5. Andreas Mueller and Margaretha Funck, Lancaster.

Nov. 5. Thomas Bumpas and Anna Toward, Lancaster.

Nov. 7. Jacob Greter and Maria Barara Hart, Moden Creek.

Nov. 10. Lazarus Wagner and Anna Catarina Bauck, Tulpehocken.

Nov. 24. John Heinrich Traut and Anna Maria Baum, Monakesen.

Nov. 26. Peter Habach and Catarina Berg, Monakesen.

Dec. 3. Michael Proops and Maria Margaretha Corell, Lancaster.

Dec. 12. Francis Reynolds and Elenore Thistle, Quittapahilla.

Dec. 16. Samuel Swaller and Margaretha Kroh, Conestoga.

Dec. 31. Johannes Noll and Elizabetha Catharine Schaeffer, Tulpehocken.

1739.

Jan. 2. George Philipp Dollinger and Maria Ferry, Pequea.

Jan. 20. Alexander Grahem and Sarah Grahem, Earl Town.

Jan. 21. Johann Ludwig Suesz and Eva Engelsch, Lancaster.

Jan. 21. Philipp Stuertzer and Barbara Huber, Lancaster.

Jan. 22. Patrick Clark and Anne Steward, Hempfield.

Jan. 23. Wendel Traut and Magdalena Walter, Strasburgh.

Jan. 29. Johann Christian Lauer and Anna Catarina Sterf, Tulpehocken.

Jan. 29. Peter Heylman and Salome Frey, Lebanon.

Feb. 6. Balthasar Wendrich and Catarina Weider, Leacock.

Feb. 6. Balthasar Boesshaar and Johanna Dorothea Weider, Leacock.

Feb. 15. Jacob Welsch and Elizabetha Wolf, Codorus.

Feb. 25. John Bontz and Magdalena Hatt, Earl Town.

Feb. 26. Johann Friederich Kapp and Eva Maria Graff, Tulpehocken.

Feb. 26. Johannes Hoehmann and Magdalena Hehnlin, Tulpehocken.

Feb. 26. John Jacob Seibert and Maria Elizabetha Teiss, Tulpehocken.

Feb. 27. Martin Braun and Catharina Heuser, Warwick.

March 13. John David Buehler and Margaretha Stoer.

March 18. Andreas Borth and Anna Barbara Klein, Lancaster.

March 18. Christian Geiger and Anna Maria Esskuchin, Lancaster.

March 23. Stephen Gutman and Eva Margaretha Schmidt, Tulpehocken.

March 26. Andreas Graff and Maria Magdalena Kreutzer, Tulpehocken.

March 27. Joseph David Triessler and Maria Drusiana Rautenbusch, Lancaster.

March 27. Johann Stephan Tranckel and Eva Catarina Hambrecht, Lancaster.

March 27. Jacob Eichholtz and Elizabetha Klein, Lancaster.

March 27. John George Graff and Maria Magdalena Braumwaehrt, Lancaster.

April 10. Philipp Adam Endtler and Margaretha Gaeiss, Leacock.

April 23. Leonhardt Breitenstein and Anna Maria Buengel, Earl Town.

April 23. Johann Ulandt and Elizabetha Lintner, Earl Town.

April 23. John Adam Hambrecht and Elizabetha Barbara Heyl, Lancaster.

April 23. John George Quickel and Ursula Mueller, Lancaster.

April 23. John Frederick Carl and Catarina Elisabetha Olig, Lancaster.

April 30. Peter Maag and Juliana Rheinhart, Opecken in Orange county, Va.

May 25. Michael Mueller and Gertraudt Gruen, Codorus.

June 12. Andreas Kochendoerffer and Justina Catar. Kayser, Tulpehocken.

June 12. Peter Stout and Margaretha Cypher, Swatara.

June 12. James Russell and Jane Russell, Lebanon.

June 13. John George Saeger and Anna Maria Kloter, Warwick.

June 15. Johann Michael Koerber and Elisabetha Ktaepper, Codorus.

June 17. George Hutzel and Elisabetha Schweinhardt, Manokesy.

June 18. Philipp Morgenstern and Maria Eva Kuntz, Conewago.

June 18. Moritz Mueller and Dorothea Beyerstall, Codorus.

June 19. John Michael Schreiner and Anna Barbara Leonhardt, Lancaster.

June 25. John Martin Oberlin and Anna Margaretha Naess, Warwick.

June 25. John Heinrich Foltz and Maria Eva Bluem, Warwick.

July 13. John Jacob Hill and Maria Appolonia Merckling, Moselem.

July 10. John Deitrich Ulrich and Elisabetha Gaeiss, Leacock.

July 17. Thomas Whithead and Margar. Shlaughter, Earl Town.

July 24. John Heinrich Sauer and Maria Dorothea Englert, Cocalico.

August 5. Balthasar Schneider and Catharina Bader, Lancaster.

August 7. John Geo. Mohr and Anna Heckendorn, Earl Town.

August 12. John George Buerger and Anna Catarina Kuenig, Warwick.

August 19. John Wilhelm Ernst and Eva Catarina Bach, Lancaster.

August 20. George Peter Schultz and Anna Catarina Hausknecht, Hempfield.

August 27. John Wendel Braun and Maria Elisabetha Knopf, Tulpehocken.

August 2. John Heyl and Werina Roenner, Tulpehocken.

Sept. 2. John Steward and Sarah Horsebrough, Lancaster.

Sept. 9. Christoph Labengeiger and Anna Catarina Hubel, Warwick.

Sept. 10. Michael Stump and Anna Catrarina Neff, Tulpehocken.

Oct. 14. John George Ellinger and Maria Justina Lew, Earl Town.

Oct. 16. John George Honig and Maria Agnes Kretscher, Lancaster.

Oct. 16. Paul Burkhardt and Anna Eva Schwab, Earl Town.

Oct. 23. John Heinrich Stoer and Maria Barbara Bruechen, Moden Creek.

Oct. 30. John George Hatt and Maria Magdalena Staengel, Earl Town.

Nov. 30. Matthew Clark and Elisabetha Ingerham, Lebanon.

Nov. 4. Abraham Hausswirth and Anna Maria Berghoefer, Codorus.

Nov. 4. Edward Wells and Elisabetha Shmidt, Hallam.

Nov. 16. James Cunningham and Anna Shadwell, Lancaster.

Nov. 20. John Heinrich Wolf and Barbara Naess, Warwick.

Nov. 25. John Caspar Schmidt and Christian Kaufman, Lancaster.

Nov. 25. Frederich Thranberg and Maria Eva Wittmer, Lancaster.

Dec. 3. Peter Knopf and Sophia Catarina Gaemling, Tulpehocken.

Dec. 4. Andreas Wolf and Regina Klein, Warwick.

Dec. 20. John George Schaiteler, Monacasy, and Margaretha Neff, Kreuz Creek.

Dec. 22. John Marshal and Hannah Baldwin, Hempfield.

Dec. 25. Nicolaus Honig and Maria Elisabetha Fisher, Lancaster.

1740.

Jan. 8. John Adam Oberlin and Catharina Agatha Stober, Warwick.

Jan. 22. Frederich Haehnlin and Margaretha Oesterlin, Warwick.

Jan. 15. James Huggens and Isabell Pleure, Earl Town.

Feb. 5. John Adam Gaumer and Margaretha Ruscher, Hempfield.

April 18. Isaac Rautenbusch and Magdalena Frey, Codorus.

May 9. William Morgan and Margaretha Jones, Earl Town.

May 10. James McDuff and Margaretha Wood, Earl Town.

May 13. Ulrich Huebscher and Maria Margar. Chaguin, Moden Creek.

May 13. Jacob Halteman and Maria Catar. Boin, Moden Creek.

May 21. Peter Schaefer and Anna Schaub, Manaquesen.

May 22. Johannes Dierdorf and Margaretha Ehrhardt, Conewago.
May 22. John George Schmeiser and Barbara Stambach, Codorus.
May 27. John Michael Ehrhardt and Catarina Elisabetha Lesch, Tulpehocken.
May 27. George Michael Kittner and Maria Catar, Friederich, Tulpehocken.
May 27. John Philipp Maurer and Catarina Rameler, Tulpehocken.
June 8. Andreas Eul and Catarina Margar Hoffman, Warwick.
July 24. Stephan Rausch and Anna Dorothea Ziegler, Earl Town.
July 28. John George Arnold and Hannah Knopf, Tulpehocken.
August 11. John George Riedt and Margaretha Filich, Earl Town.
August 11. Jacob Bauman and Elizabetha Rueger, Earl Town.
August 20. Balthasar Schoenberger and Anna Margar. Zwickel, Conojahela.
Sept. 19. Johannes Iuengling and Margaretha Elenora Beuckert, Conewago.
Sept. 19. Friederich Kreuter and Anna Barbara Euler, Conewago.
Sept. 23. Albinus Beyer and Anna Maria Steutz, Codorus.
Oct. 5. John George Bohrmann and Agnes Doerr, Warwick.
Oct. 25. George Heard and Elenore Boyd, Warwick.
April 29. Carl Eisen and Rebecca Hamspacher. Codorus.
Nov. 9. Johannes Braun and Eva Kueffer, Tulpehocken.
Nov. 25. John Waters and Sarah Hopkins. Conewago.
Dec. 8. Andreas Kapp and Regina Sophia Siegmann, Tulpehocken.
Dec. 9. Nicolaus Geiger and Anna Margaretha Feg, Tulpehocken.
Dec. 26. John Daniel Diehl and Anna Maria Elisabetha Simon, Warwick.
Dec. 26. John Adam Simon and Maria Elisabetha Diehl, Warwick.

1741.

Jan. 19. Valentin Bentz and Maria Catarina Oberlin, Cocalico.
Jan. 23. John Heinrich Wilhelm and Catarina Haermaennin, Swatara.
Feb. 10. George Jacob Schnuerer and Catarina Bohrmann. Warwick.
Feb. 17. Jacob Holtzinger and Maria Veronica Wittmeyer, Cocalico.
March 27. John Peter Volck and Anna Maria Boetten (a Quaker), Conestoga.
March 30. John Leacock and Esther Eshender, Martick Township.
April 5. James Hinds and Margaretha Skarl, Great Conewago.
April 5. John Martin Mannsperger and Margaretha Nuesch, Codorus.

April 8. John Simon Eitlen and Anna Magdalena Kintz, Earl Town.
April 12. Thomas Greuel and Margaretha Koellmer, Tulpehocken.
April 12. Jacob Zorn and Anna Maria Gotteskind, Tulpehocken.
April 12. Gottfried Lautermilch and Anna Margaretha Meyer, Tulpehocken.
April 27. Abraham Wendel and Barbara Straup, Earl Town.
June 7. John Jacob Sauebert and Susanna Schuetz, Tulpehocken.
June 9. Michael Lauer and Maria Barbara Frey, Moden Creek.
July 6. John Weidman and Margaretha Hausshalter, Cocalico.
July 20. Christian Rotenbach and Magdalena Wagner, Cocalico.
July 26. John Michael Quickel and Barbara Mueller, Conestoga.
Aug. 4. John Michael Haagmeyer and Eva Frederica Weidman, Conestoga.
August 20. Jacob Otlinger and Anna Johanna Josie, Codorus.
August 20. George Adam Zimmerman and Anna Maria Motz, Codorus.
Sept. 29. John Flatsher and Abernie Kare, Mash Creek.
Oct. 6. Ulrich Buerger and Magdalina Binckel, Moden Creek.
Oct. 13. Engelhardt Flohry and Elisabetha Zerw, Tulpehocken.
Oct. 20. Nicolaus Roils and Catarina Margar. Schneider, Moden Creek.
Oct. 26. Adam Guellin and Rebecca Worley, Conestoga.
Nov. 10. Samuel Pickerstaff and Elisabeth Moor, Cana Shicken.
Nov. 17. John Christoph Traenckel and Anna Maria Spengler, Lancaster.
Nov. 21. James Tennin and Elisabeth Adams, of Swatara.
Nov. 26. Gehrhardt Zimmerman and Elisabetha Beyer, Lancaster.
Dec. 6. John Christian Schmidt and Juliana Pohin, Tulpehocken.
Dec. 7. Nicolaus Jungblut and Anna Maria Kappler, Tulpehocken.
Dec. 14. John Michael Biegler and Susanna Reuscher, Conewago.
Dec. 14. John Geo. Ulrich and Catarina Sell. Conewago.
Dec. 21. Jacob Kuehports and Maria Elis. Haehnlin, Pequea.
Dec. 28. Martin Stuep and Anna Susanna Wallbort, Tulpehocken.

1742.

Jan. 3. Nicolaus Kintzer and Anna Catara. Hoester, Quittapahilla.
Jan. 9. Jacob Storm and Maria Saurin. Earl Town.
Jan. 24. Johannes Mueller and Anna Barbara Schuppinger, Tulpehocken.

Jan. 25. Jacob Vollmar and Justina Kaercher, Tulpehocken.

Jan. 26. Christian Gruber and Anna Kueningunde Stulp, Tulpehocken.

Jan. 26. Stephan Cunradt and Anna Catarina Stahlschmidt, Tulpehocken.

Feb. 23. James Waite and Catarina Evans, Earl Town.

Feb. 24. George Stephan Mann and Maria Catarina Mueller, Lancaster.

March 7. Johan George Kintz and Maria Elizabetha Quickel, Lancaster.

March 9. Michael Kissinger and Catarina Roland, Cocalico.

March 16. Melchior Heiter and Anna Maria Amborn, French Creek.

March 22. John Abraham Leppo and Anna Margaretha Schueler, Swatara.

March 26. John Christian Schneider and Maria Magdalena Schaeffer, Earl Town.

March 26. Maurice Skullin and Bridgitte Conally, Salsbury.

March 29. Joseph Obold and Elizabetha Hausshalter, Cocalico.

April 7. Michael Mueller and Barbara Stucker, Codorus.

April 7. Antony Hinds and Anna Canaan, Conojohela.

April 18. Leonardt Umberger and Barbara Borst, Lebanon.

April 16. John Wendel Heyl and Anna Trotter, Bethel.

April 26. John George Emmert and Eva Maria Graff, Heidelberg.

April 26. John Immel and Anna Barbara Lay, Tulpehocken.

April 27. Christoph Witter and Christiana Roeser, Cocalico.

April 27. John Philipp Stoer and Anna Maria Holder, Warwick.

April 29. Valentin Frey and Anna Barbara Meyer, Moden Creek.

April 29. Martin Frey and Susanna Catarina Ensminger, Moden Creek.

May 11. Nicolaus Martin and Eva Stover, Warwick.

May 11. Jacob Neff and Christina Stober, Warwick.

May 16. Michael Scholl and Anna Margaretha Helwig, Tulpehocken.

May 16. Adam Helwig and Sophia Scholl, Tulpehocken.

May 16. John Gilbert and Elizabetha Pannel, Swatara.

May 16. John Kuehny and Elizabetha Cars, Swatara.

June 8. Abraham Neff and Anna Christina Loesh, Tulpehocken.

June 9. John Welsh and Anna Sharp, Lebanon.

July 4. Nicolaus Marret and Magdalena Eub, Warwick.

July 31. Philipp Linn and Catarina Buschfeld, Codorus.

July 31. Gottfrey Frey and Margaretha Linn, Codorus.

August 8. Peter Wolf and Hanna Wolf, Tulpehocken.

August 16. John Christoph Schupp and Anna Margaretha Pokin, Moden Creek.

August 17. Heinrich Spanhauer and Anna Elizabeth Linn, Lancaster.

Oct. 11. John Peter Schmidt and Eva Rosina Fauth Manakasy.

Oct. 11. James Conner and Anne Catarina Ellrodt, Manakasy.

Oct. 16. Gotthardt Dressel and Anna Maria Weill. Warwick.

Oct. 18. Michael Umberger and Anna Maria Ramler, Tulpehocken.

Oct. 19. John Heinrich Ensminger and Christina Ouir, Cocalico.

Oct. 24. Thomas McCarthy and Margaretha Dill, Conewaga.

Oct. 29. Casper Loewe and Margaret Esskuch, Lebanon.

Oct. 31. Ludwig Knopf and Margaretha Fraelich, Tulpehocken.

Nov. 19. John Michael Oberlin and Christina Zwecker, Earl Town.

Nov. 24. John Causseler and Maria Catarina Pfleuger, Codorus.

Nov. 24. John Bichszler and Magdalena Krohbiel, Codorus.

Nov. 24. Carl Thiel and Maria Elizabetha Ehrhardt, Codorus.

Nov. 28. John Peter Schmidt and Maria Margaretha Huber, Tulpehocken.

1743.

Jan. 6. Andreas Ketterle and Catarina Barbara Becher, Lebanon.

Jan 14. John Pontius and Anna Catarina Zoeller, Tulpehocken.

Jan. 17. William Crogge and Catharine Kenny, Earl Town.

Jan 18. Valentin Stober and Eva Elizabetha Beyer, Warwick.

Jan. 23. Philipp Petry and Susanna Juliana Emmert, Northkill.

Jan. 25. Martin Beyer and Anna Barbara Staehlin, Warwick.

Feb. 1. John Jacob Stober and Anna Catarina Naess, Warwick.

Feb. 8. Heinrich Bauer and Margaretha Bauer, Earl Town.

Feb. 10. John Cox and Mary Cresswell, Salisbury.

Feb. 20. John George Huber and Catarina Hoster, Tulpehocken.

Feb. 24. Sebastian Naess and Margaretha Gross, Cocalico.

Feb. 27. Jacob Reuter and Anna Maria Frey, Moden Creek.

March 13. John David Schaeffer and Anna Catarina Simon, Codorus.

March 23. Andreas Friederich and Elizabetha Shoerck, Conestoga.

April 5. John Jost Schwab and Anna Maria Bricker, Earl Town.

April 11. Michael Katz and Anna Maria Mohr, Tulpehocken.

April 17. Daniel Huber and Anna Sophia Meyer, Warwick.

April 19. Johannes Kistler and Anna Magdalena Prossman, Tulpehocken.

May 22. John Ermentrout and Anna Elizabetha Hedderich, Bern.

May 30. Mattheis Boeckle and Maria Dorothea Riedt, Earl Town.

June 20. John Callbreath and Martha Henderson, Hanover.

June 28. Peter Laucks and Anna Barbara Kuerschner, Tulpehocken.

July 3. Jacob Schaub and Barbara Heyer, Tulpehocken.

July 24. Adam Faber and Anna Maria Hautsch, Warwick.

July 31. Heinrich Meyly and Veronica Spitaler, Bethel.

August 14. George Veit Kapp and Gertraudt Friederich, Tulpehocken.

August 23. Heinrich Wilhelm and Elizabetha Scherb, Bethel township.

August 30. Heinrich Frey and Catarina Schauer, Heidelberg.

Sept. 26. John Peter Wampler and Anna Barbara Brenneiss, Swatara.

Oct. 10. George Michael Schollmeyer and Anna Barbara Huber, Warwick.

Oct. 17. John Adam Hausshalter and Maria Elizabetha Weidman, Warwick.

Oct. 18. John Philipp Kissinger and Catarina Heyl, Cocalico.

Oct. 20. Nicolaus Kintzer and Juliana Schneider, Tulpehocken.

Oct. 23. John Herman Eckel and Anna Margaretha Ohrendurf, Lebanon.

Oct. 31. Caspar Meissner and Anna Barbara Echardt, Moden Creek.

Nov. 29. John CasperEckhardt and Maria Catarina Ruhlmann, Cacoosing.

Dec. 1. Jacob Sierer and Anna Catarina Schmidt, Earl Town.

Dec. 9. John Jacob Fischer and Maria Elizabetha Friederich, Tulpehocken.

Dec. 28. Johannes Zoeller and Maria Becker, Tulpehocken.

1744.

Jan. 1. John George Wittman and Anna Barbara Hausshalter, Warwick.

Jan. 24. Philipp Meeth and Anna Maria Ebert, Northkill.

Jan. 21. John Tomson and Susannah Hammon, Lebanon.

Jan. 31. John Tomson and Susannah Margaretha Vollmar, Bethel.

Feb. 2. John Philipp Holinger and Juliana Umberger, Lebanon.

Feb. 7. Sebastian Huber and Catarina Mueller, Tulpehocken.

Feb. 8. Robert Jones and Hannah Patterson, Hanover.

Feb. 14. Hartman Verdriess and Catarina Bender, Warwick.

Feb. 28. John Philipp Strauss and Anna Margaretha Reinier, Bern Township.

March 3. Daniel Gray and Mary Patton, Lebanon.

March 12. Johann Heinrich Enssminger and Maria Barbara Crautzdorf, Cocalico.

March 25. John Jacob Haeckert and Agnes Bohrman, Warwick.

April 8. John Herman Lehn and Maria Catarina Weidman, Warwick.

May 22. John Friederich Zeh and Maria Ottilia Stempel, Swatara.

June 4. John Zerwe and Catarina Stup, Tulpehocken.

June 19. John Martin Kirstaetter and Magdalena Huckenborger, Lebanon.

July 8. Christian Bienen and Maria Sara Maennerin, Swatara.

August 14. Jacob Zartman and Maria Magdalena Rehm, Warwick.

Oct. 2. Wiliam Leadsoorth and Elizabeth Loodenton, Bethel.

Nov. 12. John George Kastnitz and Anna Maria Gottliebin Dupss, Bethel.

Nov. 20. John Philipp Schaefer and Christina Ensminger, Cocalico.

Dec. 16. John Philipp Martzeloff and Maria Sybilla Frey, Moden Creek.

1745.

Jan. 15. George Andreas Ziegeler and Anna Margaretha Madern, Swatara.

Jan. 29. Peter Negele and Maria Buenckel, Cacoosing.

March 24. Jacob Wuest and Catarina Barbara Ringel, Cocalico.

March 26. Johannes Wolleben and Anna Margaretha Wuerst, Tulpehocken.

April 7. Philipp Brendel and Maria Christman, Cocalico.

April 7. Jacob Faber and Catarina Agatha Kerlinger, Warwick.

April 9. Caspar Schaefer and Anna Margar. Erster, Tulpehocken.

April 15. John Frederich Stulp and Anna Barbara Karcher, Tulpehocken.

April 16. Michael Ruch and Anna Frantzina Merckling, Moselem.

May 7. Philipp Adam Diller and Maria Magdalena Ellmecker, Earl Town.

June 16. John Philipp Hertz and Susanna Hautz, Moden Creek.

June 18. Christoph Meyer and Catarina Braun, Warwick.

July 22. John Adam Fried and Anna Margar. Rehm, Warwick.

Aug. 4. Florian Buringer and Philippina Christian Kitzmiller, Tulpehocken.

Aug. 11. Wilhelm Spatz and Anna Elisabetha Staehler, Cocalico.

Sept. 19. James Carr and Mary Hyde Lebanon.

Sept. 24. John Cunradt Tempelmann and Maria Elisab. Buechin, Lebanon.

Dec. 10. Frederick Kraemer and Anna Maria Merckling, Moselen.

1746.

Jan. 7. Mattheis Boger and Anna Magdalena Wampsler, Lebanon.

Jan. 8. Johannes Meyer and Anna Maria Essel, Tulpehocken.

Jan. 26. John Michael Braun and Anna Karger, Warwick.

Feb. 10. George Balmer and Anna Elizabeth Sauter, Conestoga.

Feb. 11. Michael Ackermann and Anna Barbara Albert, Lebanon.

March 17. Christian Lutz and Maria Magdal. Wissenandt, Moden Creek.

April 27. Leonhardt Kern and Anna Margaretha Schmidt, Swatara.

May 11. Jacob Kanterrmann and Catarina Mueller, Swatara.

May 15. James Clarck and Margaretha Tratter, Lebanon.

May 25. Johannes Kuehny and Margaretha Schneider, Swatara.

July 6. Jacob Ramler and Eva Margaretha Franck, Tulpehocken.

July 13. George Gross and Anna Catarina Schneider, Warwick.

July 27. Heinrich Mayer and Anna Barbara Graff, Warwick.

Sept. 9. John Philipp Schreiner and Eva Catarina Boltz, Manheim.

Oct. 21. Johan Christoph Suess and Catarina Elisabetha Haager, Warwick.

Oct. 21. Johann Wilhelm Stober and Anna Margaretha Suess, Warwick.

Nov. 18. Johann George Haussbalter and Margaretha Balmer, Warwick.

Dec. 1. Wilhelm Ehrhardt and Anna Catarina Schreiner, Warwick.

Dec. 3. Dennis Druggon and Johanna Conner, Lebanon.

Dec. 15. William Packwood and Sarah Hough, Bethel.

Dec. 21. Michael Aver and Maria Barbara Spiess, Tulpehocken.

Dec. 21. John Adam Weber and Barbara Jaeger, Tulpehocken.

Dec. 22. Valentin Von Huss and Maria Barbara Zerwe, Tulpehocken.

Dec. 22. John George Meyer and Catarina Zerwe, Tulpehocken.

1747.

Jan. 13. Jacob Brenneiser and Anna Veronica Wampsler, Lebanon.

Feb. 10. Paul Ebrecht and Barbara Margaretha Sauter, Warwick.

Feb. 16. John Von Huss and Hannah Cheeck, Heidelberg.

March 16. George Michael Wildfang and Sophia Catarina Veitheim, Tulpehocken.

March 23. Balthasar Boesshaar and Anna Maria Schaefer, Leacock.

April 7. Jacob Lehnherr and Eva Maria Haager, Warwick.

May 17. William Keeper and Clara Tanner, Warwick.

June 2. Adam Wittman and Catarina Gansert, Moden Creek.

June 3. William Treese and Mary Griffith, Newberry.

August 24. George Immler and Christina Fuss, Cocalico.

Sept. 15. Wilhelm Geiger and Eva Barbara Stober, Warwick.

Oct. 12. Jacob Reess and Rachel Dyx, servants at Henry Schmidt's, Bethel.

Oct. 13. James Barnet of Conecocheague and Martha Rogers, Hanover.

Nov. 2. Michael Bauer and Anna Maria Lentz, Warwick.

Nov. 17. Joseph McCrory and Roass Feree, Hanover.

Dec. 14. William Grace and Mary McNealy, Hanover.

Dec. 29. Valentin Herchelrodt and Elisabetha Meusser, Lebanon.

Dec. 29. Jacob Schober and Maria Dorothea Zimmerman.

1748.

Feb. 1. Mattheis Pflantz and Elisabetha Balmer, Warwick.

Feb. 7. Mattheis Kaempfer and Maria Magdla. Reimer, Northkill.

Feb. 7. George Wolfert and Elisabeth Zimmerman, Atolhoe.

March 15. David Zeller and Maria Christina Hoerner, Warwick.

March 21. Thomas Mackey and Mary Meben, Hannover.

March 29. John Heinrich Deck and Catarina Barbara Froehlich, Tulpehocken.

April 3. Heinrich Berger and Anna Rosini Fohrer, Tulpehocken.

May 1. Martin Eisenhauer and Anna Barbara Graff, Atolhoe.

May 2. Peter Goettel and Eva Friederich, Bethel.

May 10. Moses Moor and Jane Gillighin, Lebanon.

May 10. Johannes Michael Gundtacker and Maria Margar. Scheidt, Warwick.

June 15. Abraham Richardson and Mary Margaretha Mintz, Lebanon.

June 20. Christoph Wittman and Mary Adams, Cocalico.

June 21. Adam Schneider and Anna Maria Bort, Lebanon.

June 21. George Michael Bronner and Barbara Tempelmann, Lebanon.

July 3. George Broeckle and Juliana Adam, Earl Town.

June 21. George Michael Bronner and Barbara Templemann, Lebanon.

July 14. Samuel Jones and Rachael Tittle, Bethel.

Sept. 8. John Cooper and Jane Varner, Hannover.

Sept. 24. John Carr and Margaretha Ross, Lebanon.

Sept. 26. Jonas Adam and Anna Eva Meipel, Earl Town.

Oct. 10. Wolf Heinrich Bronner and Anna Catarina Eussminger, Cocalico.

Oct. 13. Peter Tittle and Mary Hough, Lebanon.

Oct. 24. Jacob Schmidt and Maria Catarina Enssminger, Cocalico.

Oct. 25. John Michael Wagner and Elisabetha Madern, Swatara.

Oct. 30. Leonhardt Faber and Catarina Barbara Roesser, Swatara.

Oct. 31. Joseph Roth and Maria Margaretha Zerwe, Tulpehocken.

Nov. 29. Sebastian Brosius and Margaretha Roth, Tulpehocken.

Dec. 11. Johann Leonhardt Foerster and Catarina Fischer, Tulpehocken.

Dec. 21. Johann Jacob Dietz and Catarina Holtzwart, Lebanon.

1749.

Jan. 8. George Borden and Anna Catarina Umbehauer, Lebanon.

Jan. 9. Balthasar Stammgast and Elisabetha Sterneberger, Atolhoe.

Jan. 12. Robert Ellit and Elisabetha Aar, Lebanon.

Jan. 17. Rudolph Brenneisen and Anna Barbara Schaeffer, Cocalico.

Jan. 18. Peter Lessle and Susanna Walther, Warwick.

Jan. 30. Joseph Neu and Anna Eva Luct, Moden Creek.

Feb. 9. William Wilson and Sarah Allen, Lebanon.

March 2. Samuel Packwood and Mary Pannel, Bethel.

March 3. William Gibson and Anna Paxtang, Bethel.

March 14. Johannes Schwab and Eva Margar. Ramler, Tulpehocken.

May 1. William Morris and Rebecca Oliphants, Lebanon.

May 7. Cornelius Macarty and Elisabeth Codougan, Nantmeal.

June 1. David Pitts and Welsh Lewis, Lebanon.

June 4. Jno. Heinrich Hansz and Maria Barbara Franck, Warwick.

June 20. Domincus Bartholomaei and Adelheit Paffenberger, Tulpehocken.

June 26. Andrew Nelson and Elisabeth Brooth, Paxtang.

July 23. John Peter Strahl and Anna Margar. Geblin, Northkill.

Sept. 12. Samuel Beight and Anna Corry, Paxtang.

Oct. 24. George Velty and Anna Maria Meyer, Bethel.

Nov. 14. Vincens Kuefer and Eva Maria Hubeler, Derry.

Dec. 31. Johann Adam Kroeber and Anna Elisab. Fischgess, Cocalico.

1750.

Jan. 30. Samuel Welsh and Sarah Reynolds, Bethel.

Feb. 4. Heinrich Stein and Juliana Andre, Atolhoe.

Feb. 7. John Syllaben and Anna Old, Warwick.

Feb. 11. Hansz George Hoells and Anna Barbara Hoff, Cocalico.

Feb. 20. John Jacob Roehrer and Maria Elisab. Brosius, Atolhoe.

Feb. 26. Herman Lattur and Barbara Spickler, Warwick.

April 1. Johannes Eberth and Maria Elisab. Riehm, Northkill.

April 24. Leonhardt Mueller and Maria Barbara Eichelberger, Warwick.

April 26. Adam Buerger and Maria Barbara Meyer, Lebanon.

May 10. Michael Zimmerman and Eva Kuenig, Swatara.

May. 20. Johannes Roop and Margaretha Frey, Moden Creek.

May 27. John Oberlin and Anna Maria Eva Wolf, Atolhoe.

May 28. Gottfried Baumgartner and Anna Catarina Kueffer, Lebanon.

June 1. James Old and Margaretha Davies, Lancaster.

June 25. John Henderson and Anna Simple, Lebanon.

August 14. John Mattheis Bohr and Maria Elizabeth Neu, Lebanon.

Sept. 16. John Abraham Stein and Anna Maria Roehrer, Atolhoe.

Sept. 25. George Maess and Anna Maria Kreuber, Bethel.

Oct. 7. John Heinrich Krum and Anna Catraina Giesser, Warwick.

Oct. 9. Jacob Wagner and Magdalena Gehrhardt, Lebanon.

Oct. 9. Johann Wolf Kissner and Anna Sabina Bindtnagel, Lebanon.

Oct. 23. Johann Frederich Zimmerman and Maria Margar. Lutz, Warwick.

1751.

Jan. 8. Noah Frederich and Margaretha Becker, Bethel.
Jan. 8. Peter Gutman and Anna Maria Hauck, Bethel.
Jan. 10. Johannes Becker and Catarina Umberger, Lebanon.
Jan. 10. Thomas Davies and Nels Read, Lebanon.
Jan. 15. Andreas Schweickhardt and Maria Catarina Schaeffer, Cocalico.
Jan. 21. John Brenneisen and Christina Minier, Bethel.
Jan. 31. David Stewart and Sarah Sinken, Hanover.
Feb. 5. Johann Peter Falten and Maria Catarina Neu, Lebanon.
Feb. 12. Philipp Adam Bahmer and Margaretha Oberlin, Warwick.
Feb. 19. Hanns Martin Ergebrecht and Susanna Forr, Lebanon.
Feb. 24. Bernhardt Adam and Margaretha Doerr, Cocalico.
April 19. John Adam and Maria Eva Schmidt, Moden Creek.
April 27. James Jeffreys and Rachel Grays, of Paxtang.
April 28. Peter Riedt and Maria Catarina Biegler, Tulpehocken.
May 16. Joseph Zieffle and Maria Catarina Guenthuer, Lebanon.
May 21. Jacob Riedt and Maria Eva Killhoeffer, Warwick.
May 21. Johannes Staengele and Anna Elisab. Oberholzer, Warwick.
June 11. Sebastian Kirstaetter and Magdalena Derver, Lebanon.
June 18. John George Eichelberger and Christina Dorothea Best, Lebanon.
June 18. Melchior Winckelmann and Barbara Sigrist, Lebanon.
July 16. Clemence Gilligham and Margaretha Patty, of Middle Pensborough, Cumberland county.
July 21. Friederich Wolf and Anna Barbara Meyer, Atolhoe.
Sept. 8. John George Meyer and Maria Catarina Reyer, Warwick.
Oct. 8. Frantz Caspar Wagner and Margar. Kirstaetter, Lebanon.
Nov. 7. John Valentin Schreiner and Anna Elisabetha Wolf, Lancaster.
Nov. 8. Jacob Backestoss and Elisabetha Kulin, Lancaster.
Nov. 10. Daniel Lucas and Eva Margaretha Ulrich, Atolhoe.
Nov. 17. Cunradt Wagner and Anna Maria Malvir, Warwick.
Nov. 17. Geo. Peter Wielandt and Anna Margar. Weiss, Warwick.
Dec. 17. Joseph Stout and Catarina Meylie, Bethel.
Dec. 17. James Rafler and Barbara Meylie.

1752.

Jan. 1. John Heinrih Weidtmann and Catarina Bassler, Warwick.
Jan. 2. Peter Kraemer and Magdalena Leidyn, Lebanon.
Jan. 5. George Muench and Catara. Margar. Guthman, Northkill.
Jan. 7. George Michael Graff and Maria Margar. Meyer, Bethel.
Jan. 7. Johannes Eisenhardt and Veronica Meyer, Bethel.
Feb. 11. Johann Jacob Vierling and Catarina Schlack, Warwick.
Feb. 24. Johannes Kissinger and Catarina Sauermilch, Cocalico.
March 8. Johannes Haehnlein and Anna Catar. Kuntz, Cocalico.
March 17. John Welsh and Margaretha Irving, Paxton.
March 20. Daniel McCardy and Nancy Weackly, Yellow Breeches, Cumberland county.
March 31. Leonhardt Mueller and Anna Maria Raetelsperger, Lebanon.
April 19. Nicolaus Brosius and Anna Barbara Schaeffer, Atolhoe.
April 19. Simon Eschbach and Eva Kautzmann, Atolhoe.
April 19. Christian Benteler and Catarina Mueller, Warwick.
June 17. Abraham Irbin and Anna Enys, Hanover.
June 23. William Coppels and Jane McMollon, Hanover.
June 29. Humphry Cuningham and Rhoda Zemmeral, Hanover.
July 5. Adam Brecht and Margaretha Battesteld, Bethel.
July 5. Adam Baum, of Derry, and Veronica Gingerich, Warwick.
Sept. 14. George Osborn and Margaretha Clark, Paxtang.
Sept. 24. Heinrich Fryman and Anna Catarina Gesell, Heidelberg.
Oct. 24. Christian Bechtel and Anna Margaretha Beutelstein, Tulpehocken.
Nov. 7. Samuel Bell and Jane McLean, of Middle Pensboro'.
Nov. 17. Henry Swaney and Barbara Ferguson, Paxtang.
Nov. 14. Phillipp Weigandt and Magdalena Baur, Lebanon.
Dec. 12. John Ludwig Ensminger and Eva Christina Philipp, Cocalico.
Dec. 12. Christian Philippy and Anna Maria Ensminger, Cocalico.
Dec. 20. James McNeese, of Bethel, and Margaretha Allen, Lebanon.

1753.

Jan. 23. Jacob Schnaebele and Susanna Hurter, Bethel.
Jan. 23. John Nicolaus Franck and Mara Catarina Fuchs, Hanover.

Jan. 30. John Adam Barth and Elisabetha Weisenkind, Lebanon.

Feb. 12. Johannes Schock and Margar. Wagner, Bern Town.

Feb. 26. Michael Kally and Mary Kuhny, Bethel.

Feb. 27. Henry Cowen and Jane Varner, Lebanon.

March 4. Frederich Klingel and Catarina Haug, Cocalico.

March 25. Philipp Armbruester and Anna Christina Tennewald, Swetl.

March 27. Michael Wohlfarth and Elisabetha Sommer, Atolhoe.

April 8. Andreas Schaeffer and Catarina Henning, Atolhoe.

May 6. Johannes Huber and Maria Elisab. Ritscher, Lebanon.

May 29. John Gillighan and Margaretha Clark, Hanover.

June 5. Johan Michael Kirstaetter and Maria Dorothea Dietz, Lebanon.

June 5. Peter Gelaspi and Sarah Enson, Paxtang.

July 19. Robert McCellan and Mary Merans, Paxton.

Aug. 14. Heinrich Hortle and Catarina Firnssler, Lebanon.

Sept. 10. Richard Benson and Mary Dereb, Derry.

Sept. 11. Philomey Kienen and Eleonore Kiefe, Hampfield.

Oct. 21. Heinrich Adam Schneider and Anna Margar. Schneber, Atolhoe.

Nov. 4. John Martin Schmidt and Maria Appollonia Tennewald, Derry.

Nov. 27. John Peter Dinnies and Anna Johanna Luecker, Warwick.

Nov. 27. Christoph Friederich Weegman and Anna Maria Keller, Derry.

Nov. 29. James Wallace and Elisabeth Elder, Hanover and Paxtang.

Dec. 16. John George Flohr and Maria Catarina Motz, Atolhoe.

Dec. 17. John Nicolaus Schaeffer and Maria Susanna Haag, Northkill.

Dec. 18. George Wendel Keller and Barbara Straup, Bethel.

Dec. 30. Jacob Huber and Anna Catarina Anton, Derry.

1754.

Jan. 12. Johannes Ache and Anna Margaretha Kraft, Bern.

Jan. 23. William Galbreath and Margaretha Buchanon, Carlisle.

Jan. 25. James Low and Isabell French, Hanover.

Feb. 10. Johannes Herr and Anna Margaretha Dietz, Tulpehocken.

Feb. 10. Andreas Schaat and Maria Elisabeth Kraft, Bern.

March 1. Johannes Nicolaus Holder, jr., and Catarina Brecht, Bern.

March 10. Johann Heinrich Beyer and Salome Suess, Tulpehocken.

April 7. Johann Friederich Wieland and Ana Eva Soerer, Atolhoe.

April 15. Cunradt Roenninger and Susana Margr. Sshuetz, Paxtang.

May 2. William Clark and Elizabeth Hough, Lebanon and Hanover.

May 18. John Nicolaus Ensminger and Christ. Elisab. Philippin, Cocalico.

May 23. Robert Gibson and Els. Davies, Lebanon.

June 2. Johannes Kloosz and Maria Barbara Strauss, Bern.

June 2. John Jacob Matz and Anna Magdal Sophia Koenig, Tulpehocken.

June 3. Johann George Obermeyer and Maria Magdl Rosenbach, Bethel.

June 25. Caspar Heussler and Rosina Schrellbecker, Lebanon.

June 28. William James and Margaretha Rogers, Hanover.

August. 5. George Hansz Dietrich and Veronica Meyer, Lebanon.

August 10. Peter Rosenberger and Maria Albrecht, Hanover.

Aug. 12. John Nicolaus Hennicker and Anna Roeser, Warwick.

Aug. 12. Casper Riedt and Anna Schaefer, Atolhoe.

Aug. 25. Johannes Kuemmerly and Catarina Margaretha Dieb, Bethel.

Aug. 27. Simon Burckard and Catarina Brandes, Lebanon.

Sept. 9. Benjamin Ainsworth and Mary Oar, of Hanover.

Sept. 12. James Woodside and Margaretha Trotter, Derry.

Sept. 16. Johannes Meyer and Margaretha Grojean, Derry.

Oct. 8. Jacob Zerwe, jr., and Anna Elizabetha Spiess, Atolhoe.

Nov. 3. Ludwig Weidner and Maria Engel Gerst, Heidelberg and Bethel.

Nov. 25. George Michael Eichelberger and Christina Elser, Warwick.

Nov. 28. William Williams and Rebecca McCaddoms, Bethel.

Dec. 2. Michael Bunert and Barbara Schnelb, Bethel.

Dec. 15. John George Haag and Anna Margaretha Bechtel, Bern.

Dec. 22. Laurence McCarthy and Sarah McCafferty, Warwick.

1755.

Jan. 5. Adam Hiesner and Magdalena Weidman, Moden Creek.

Jan. 9. Wilhelm Lutz and Catarina Deininger, Derry Township.

Jan. 13. Andreas Morr and Catarina Roenninger, Bethel.

Jan. 13. Christian Kaufman and Magdalena Schnaebele, Bethel.

Jan. 30. Samuel Kent and Isabel Schmidt, Paxton.

Feb. 9. Dieter Gerberich and Anna Margaretha Rudolph, Atolhoe.

Feb. 13. John Dieben and Anna Margaretha Ramler, Hanover and Heidelberg.

Feb. 24. Thomas Walcker and Sarah McCaughlin, Hanover.

Feb. 25. John Caspar Obermann and Magdalena Seubler, Warwick.

Feb. 25. Ludwig Wohlfahrdt and Anna Margaretha Hoeg, Warwick.

March 10. Johann George Ludwig and Maria Christina Beutelstein, Tulpehocken.

March 11. Jacob Pretzius and Maria Magdalena Aulenbach, Tulpehocken.

March 11. Johannes Oehrle and Regina Siechelin, Derry.

March 30. George Mueller and Anna Margaretha Augenstein, Warwick.

April 9. Adam Riesz and Anna Margaretha Seemahr, Bethel.

April 28. James Johnson and Ruth Ellet, Upper Paxtang in the Narrows.

April 28. Jacob Weltz and Magdalena Bird, Paxtang.

May 15. Robert Montgomery, Bethel, and Chrysy Walker, Derry.

May 19. Johannes Stein and Maria Barbara Gebhardt, Atolhoe.

May 25. Johannes Haeker and Dorothea Wirschumer, Moden Creek.

May 28. George Sprecher and Eva Margaretha Schwab, Lebanon.

June 10. William Roger and Margaretha Collweil, Hanover.

June 29. Philipp Hauss and Anna Elizabetha Friederich, Tulpehocken.

July 21. Johann Adam Bohr and Anna Barbara Labengeiger, Lebanon.

July 21. Johann Peter Pannekuchen and Catarina Dietz, Lebanon.

August 3. Johann Adam Wirth and Eva Elizabetha Schnug, Lebanon.

August 12. Johann Michael Kessinger and Anna Maria Grasser, Derry.

August 26. Johann George Stang and Anna Maria Deck, Tulpehocken.

August 26. John George Roessler and Elizabetha Catarina Aras, Lebanon.

Sept. 23. Jacob Dobler and Anna Hough, Bethel.

Sept. 23. Samuel Stout and Mary Elizabeth Thomas, Bethel.

Sept. 23. Lorentz Fischer and Catarina Boner, Bethel.

Sept. 25. John Daugherty and Juliana Shuel, Paxtang.

Oct. 5. Lorentz Kurtz and Maria Elizabetha Saur, Lebanon.

Oct. 14. Martin Oberlin and Eva Nagel, Atolhoe.

Oct. 16. George Kleinfelter and Anna Barbarina Keller, Susquehanna.

Oct. 19. Martin Weszner and Elizabetha Sprecher, Hanover.

Oct. 20. Joseph Brix and Rosina Barbara Despenet, Tulpehocken.

Oct. 27. Michael Lentz and Catarina Kaufman, York.

Nov. 2. Peter Balmus and Anna Maria Pretz, Derry.

Nov. 9. Balthaser Hetzler and Anna Barbara Dohm, Heidelberg.

Nov. 18. Johann Adam Stoehr and Eva Catarina Ietter, Lebanon.

Dec. 19. Ulrich Volck and Maria Elizabetha Ebert, Derry.

1756.

Jan. 7. Thomas Welsh and Agnes Alexander, Paxtang.

Feb. 8. John George Roth and Maria Barbara Spieler, Tulpehocken.

Feb. 10. George Rein and Anna Maria Meyer, Lebanon.

Feb. 15. Johannes Hey and Juliana Maul, York.

March 8. Johannes Werner and Christina Grossmann, Bethel.

March 9. William Breaden and Isabella Wallace, Derry.

March 23. Abraham Clark and Jane Clark, Lebanon.

March 25. Michael Malfir and Anna Eva Schnug, Lebanon.

March 30. Iost Iotter and Eva Catarina Hubeler, Lebanon.

April 20. Peter Maurer and Catarina Elizabetha Kniesz, Bethel.

May 18. Adam Wilson and Mary Brown, Derry.

May 30. John Nicolaus Haag and Anna Maria Redebach, Northkill.

May 30. Peter Muench and Eva Maria Ritzmann, Atolhoe.

June 1. Johann Martin Kirstaetter and Elizabetha Bickel, Lebanon.

June 2. Samuel Reed and Agnes Braeden, Derry.

June 13. Melchior Webert and Elizabetha Biener, Bethel.

June 13. Heinrich Mueller and Catarina Frey, Derry.

June 15. George Hansz Dietrich and Dorothea Boltz, Lebanon.

July 4. Wendel Keller and Elizabetha Fuchs, Bethel.

July 6. John Walker and Jane Wilson, Derry and Heidelberg.

July 6. John Michael Pfrang and Anna Catarina Gring, Lebanon.

July 11. John George Kupper and Elizabetha Zimmerman, Lebanon.

July 25. John Peter Heberling and Anna Maria Kendel, Atolhoe.

July 25. George Schenck and Barbara Lang, Atolhoe.

July 27. Erasmus Rosenberger and Anna Catarin Baumgaertner, Hanover and Bethel.

August 22. Jacob Soerer and Maria Catarina Bender, Atolhoe.

August 23. Bartholomaeus Heck and Margaretha Aulenbach, Heidelberg.

August 24. John Nicolaus Schmidt and Barbara Suess, Warwick.

August 24. William Thrennin and Jane Tweed, Derry and Donegal.

August 26. Joseph Scot and Anna Kalliah, Lebanon.

August 26. Robert Hueston and Elizabeth Wacker, Hanover and Derry.

Oct. 7. James Black, of Derry, and Elizabetha Rogers, Hanover.

Dec. 29. Christian Ewig and Anna Magdalena Schmidt, Warwick.

Dec. 29. Philipp Hofmann and Catarina Balmer, Warwick.

1757.

Jan. 6. Christoph Schomm and Anna Elizabetha Hausz, Atolhoe.

Jan. 6. John Peter Ritzmann and Anna Christina Stuepp, Atolhoe.

Jan. 11. Johannes Wunderlich and Maria Elizabetha Siechelin, Derry.

Jan. 18. George Drapel and Margaretha Drember, Warwick.

Jan. 25. Johannes Weidner and Maria Salome Guenther, Hanover.

Feb. 6. Jacob Fehler and Anna Weiss, Atolhoe.

Feb. 10. Johannes Mueller and Elizabetha Magdalena Fuechs, Hanover.

Feb. 15. John Peter Ritscher and Anna Margaretha Kirber, Lebanon.

March 1. Michael Fischer and Maria Magdalena Eisenhauer, Bethel.

March 2. Mattheis Schmutz and Regina Zwerontzor, Lebanon.

March 6. John Christoph Muench and Maria Barbara Holder, Bern.

March 8. John Gahus and Elizabeth Straghorn, Hanover.

March 14. John Lerkin and Margaretha Thompson, Lebanon.

March 14. Wendel Keller and Catarina Dorothea Haberland, Lebanon.

March 15. Andreas Kochendoerfer and Elizabetha Nagel, Bethel.

March 22. John Jacob Boltz and Catarina Madern, Lebanon.

March 29. Johannes Krueger and Anna Margaretha Heydt, Lebanon.

April 13. Jacob Zimpfer and Anna Maria Lorentz, Lebanon.

April 14. John Crocker and Mary Chambers, Paxtang.

April 14. Samuel Gowdy and Sarah Morton, Paxtang.

April 19. Johann Martin Kuefer and Elizabetha Meyer, Bethel.

April 26. Johann Casper Stoever, jr., and Anna Maria Barbara Nagel, Lebanon.

May 30. Johannes Schneider and Eva Oberlin, Derry.

May 31. Johannes Kuemmerling and Anna Maria Pfrang, Lebanon.

May 31. George Hatz and Anna Margaretha Dieb, Lebanon.

July 24. Jacob Walther and Anna Maria Kaufman, Bern.

July 24. Asahel Bayer and Maria Eva Spieler, Atolhoe.

Aug. 2. Johannes Philippy and Maria Eva Barbara Eichelberger, Warwick.

Aug. 7. Martin Schmidt and Catarina Fischer, Lebanon.

Aug. 15. Emanuel Suess and Susanna Mueller, Warwick.

Sept. 4. Hansz Ulrich Huber and Elizabeth Firnsler, Lebanon.

Sept. 20. James Crampton and Susanna Likens, Paxtang.

Sept. 27. Patrick McCrannighan and Catarina Daugherty, Paxton.

Oct. 16. John David Fiess and Anna Maria Kaufman, Bern.

Oct. 18. Peter Kraemer and Anna Margaretha Ernst, Lebanon.

Oct. 25. John Adam Neu and Veronica Barbara Koemmet, Lebanon.

Nov. 22. John Heinrich Hertle and Catarina Kuehn, Lebanon and Bethel.

Nov. 24. John Nicolaus Brechtbiel and Juliana Diller, Lebanon.

Nov. 24. Sebastian Nagel and Maria Magdal. Diller, Bethel.

Dec. 11. Frederich Schnock and Elisab. Gerbrig, Atolhoe.

Dec. 20. Adam Stephan and Maria Agnes Pfrang, Lebanon.

1758.

Jan. 3. George Fischer and Anna Elisabeth, Knopf, Lebanon.

Jan. 5. Mattheis Weinmar and Catarina Volemer, Derry.

Feb. 5. Adam Koch and Anna Catarina Duckner, Bern.

Feb. 6. George Loos and Anna Barbar. Uhrich, Tulpehocken.

Feb. 14. John Jacob Bickel and Eva Margaretha Ietter, Lebanon.

Feb. 14. Antonius Ditzler and Anna Magdalena Mader, Bethel.

Feb. 27. Antonius Karmenie and Anna Christina Hetzler, Lebanon.

Feb. 28. Johannes Berger and Anna Barbara Hoerchelrodt, Heidelberg.

March 29. Andreas Bartruff and Christina Sophia Klein, Lebanon.

April 2. Johannes Hebberling and Maria Elisab. Pressler, Lebanon.

April 4. John Martin Kuemmerling and Elisabetha Kirstetter, Lebanon.

April 10. Christoph Heinrich Reinholdt and Sophia Louisa Amweg, Cocalico.

April 10. Jacob Schmidt and Elisabetha Hoerchelrodt, Heidelberg.

April 24. Abraham Heydt and Elisabtha Sieg, Lebanon.

May 1. David Purviance and Margaretha McEntyre, Paxtang.

May 15. George Adam Geiss and Anna Barbara Haag, Bern.

May 23. Johann Stroh or Strauss and Anna Maria Fischer.

May 28. Caspar Hinckel and Maria Eva Vollmar, Tulpehocken.

May 28. Jacob Strauss and Elisabetha Brecht, Bern.

June 19. John George Dumm and Anna Catarina Pflantz, Derry.

June 15. Robert Rogers and Anna Christina Ramberg, Lebanon.

July 2. Peter Fischer and Catarina Bockle, Lebanon.

July 16. Johannes Busch and Anna Maria Huber, Heidelberg.

July 23. Johannes Lescher and Anna Catarina Wohlfahrt, Atolhoe.

August 17. Johann Sebastian Stiegler and Catar. Margr. Seidenbinder, Moden Creek.

August 29. Carolus Scheidt and Maria Eva Selzer, Warwick.

Sept. 22. Benedict Ledig and Maria Juliana Boehmer, Heidelberg.

Oct. 15. Melchior Ditzler and Maria Eva Lerter, Atolhoe.

Nov. 6. George Stober and Eva Elszer, Warwick.

Nov. 13. John Jacob Stiegeler and Maria Catar. Stobler, Moden Creek.

Nov. 14. Johann Schweickhardt Innboden and Eleanora Diller, Lebanon.

Nov. 21. Samuel Adam and Catarina Gansert, Moden Creek.

Nov. 30. Benjamin Varner and Mary Homes, Yellow Breeches, Cumberland county.

1759.

Jan. 29. Johannes Stohler and Anna Maria Glassbrenner, Heidelberg and Lebanon.

Feb. 1. Robert Whitehill and Elenore Reed, Pequea and Hanover.

Feb. 5. Johannes Reid and Dorothea Roehrer, Atolhoe.

Mch. 4. Johannes Deck and Anna Schnaebel, Atolhoe.

Mch. 5. Jacob Sprecher and Dorothea Blecher, Lebanon.

April 16. Johann Christoph Kern and Maria Catarina Wagner, Tulpehocken.

My 20. Johannes Schwartz and Catarina Esther Mueller, Moden Creek.

May 27. Christian Ramberg and Elizabeth Lang, Hanover.

July 9. Heinrich Gerhardt and Catarina Bendter, Lebanon.

Aug. 21. Peter Brechbiel and Maria Catarina Franck, Lebanon.

Aug. 21. Jacob Strauss and Elizabetha Brecht.

Aug. 30. Thomas Clark and Margaretha Heydt, Lebanon.

Sept. 18. Martin Herman and Anna Dorothea Borst, Lebanon.

Oct. 28. Philipp Baasz and Anna Weimer, Lebanon.

Oct. 28. John Ernst Curt and Margaretha Riedt, Lebanon.

Nov. 4. Matthias Hess and Eva Catarina Stober, Warwick.

Nov. 11. John Leonhardt Fischer and Barbara Gerhardt, Bethel.

Dec. 13. James Huens and Maria Sabina Felleberger, Lebanon.

1760.

Jan. 13. Simon Berger and Anna Maria Dorothea Frederica Busser, Atolhoe.

Jan. 13. Jacob Saltzer and Anna Maria Truckenmueller, Atolhoe.

Jan. 15. Andreas Beck and Anna Weber, Donegal and Hanover.

Jan. 21. Jacob Ziegeler and Juliana Kirstetter, Lebanon.

Jan. 21. Abraham Schaeffer and Maria Barbara Sirer, Lebanon.

an. 22. Adam Dumm and Catarina Heydt, Lebanon.

Feb.19. David Herbster and Anna Maria Barbara Hacker. Lebanon.

Feb| 26. Frantz Caspar Wagner (widower), and Elizabetha Wirtz, Lebanon and Cocalico.

Mch. 12. Johannes Meyer and Eva Catarina Hoegien, Conestoga and Warwick.

April 6. Peter Thomas and Eva Maria Sip, Bethel. Berks county.

May 4. John Daniel Madern and Maria Elisab. Strauss, Bern Township.

May 6. John George Seidelmeyer and Magdalena Wagner, Bethel.

May 6. Antonius Hemperle and Juliana Baumann, Derry.

May 9. John Hume and May Cunningham, Hanover.

May 13. John Sturtzen and Elenore Ferrys, Paxtang.

May 20. Wendel Hautz and Catarina Elizaba. Riegel, Bethel, Leb. Co., and Tulpehocken.

May 20. Geo. Michael Muench and Maria Magdal. Wagner, Bern. and Tulpehocken, B. C.

June 2. Geo. Obermeyer and Anna Barbara Vogt, Hanover.

June 9. Peter McCarthy and Nancy Thompson, Lebanon.

June 9. Laurence Rack and Brigitta Strattel, Lebanon.

June 16. Wilhelm Weyhrich and Maria Elizaba. Simon, Hanover.

June 17. Michael Lindenmuth and Maria Eve Noecker, Heidelberg.

June 26. Michael Kirber and Anna Maria Schlatter, Lebanon.

June 29. Michael Bayer and Catarina Elizabetha Haag, Bern.

June 29. Jacob Wagner and Maria Appolonia Muench, Bern.

July 3. James Andrew and Jane Campbell, Hanover.

July 6. Adam Bayer and Maria Sara Ritschor, Lebanon.

Aug. 14. Isaac Martin and Elenore Clark, Hanover.

Aug. 19. Philipp Jacob Bortner and Maria Elizabetha Velt, Bethel.

Aug. 24. Johannes Pfaffenberger and Otillia Margar. Boetzel, Atolhoe.

Aug. 26. Thoas McKee and Else Whitside, Yellow Breeches.

Aug. 31. Abrahnm Kroh and Maria Schaeffer, Bethel. Lebanon Co.

Sept. 2. John Christoph Friederich and Ana Maria Wagner, Lebanon.

Sept. 15. Joseph Killgore and Isabell Stephens, Paxtang.

Sept. 16. John Brown and Anna Maria Moser, Bethel.

Sept. 16. Christian Mueller and Elizabeth Ried, Lebanon.

Sept. 23. Robert Dixon and Mary Gelaspie, Derry.

Sept. 29. Edward Steans and Mary Martin, Lebanon.

Oct. 7. John Martin Gross and Catarina Schuetz, Paxtang.

Oct. 14. Peter Benedict and Maria Elizabetha Lauckster, Lebanon.

Oct. 23. John Michael Firnssler and Maria Catar. Hedderich, Lebanon and Hanover.

Oct. 23. Peter Hedderich, jr., and Margar. Hoerchelradt, Hanover and Heidelberg.

Oct. 28. Matthies Staub and Sophia Fischer, Lebanon.

Nov. . John Hitze and Catarina Sharp, Hanover.

Nov. 10. John Heinrich Ache and Maria Catarina Philbert, Cocalico and Bern.

Nov. 16. Peter Elsser and Anna Margaretha Stoever.——

Nov. 18. George Ulrich and Elizabeth Naess, Lebanon and Cocalico.

Nov. 18. James Atkinson and Anne Carnill or Camell Lebanon and York county.

Nov. 25. John Friederich Kuefer and Sabina Vollmar, Derry and Bethel,

Nov. 25. Heinrich Mueller and Jacobina Wagner, Bethel.

Dec. 2. Mattheis Schwertzel and Catarina Barbara Laey, Lebanon.

Dec. 4. John Crawford and Elizabeth Bell, Hanover.

Dec. 7. Geo. Adam Vollmar and Catharine Walther, Tulpehocken.

Dec. 30. William Graham and Jane Hill, Hanover.

Dec. 30. John Christian Demmen, or Dennam, and Margar. Magdal. Mueller, Lebanon.

1761.

Jan. 10. David Harris and Mary Magham, of Paxtang.

Jan. 22. James Millighan and Agnes Strain, Derry.

Jan. 22. John Edwards and Sarah Strain, Derry.

Jan. 27. Johann Wendel Weber and Elizab. Magdalena Eichelberger, Lebanon.

Feb. 3. John George Held and Maria Magdalena Wolf, Lebanon.

Feb. 5. John Collins and Catarina Finley, Lebanon.

Feb. 17. Thomas Kintzel and Ana Maria Holderbaum, Lebanon.

Mch. 1. David Meuerle and Maria Magdalena Kaufmann, Bern.

Mch. 19. Thomas Atkinson and Elizabeth Williams, Lebanon.

Mch. 20. John Campbell and Jane Stuart, by license, Hanover.

April 5. Johann Ludwig Traber and Maria Magdal. Willich, Derry.

April 7. Johann Ludwig Kleber and Anna Magdalena Ellinger, Lebanon.

April 28. John Martin Bindtnagel and Maria Elizabetha Sprecher, Derry.

April 30. Johann Friederich Kuhbauch and Anna Catarina Felt, Lebanon and Bethel.

April 30. George Meyer and Barbara Felt, Lebanon and Bethel.

May 11. Christian Goellnitz and Maria Elizab. Steg, Lebanon.

May 19. Peter Kuefer and Anna Waibel, Bethel and Lebanon.

June 2. Robert Karr and Martha Karr, Donegal.

June 3. Timothy Brannen and Elizabeth Boid, Paxton.

June 4. Abraham M'Clunty and Sarah Bard, Lebanon and Hanover.

June 11. George Williams and Jennet Beans, Hanover.

June 16. John Daniel Stroh and Catarina Barbara Uhler, Lebanon.

June 16. Heinrich Schnatterle and Anna Barbara Uhler, Lebanon.

June 21. Johann Nicolaus Deck, jr., and Maria Magdalena Wendrich, Atolhoe.

Aug. 1. John Cantzon and Sarah Diggy, Paxtang.

Aug. 11. John Strain and Sarah Glillin, Derry.

Aug. 27. John Dunkin and Elenore Sharp, Salisbury and Hanover.

Aug. 31. William Wallace and Mary Clark, Upper Paxtang.

Sept. 22. William Reed and Ruth Williams, Hanover.

Sept. 30. Benjamin Sterret and Margaretha Shealds, Hanover and Derry.

Oct. 6. Jno. Jacob Kitzmueller and Catarina Peter, Lebanon.

Oct. 20. James Crafford and Rossanna Allison, Hanover and Donegal.

Nov. 10. Joseph Robinson and Margaretha Williams, Hanover.

Nov. 12. John McGomery and Christian Foster, Hanover.

Nov. 23. Hugh Hall and Sarah Liske, Lower Paxtang.

Nov. 26. Henry Little and Margaretha Reed, of Paxtang.

Dec. 22. William Craig and Elizabeth Gilliman, Derry and Hanover.

1762.

March 23. Samuel Forgy and Sara Wilson, Paxtang.

April 18. Johann Philipp Firnssler and Anna Christina Stoever, Lebanon.

April 20. Frantz Caspar Wagner and Elisabetha Haehlin, in Rapho.

April 20. Jacob Friederich Danninger and Anna Maria Balmus, in Rapho.

April 22. John Hudchinson and Welshburn Pitts, Derry.

April 22. Jonathan Cummins and Mary Carr, Paxtang.

April 27. Owen Davies and Anna Maria Weber, Lebanon.

May 17. John Robinson and Mary Beset, Lebanon.

May 18. Benjamin Davies and Lyddia Cloward, Lebanon.

June 7. William Bear and Sarah Boile Lebanon.

Jue 29. Peter Guenther and Maria Catarina Williams, Derry.

July 22. Thomas Kees and Rebecca Shmidt, Midletown and Paxtang.

August 24. George Fischer and Elisabeth Cunradt, Bethel and Lebanon.

August 29. Wilhelm Stein and Catarina Scheidt, Atolhoe.

Sept. 2. Laurence Clark and Susanna Clark, by license, Lebanon.

Sept. 6. James Pettigrew and Jane Ainsworth, by license, Hanover.

Sept. 7. Jacob Egler (?) and Catarina Biliams (?), Lebanon and Lancaster.

Sept. 12. Wilhelm Bendig and Anna Christina Lang, Halifax and Middletown.

Sept. 12. John Jacob Burchhardt and Anna Weber, Paxtang and Middletown.

Sept. 12. Adam Gutman and Regina Mooser, Hanover.

Sept. 28. John Michael Fischer and Anna Magdalena Fischer, Bethel.

Sept. 30. William McCrabbord and Hannah McCullock, Paxtang.

Oct. 5. John Lauglin and Mary Preece, Hanover.

Nov. 9. Christoph Schaber and Maria Eva Rosina Strauss, Tulpehocken.

Nov. 9. Johannes Lang and Maria Catarina Strauss, Bern.

Nov. 16. Michael Lawleer and Mary Preece, Bethel and Hanover.

Nov. 22. Jacob Looser and Margaretha Schmidt, Bethel and Heidelberg.

Nov. 23. George Weyhrich and Eva Barbara Mooser, Hanover.

Nov. 30. Theobaldt Mueller and Catarina Elisab. Enssminger, Cocalico.

Dec. 18. Paulus Brickle and Catarina Kupper, other side of Blue Mountain.

Dec. 18. James Rough and Anna Elisabetha Appel, Bethel, Berks county.

Dec. 19. Johannes Kraemer and Anna Margar. Gebhardt, Bethel, Berks county.

Dec. 27. Peter Schmeltzer and Catarina Thau, Bethel, Berks county.

1763.

Jan. 18. William Walker and Agnes Walker, by license, Derry.

Feb. 22. Daniel Wunderlich and Eva Barbara Siechlin, Paxtang.

April 23. James Forster and Dorcas Forster, Paxtang, up Narrows.

May 12. Conradt Iauch and Emma Margar. Sip. Bethel, Berks county.

May 16. Thomas Filbert and Catarina Batteiger. Bern.

May 16. Heinrich Weber and Elisabetha Filbert, Bern.

May 17. Johannes Messerschmidt and Catarina Becker, Derry.

May 21. Caspar Roeder and Regina Gerhardt, Bethel.

June 16. William Dean and Martha McNut, by license, Hanover.

June 20. Johannes Partemer and Anna Catarina Schupp, Derry.

July 1. Samuel Martin and Margaretha McCarthy, Derry.

July 18. Peter Balmer and Magdalena Hoeg, Warwick.

July 24. Johannes Fehler and Eva Catarina Raup, Bethel.

Aug. 14. Daniel Losch and Elisabetha Stang or Staug, Derry.

August 15. Thomas McNitt and Elisabeth Steel, Derry.

August 23. Thomas Preece and Jane Loughlin, by license, Hanover.

August 25. John Mourdagh and Jane Sheals, by license. Paxtang.

August 30. Christian Lehman and Eva Maria Koppenhoefer, Tulpehocken.

Sept. 1. Robert McLung and Elisabeth Kearsen, Paxtang.

Oct. 4. Jno. Burchardt Bohr and Lucia Henrietta Bartholuss, Bethel and Hanover.

Oct. 23. Jacob Scheretz and Elisabetha Rausch, Lebanon.

Nov. 5. George Philipp Chagrin and Catarina Hemberlin, Middletown.

Nov. 5. Lorentz Huebscher and Magdalena Schaeffer, Middletown.

Dec. 4. Heinrich Albrecht and Maria Barbara Haepplin, Middletown.

Dec. 11. Samuel Laney and Chryssil Scot, Paxtang.

Dec. 13. Nicolaus Kihmer and Elisabetha Teiss, Lebanon.

Dec. 25. Conradt Redman and Anna Catarina Sier, Tulpehocken.

Dec. 25. Heinrich Koeller and Elisabetha Fischer, Tulpehocken.

1764.

Jan. 23. Johannes Feistenauer and Salome Winter, Reading.

Feb. 7. John Craighton and Marraretha Crafford, Hanover.

Feb. 16. Moses Cavet and Agnes Meetch. Paxtang.

March 6. Jacob Firnssler and Magdalena Peter, Lebanon.

March 7. Philipp Lorentz Hautz and Anna Maria Mueller, Lebanon.

March 17. Frantz Hubeler Hautz and Anna Margar. Troester, Atolhoe.

March 17. Philipp Christian Tauber and Eva Catarina Harteich, Heidelberg.

March 20. George Balmer and Barbara Olinger, Lebanon.

April 5. George Dumm and Anna Maria Geiger, Derry and Lebanon.

April 10. Christian Schnug and Catarina Boyer, Lebanon.

April 5. Johannes Peter and Barbara Firuszler, Lebanon.

April 25. William Owens and Mary Swan, Hanover.

April 30. John Adams and Elisabeth Blackburn, Derry.

May 8. William Rogers and Elenore Rogers, Hanover.

May 390. William Whitside and Elenore McNees, Bethel.

June 12. Hugh Cunningham and Agnes Tucker, Paxtang.

July 3. William Thornton and Elizabeth Clark, Hanover.

July 10. John Jacob Bohrmann and Anna Elisabeth Pflautz, Donegal.

July 15. Friederich Deck and Maria Veronica Soerer, Atolhoe.

July 23. Christoph Friederich Wegman and Maria Eva Pfrang, Lebanon.

July 31. David Allison and Sarah Rea, Derry.

August 7. Jno. Atkinson and Catarina Dieb, Bethel.

August 20. Michael McCleere and Jane Kinkead, Hanover.

August 16. John Moor and Rebecca Maxell, York county.

Sept. 9. Conradt Henne and Catarina Elisabetha Mattern, Bern.

Oct. 9. John Heinrich Firnssler and Juliana Simon, Lebanon and Hanover.

Oct. 9. Heinrich Weiss and Eva Catarina Fuchs, Lebanon and Hanover.

Oct. 9. Peter Kober and Margaretha Stroher, Lebanon.

Oct. 16. Heinrich Meyer and Juliana Emrich, Bethel.

Oct. 16. Johannes Seydelmeyer and Rosina Layblin, Bethel.

Oct. 22. Geo. Adam Bueckle and Maria Salome Huber, Reading and Derry.

Oct. 28. George Federhoff and Anna Elisabetha Schnaebelin, Lebanon.

Nov. 6. Christian Kaufman and Elizabeth Clerck, Bethel and Hanover.

Nov. 20. Adam Solomon and Dinah Backer, Lebanon.

Nov. 27. Johannes Reichembach and Anna Maria Reiber, Hanover and Bethel.

Dec. 11. Carl Buerger and Anna Elisabetha Henninger, Bethel.

1765.

Jan. 3. Jno. Ainsworth and Margaretha Mays, Hanover.

March 5. John Adam Maennig and Anna Margaretha Holtz, Rapho and Lebanon.

March 5. Christian Michael and Maria Barbara Eisenhauer, Bethel.

March 12. Tobias Lohman and Maria Margar. Bickel, Heidelberg.

March 19. Andreas Kastnitz and Elisabetha Gockel, Lebanon.

April 15. George Ellinger and Anna Maria Catarina Weyhrich, Lebanon.

April 23. Heinrich Boebel and Anna Maria Ellinger, Lebanon.

May 7. Peter Eisenhauer and Anna Maria Fischer, Bethel.

May 14. Jacob Schock and Anna Elisabetha Angst, Lebanon and Hanover.

May 21. William Karnoughan and Mary Shmidt, Derry.

May 30. David Caldwell and Rebecca Finney, Paxton and Hanover.

June 10. William Dunn and Grace Greys, Paxtang.

June 20. Dennis Hoellen and Elisabetha McMollen, Derry and Hanover.

June 25. Jno. George Schock and Anna Catarina Maurer, Lebanon and Heidelberg.

June 27. Edward I. Praello and Martha Pettigrew, Hanover.

Sept. 8. Johannes Raup and Catarina Agatha Faber, Warwick.

Sept. 26. Lazarus Stewart and Martha Espy, Hanover.

Sept. 29. Christian Frendling and Anna Wolf, Lebanon.

Oct. 8. John Jacob Wolf and Anna Margar. Schnug, Lebanon.

Oct. 22. John George Schaeffer and Maria Catarina Loresch, Bethel and Tulpehocken.

Oct. 22. Robert Hill and Agnes Morton, Hanover.

Nov. 26. Christian Korr and Barbara Hauck, Bethel and Hanover.

Nov. 26. Philipp Rauh and Anna Maria Regina Braun, Bethel.

Dec. 10. James Williams and Magdalena Haehmlin, Bethel.

Dec. 16. Heinrich Muench and Catarina Ried, Heidleberg and Tulpehocken.

Dec. 17. John Cooper and Agnes Currey, Paxtang and Hanover.

1766.

Jan. 7. Robert Clunty and Mary Cunningham, Lebanon and Hanover.

Feb. 3. Jacob Friederich Danninger and Anna Maria Fauler, Rapho.

Feb. 6. Johannes Stein and Eva Barbara Kucher, Lebanon.

March 4. Jacob Bickel and Maria Catarina Braun, Lebanon.

March 4. John Nicolaus Bohr and Maria Margaretha Kobnar (Kolmar), Lebanon.

March 4. John Martin Kolmar and Anna Margdalena Hetzler, Lebanon.

April 1. Peter Schumacher and Anna Dorothea Schaaf, Lebanon.

April 8. Jno. Martin Knemmerling and Anna Margar. Edelmann, Bethel.

April 8. Anastasius Heylmann and Rosina Barbara Maurer, Lebanon and Heidelberg.

April 8. Geo. Maurer and Magdalena Heylmann, Lebanon.

April 8. John Cowden and Agnes Allen, by license, Paxtang and Hanover, married in Derry.

April 14. Caspar Elias Diller and Eva Magdalena Meyer, Lebanon.

April 15. Isaac Hanna and Martha Bell, Paxtang.

April 15. Andrew Mays and Mary Rutherford, Paxtang.

April 15. George Heinrich Ziegler and Dorothea Schnug, Lebanon.

April 29. John Brown and Sarah Cunningham, Hanover.

May 13. Robert White and Isabell Brown, Hanover.

May 27. John Nicolaus Biohl and Elisabetha Kuefer, Bethel.

May 27. John Adam Balmer and Barbara Schauffler, Lebanon.

June 4. John Schnug, widower, and Catarina Duliban, Lebanon.

June 17. Antonius Hauer and Barbara Kueffer, Bethel.

July 8. Johannes Klein and Maria Magdalena Bartholomaey, Bethel and Hanover.

July 29. John Hicks and Elisabetha Holderbaum, Lebanon.

August 4. John Adam Weiss and Maria Eva Meyer, Lebanon.

Aug. 11. Johannes Brechtbiel and Elisabetha Uhrich, Hanover and Tulpehocken.

Aug. 26. John Simson and Agnes Brown, Hanover.

Sept. 5. Andreas Bayer and Anna Margaretha Kraemer, Derry.

Sept. 9. Heinrich Bickel and Catarina Gerhardt, Bethel.

Sept. 11. William McNutt and Jane McNutt (by license), Paxtang.

Sept. 23. Andreas Patz and Catarina Stuck, Bethel and Lebanon.

Sept. 30. Conrad Hornberger and Catarina Maag, Bethel.

Sept. 30. Johannes Zimmerman and Anna Maria Derr, Derry and Donegal.

Oct. 20. George Kuntz and Elisabetha Rauch, Hanover and Bethel.

Oct. 28. Martin Koch and Elisabetha Schantz, Lebanon.

Nov. 11. Daniel Angst and Magdalena Fischer, Hanover and Tulpehocken.

Nov. 11. Edward Tate and Anna Camron, Lebanon and Hanover.

Nov. 15. Thomas Steel and Isabell Steel, Paxtang.

Nov. 18. Andreas Karg and Anna Maria Heinrich, Lebanon.

Nov. 18. Daniel Jungblut and Anna Maria Elizabeth Heinrich, Lebanon.

Nov. 25. John Leonhardt Kirstaetter and Anna Elisabetha Zehrung, Lebanon.

Dec. 9. John Christoph Uhler and Margar. Barbara Spicker, Lebanon.

Dec. 16. Daniel Weber and Mary Manningham, Hanover and Bethel.

1767.

Jan. 26. Johann Wendel Wolf and Anna Dorothea Endress, Lebanon.

March 10. Christoph Ulrich and Juliana Umberger, Lebanon.

March 17. John Nicolaus Fehler and Barbara Leonhardt, Bethel.

April 2. James Morton and Catarina Crow, Derry Township.

April 15. Thomas Allen and Jane Cassen, Hanover and Paxtang.

April 21. George Meyer and Maria Elisabetha Stoehr, Rapho and Lebanon.

May 1. John Thome and Anna Maria Reiss, Lebanon.

May 12. Ambrosius Crain and Sarah Cunningham, Lebanon and Hanover.

May 18. John George Dollinger and Margaretha Jones, Williamsborough.

May 22. Philipp Faber and Rachael English, Paxtang.

June 11. Arthur Mollen and Jane Mc-Mollen, Hanover and Paxtang.

June 30. John George Schuetz and Anna Margar. Wolfkiel, Paxtang and Earl Town.

July 21. Moses Dunlap and Mary Wilson, Hanover and Paxtang.

July 28. Jacob Raisch and Anna Margar. Kessinger, Derry.

Aug. 11. Samuel Zerfass and Sabina Baltz, Cocalico and Lebanon.

Aug. 19. John Christoph Zoll and Veronica Eberly (by license), Cocalico.

Aug. 25. George Peter and Anna Catarina Siechlin, Lebanon and Hanover.

Aug. 27. John Bowman and Mary Lusk. Paxtang.

Aug. 27. William McClure and Hanna Bell, Hanover.

Sept. 1. Johannes Petry and Catarina Oehler, Williamsburg and Lancaster.

Sept. 15. Michael Stroh and Eva Barbara Goettel, Heidelberg and Hanover.

Oct. 2. Robert Stuart and Agnes Drumming, Derry.

Oct. 8. John Fleming and Jane Ramsey, Derry.

Oct. 12. Johannes Scharf and Susanna Michael, Bethel.

Oct. 18. Jacob Oberholtzer and Barbara Faber, Bethel.

Oct. 20. Johannes Reyer and Ma.1 Elisabetha Neu, Warwick and Lebanon.

Oct. 25. Heinrich Keim and Catarina Reiber, Bethel.

Oct. 26. Jacob Fehler and Anna Eva Benin, Heidelberg.

Oct. 27. Andreas Kueffer and Elisabetha Bickel, Lebanon.

Nov. 10. James Wilson and Anna Bell, Hanover and Derry.

Nov. 30. Christoph Mueller and Catarina Stober, Warwick and Cocalico.

Dec. 8. John Boggs and Jane Hays Hanover.

Dec. 3. Alexander McClunty and Mary Aston, Derry.

Dec. 31. William Crain and Annie Hill, Hanover.

1768.

Jan. 4. John McCurry and Sarah Johnston, Hanover.

Jan. 5. Lucas Schally and Maria Elisabetha Boger, Lebanon.

Jan. 19. Christoph Meyer and Anna Margaretha Ilin, Lebanon.

Jan. 26. Heinrich Simund and Elisabetha Holtz, Elisabetha Township.

March 4. John George Feltin and Catarina Elisabetha Burckhardt, Bethel.

March 8. Alexander Kennedy and Margaretha Watson, Hanover.

March 15. John Martin Uhler and Ana Elisabetha Stroh, Lebanon Town.

March 22. Rudolph Koellicker and Anna Maria Weidman, Lebanon Town.

March 24. William Mahorder and Jane Boyd, Paxtang.

April 17. Jacob Fischer and Sabina Rauch, Bethel.

April 18. Samuel Humphreys and Gryssel Cavet, Hanover.

April 26. Anthony McCraight and Abigail Hill, Hanover.

May 27. John George Walmer and Eva Barbara Weyrich, Hanover.

May 30. George Thany and Margaretha Elisabetha Truckemueller, Bethel.

June 7. Christian Koch and Maria Magdalena George, Hanover and Heidelberg.

June 17. John Farrell and Isabell Barnet, Hanover and Paxtang.

June 21. George Volck and Catarina Germann, Lebanon.

June 28. Martin Hoeger, widower, and Maria Elisabetha Beamensdoerfer, Warwick.

July 5. John Cunradt Bingeman and Catarina Barbara Feuerbach, Bethel.

July 5. Johannes Herman and Catarina Herman, Lebanon.

Aug. 2. Christoph Ernst and Anna Margaretha Siechlin, Derry and Paxtang.

Aug. 10. Peter Read and Hanna or Anna Herr, Warwick and Elisabeth.

Aug. 16. Leonhardt Albrecht and Anna Catarina Stroher, Lebanon.

Aug. 21. Johannes Wagner and Maria Elisabeth Gur, Conestoga and Bethel.

Sept. 13. William Snodgrass and Elisabetha McClunnighen, Hanover.

Nov. 14. Heinrich Naess and Christina Heyl, Bethel.

Nov. 14. Jacob Fischer and Anna Maria Steinmann, Bethel and Lancaster.

Nov. 14. Jacob Schwenck and Margaretha Mueller, Lebanon and Hanover

Nov. 22. John Frantz Helm and Anna Maria Koch, Lebanon.

Nov. 22. Jacob Stober and Eva Weber, Hanover.

Nov. 22. Johannes Weber and Maria Elisabetha Bassler, Hanover and Tulpehocken.

Nov. 24. James Ross and Christina Williams, Hanover.

Nov. 25. Samuel Post and Alice Bell Derry.

Nov. 29. Johannes Mohr and Margaretha Gallmeyer, Lebanon.

Dec. 5. Christian Bamberger and Maria Magdalena Held, Hanover.

Dec. 5. Benajamin Still and Mary McElhenny, Paxtang.

Dec. 12. Andreas Endress and Anna Maria Gingrich, Lebanon.

Dec. 13. Christoph Neiss and Barbara Stober, Heidelberg andHanover.

Dec. 30. John Scannel and Mary McManus, Paxtang.

1769.

Jan. 2. John Peter Fischer and Anna Elizabetha Heylman, Lebanon.

Jan. 8. Frantz Mueller and Catarina Mueller, Elizabeth township.

Jan. 17. Augustus Stahl and Ana Elizabetha Nufer, Derry.

Jan. 17. Jacob Kaufmann and Elizabetha Bayer, Derry.

Jan. 17. Johann Martin Riess and Catarina Schmidt, Heidelberg.

Jan. 24. Andrew Carson and Nancy Dixon, Lebanon and Hanover.

Feb. 7. Balthaser Laber and Rosina Wentz, Lebanon.

Feb. 12. Anastasius Ellinger and Catarina Ollinger, Lebanon.

Feb. 2. Michael Traner and Agnes Neal, Hanover.

March 14. Andrew Vogel and Anna Maria Ramberger, Hanover.

March 16. Michael Bosch and Elizabetha Koch, Lebanon.

March 16. John George Lentz and Anna Rosina Reiber, Hanover.

March 16. Heinrich Baumgaertner and Rosina Laedin, Hanover.

March 28. Gottlieb Roth and Anna Elizabetha Brecht, Bethel.

March 30. James Innis and Mary Phaghon, Hanover.

April 10. Conradt Braun and Agnes Schneider, Lebanon.

April 10. John Wilhelm Neu and Juliana Firnssler, Derry and Lebanon.

April 25. Daniel Scherertz and Maria Catarina Meyer, Lebanon.

April 25. Robert Hunter and Isabel Waters, Lebanon.

May 2. Adam Bach, jr., and Barbara Flohr, Lebanon and Rapho.

May 9. John Melchior Abmeyer and Anna Maria Kuemmerling, Lebanon.

May 16. Jacob Blanck and Magdalena Boesshaer, Williams borough and Hanover.

May 16. John Dieterich Koester and Anna Elizabetha Bopp, Reading.

May 23. Johann Heinrich Frey and Anna Maria Boger, Lebanon.

June 15. Andrew Thompson and Elizabetha Bell, Hanover.

June 20. John Heinrich Rheinoehl and Juliana Gebhardt, Lebanon.

Aug. 15. Jacob Schenk and Dorothea Speck, Heidelberg.

Aug. 19. Samuel Jones and Rachael Willis, of Newberry, York county.

Aug. 22. Caspar Jungblut and Catarina Felleberger, Lebanon.

Aug. 31. James Carnaghan and Mary Buck, Derry.

Oct. 20. Johannes Schnaebele and Anna Barbara Hauck, Bethel and Hanover.

Nov. 2. Johann Friederich Hummel and Elizabetha Barbara Blessing, Derry.

Nov. 2. Philipp Mattheis and Catarina Kintzel, Derry.

Nov. 9. Alexander Loughlin and Anne Sharp, Hanover.

Nov. 28. John Bigham and Catarina Watson, Lebanon.

Dec. 12. Michael Kleber and Catarina Holderbaum, Lebanon.

Dec. 12. Peter Neuschwanger and Agnes Mueller, Codorus and Bethel.

Dec. 14. Patrick Cunningham and Elizabetha Brown, Hanover.

Dec. 28. John Nicholaus New and Anna Margaretha Schaefer, Lebanon and Hanover.

1770.

Jan. 5. Peter Boeszhaar and Maria Eva Heyl, Hanover and Bethel.

Jan. 25. Gilbert Kennedy and Mary McKut, Hanover.

Feb. 6. Alexander Fulton and Susanna Scot, Londonderry..

March 6. Peter Deissinger and Margaretha Roth, Bethel.

March 27. Johann Ulrich Ohlinger and Catarina Roeszlin, Lebanon.

March 27. Christian Long and Sarah Brown, Hanover.

April 16. Friederich Boeszhaar and Barbara Heyl, Bethel.

April 24. Michael Hoerner and Margaretha Loresch, Bethel.

April 24. John Adam Stoever and Catarina Elizabetha Heylman, Lebanon.

May 8. Thomas Atkinson and Magdalena Kintzel, Lebanon.

May 20. Peter Thomas and Dorothea Strohfuss, Hanover and Lebanon.

June 6. Nicholaus Enderes and Barbara Ritter, Heidelberg.

July 3. Johann Christoph Fuchz and Susanna Maria Bayer, Hanover and Lebanon.

July 5. George Egis and Elizabetha Oberfeld, Elizabeth Furnace.

July 29. John George Haessler and Elizabetha Rebmann, Tulpehocken.

August 21. Andreas Lay and Hannah Dinniss, Lebanon.

August 21. Johannes Heckendorn and Maria Catarina Hammann, Lebanon.

August 21. Peter Eisenhauer and Maria Elizabetha Schmidt, Bethel.

August 28. Isaac William and Maria Elizabetha Falck, Bethel.

Nov. 12. Johann Gall and Elizabetha Jameson, Paxtang and Hanover.

Nov. 13. Johannes Schirck and Catarina Schnaebelin, Bethel.

Nov. 20. Christoph Friederich Seiler and Maria Elizabetha Kintzel, Lebanon.

Nov. 20. William Kirckwood and Elenore Bryan, Hanover and Lebanon.

Dec. 20. John Campell and Jane Cleellan, Londonderry and Hanover.

1771.

Jan. 15. Johannes Wepner and Catarina Bauman, Lebanon and Bethel.

Jan. 29. Alexander Greenlee and Anne Henry, of Hanover.

Feb. 3. Jacob Roth and Maria Elizabetha Stoltz, Bethel.

Feb. 19. Martin Ulrich and Regina Feltin, Lebanon and Bethel.

Feb. 26. Joseph McLyntie and Margaretha McQuien, Lebanon and Londonderry.

March 19. Michael Decker and Margaretha Hofman, Tulpehocken.

March 21. John Sharp and Elizabetha Laughlin, Hanover.

March 26. John Nicolaus Neu and Eva Catarina Rudiesiehl, Derr and Lebanon.

April 1. Michael Bartholomae and Barbara Grosz, Londonderry.

April 1. Melchior Ruecker and Catarina Mueller, Hampfield.

May 2. George Sprecher and Margaretha Boger, Lebanon and Hanover.

May 9. Hugh Watson and Isabell Craigh, Hanover.

May 16. Matthew McKiney and Elizabetha Lard, Paxtang and Derry.

May 20. Philipp Buchman and Salome Stiebich, Derry.

May 28. Andreas Beistel and Christina Pflantz, Lebanon.

May 28. Jacob Sauter and Philippina Beistel, Lebanon.

June 6. Cornelius McMurphey and Mary Dougless, Hanover.

June 13. James Lock and Agnes Brown, Hanover.

June 18. Jacob Klesmann and Elizabetha Catarina Bayer, Hanover and Lebanon.

July 1. Alexander Martin and Martha Grimes, Hanover.

August 27. Johannes Bickel and Maria Feltin, Bethel.

Sept. 3. Johannes Scherer and Magdalen Staufer, Donegal and Derry.

Oct. 1. John Martin Lang and Elizabetha Huber, Lebanon.

Oct. 1. Peter Weyrich and Catarina Simon, Hanover.

Oct. 19. Thomas Owens and Dorothea Zieger, Lebanon.

Nov. 12. Daniel Birckie and Catarina Dauter, Hanover.

Nov. 14. Daniel Leng and Maria Barbara Koerner, Bethel.

Nov. 19. Leonhardt Schuetz and Clara Deiss, Paxtang.

Dec. 8. Christoph Scheretz and Magdalena Rausch, Hanover.

Dec. 8. Nicolaus Gebhardt and Anna Appolonia Kornmann, Lebanon.

Dec. 15. Valentin Schneider and Elizabetha Wagner, Paxtang.

Dec. 31. Peter Etter and Elizabetha Daut, Lebanon and Hanover.

1772.

Jan. 5. Christian Meyer and Margaretha Eisenhauer, Bethel.

Jan. 7. Daniel Brians and Elizabetha Reush, Lebanon.

Jan. 19. Christian Seltzer and Maria Diewing, Bethel and Hanover.

Feb. 11. Amos Jones and Anna Jordan, Conewago.

March 18. Curtis Grubb and Elizabetha Carpenter, Cornwall Furnace.

April 21. Tobias Stoever and Hannah Zimmerman, Lebanon.

May 1. Jacob Bronner and Anna Stoppelbein, Hanover and Lebanon.

May 19. Johannes Schnug and Anna Christina Heylmann, Lebanon.

May 31. Stephan Huck and Christina Decker, Lebanon.

June 4. James Robinson and Mary Lock, Hanover and Derry.

June 16. Johannes Schmidt and Christina Nunnenmacher, Lebanon.

June 21. Michael Karmenie and Catarina Meyer, Lebanon.

June 21. Andreas Heckman and Susanna Gerhardt, Bethel.

Sept. 18. Martin Guntrum and Maria Catarina Boesshaar, Bethel.

Sept. 22. Albrecht Siechle and Maria Priess or Pruess, Lebanon and Hanover.

Spet. 27. Michael Schudy and Elizabetha Fleck, Heidelberg.

Oct. 5. Michael Zoeller and Catarina Dillman, Heidelberg.

Oct. 14. John Glover and Sophia Duncan, Derry.

Nov. 10. Cunradt Scherertz and Maria Margaretha Laed, Hanover.

Nov. 17. Michael Haehnle and Catarina Looser, Bethel.

Dec. 15. David Merckir and Catarina Kintzler, Bethel, Berks county.

Dec. 15. Peter Koch and Juliana Heinrich, Lebanon.

Dec. 28. Zacharias Ralph and Hannah Danin, Londonderry.

1773.

Feb. 1. John Cunning and Anna Hillis, Hanover.

Feb. 9. John Michael Neu and Justina Bart, Lebanon.

April 13. John Clarck and Magdalena Litsch, Bethel, Berks county.

April 18. Johann Frantz Boehler and Catarina Breit, Lebanon.

April 20. John Michael Uhler and Anna Maria Elizabetha Stroh, Lebanon.

May 17. James Long and Anna Charrin, Hanover.

June 6. Christian Fremdling and Susanna Maria Glasser, Lebanon.

June 8. Samuel Man and Elizabetha Allen, Hanover.

June 22. Martin Friedle and Magdalena Ruecker, Derry.

June 22. Samuel Irwin and Jane Grimes, Hanover.

June 29. John Martin Wagner and Charlotta Kintzel, Lebanon.

Aug. 22. Heinrich Bucher and Maria Barbara Schmidt, Hanover and Bethel.

Sept. 23. James Porterfield and Jenny Hillis, Hanover.

Sept. 26. David Mueller and Elizabetha Catarina Wild, Bethel.

Sept. 28. Johannes Meyer and Anna Maria Rehwald, Lebanon.

Oct. 1. John Walcker and Mary Gashens, Upper Paxton.

Oct. 18. John Scott and Susannah McClure, Hanover.

1774.

Jan. 18. Robert Murhead and Anne Evans, Hanover.

Jan. 25. John Michael Conradt and Margaretha Eschbach, Bethel.

Feb. 3. William Asherast and Jane Wauce, Hanover.

Feb. 22. John Adam Fischer and Maria Elizabetha Becker, Lebanon.

March 10. John McElhanny and Margaretha McCord, Hanover.

May 1. Johannes Brubacker and Anna Meyer, Cocalio.

May 1. Heinrich Brubacker and Elizabetha Hundsraecker, Cocalio.

May 2. Andrew Armstrong and Jane Forester, Hanover.

May 17. William Grimes and Mary Brown, Hanover.

May 24. Johannes Stoever and Anna EngelKissecker, Lebanon.

May 31. Martin George Leonhardt and Maria Barbara Eschebach, Bethel.

May 31. James Miley and Margaretha Brown, Williams borough.

June 1. Richard Fosset and Margaretha Williams, Hanover and Bethel.

July 17. John Philipp New and Elizabetha Preiss, Lebanon.

July 26. Heinrich Diettel and Margaretha Pilgrum, Bethel.

August 30. John Christoph Franck and Anna Margaretha Maurer, Lebanon.

Nov. 10. Daniel Mueller and Catarina Lang, Derry.

Nov. 13. Patrick Darby and Molly Rice, Hanover and Derry.

Nov. 22. Frederich Helm and Barbara Altig (or Albig), Hanover.

Nov. 22. Johannes Philipp Loeffler and Catarina Riedt, Bethel.

Dec. 20. Johannes Nicolaus Bopp and Catarina Margaretha Felt, Lebanon and Hanover.

1775.

Feb. 3. John Friederich Weber and Anna Margaretha Iauch, Bethel, Berks county.

Feb. 15. Walther McFarling and Hannah Clarck, Hanover.

March 21. Mattheis Stroeher and Anna Barbara Brechtbiel, Lebanon.

March 28. Leonard Presby and Agnes Makee, Hanover.

May 12. Michael Meck and Margaretha Motz, Muehlbach.

August 30. Richard Kasey, and Sarah Pits, Hanover.

Sept. 5. George Adam Eckhardt and Maria Margaretha Kraemer, Lebanon.

Sept. 5. John David and Rebecca Turner, Hanover.

Sept. 21. William Hall and Frances Starret, Hanover.

Sept. 27. Robert Lewers and Elenore Wier, Hanover.

Sept. 28. Benjamin McRentzie (or McKentzie) and Margary Cunningham, Hanover.

Sept. 28. Peter Bucher and Maria Barbara Kuntzlemann, Hanover.

Nov. 23. James Taylor and Jane Moor, Hanover.

Dec. 12. Christian Schweitzer and Maria Huber, Cumberland and Lancaster county.

Dec. 19. Andreas Braun and Magdalena Malfir, Hanover and Lebanon.

1776.

Jan. 18. Daniel Clarck and Anna Maria Bilgeram, Bethel.

Jan. 18. Michael Haehnle and Anna Maria Boltz, Bethel.

Jan. 31. John Stuebich and Anna Langenecker, Derry.

March 19. William Cunningham and Nancy Glascow, Lebanon.

March 26. Heinrich Peter and Anna Christian Imbode, Lebanon.

April 30. Theobolldt Wildt and Anna Maria Achelbach, Bethel and Lebanon.

May 29. Jacob Long and Elisabeth Coole, Northumberland county.

Oct. 11. William Sawyer and Jane Rotch, Londonderry.

Oct. 13. Jno. Cunradt Kachel and Margaretha Schwalb, Lebanon.

Oct. 20. John Schnug, jr., widower, and Anna Margaretha Bohr, Lebanon and Hanover.

Nov. 28. Jno. Jacob Bickel and Christina Schindel, Lebanon.

1777.

Feb. 18. Jacob Epprecht and Elizabetha Weitzel, Lebanon.

Feb. 18. Jacob Sichle and Susanna Muench, Lebanon and Hanover.

March 30. John George Glassbrenner and Catarina Rudy, Lebanon.

April 8. John Peter Neu and Mary Regina Reusch, Lebanon and Londonderry.

April 14. Andreas Eckert and Sabina Sauter, Bethel.

April 22. Geo. Boeszhaar and Catarina Kraeht, Hanover and Williamsborough.

May 4. Johannes Schultz and Barbara Korr, Bethel.

May 20. John Stehrer and Magdalena Bickel, Cumberland and Lancaster counties.

June 17. Jacob Wolandle and Catarina Bickel, Lebanon.

June 23. Joseph Flory and Catarina Dub, Paxtang.

June 24. Michael Meyer and Catarina Koppenhoefer, Hanover.

June 24. Wilhelm Balm and Margaretha Bishoff, Derry and Hanover.

July 29. William Wilkinson and Mary Maghen, Derry.

Aug. 26. Nicolaus Cassel and Anna Margara. Braun, Middletown and Hanover.

Aug. 28. James Stuart and Precilla Ashby, Hanover.

Sept. 2. Johannes Buchs, or Bucks, and Margara. Baurin, Derry.

Sept. 4. John Oehrle, jr., and Margaretha Deininger, Londonderry.

Sept. 11. Abraham Alles and Anna Maria Ried, Hanover.

Dec. 23. Mattheis Boyer, jr., and Barbara Foerster, Lebanon.

1778.

Jan. 19. Engel Martin and Barbara Ehrhardt, Elizabeth and Rapho.

March 13. Michael Battorff and Catarina Emmerich, Bethel, Berks county.

March 17. Simon Muench and Anna Maria Weber, Hanover.

March 18. Johannes Staehly and Eva Maria Schedt, Bethel.

March 19. Christian Stutzmann and Catarina Ecket, Berks county, across the Blue Mountain.

March 21. Valentin Schauffler and Cattarina Heyl, Bethel.

March 31. Michael Leutz and Anna Elisabetha Uhrich, Bethel.

April 20. John Adam Zimmerman and Elisabetha Baumgartner, Derry.

April 20. John Stober and Juliana Barbara Wolf, Hanover.

June 8. Patrick McNight and ——— McNight, Hanover.

June 23. Heinrich Miller and Maria Magdal. Braun, Hanover.

June 30. Thomas Gordon and Susannah McLinty, Lebanon.

July 9. Heinrich Naess and Margar. Bucher, Bethel and Hanover.

July 13. George Machon and Margaretha Clerck, Derry.

July 23. John Hollenbach and Elisabetha Stanbury, Middletown.

July 28. Andreas Braun and Christiana Weber, Hanover.

Aug. 23. Heinrich Meyly and Magdalena Kroh, Bethel.

Sept. 22. Johannes Peter and Salome Bender, Lebanon.

Sept. 22. Hugh Morris and Margaretha Rammiage, Hanover.

Oct. 1. John Jacob Voltz and Christina Koch, Warwick.

Oct. 6. Hartman Deutsch and Elisabetha Huber, Warwick.

Oct. 27. Johannes Beltz and Maria Heyer, Lebanon.

Oct. 27. Thomas Koppenhoefer and Elisabetha Miess, Hanover and Bethel.

Dec. 1. Duncan McGregor and Anne Kezey, Elizabeth.

Dec. 9. Christian Schauffeler and Barbara Lehman, Williamsborough.

1779.

Feb. 16. Jacob Palm and Maria Dorothea Bischoff, Londonderry.

Feb. 16. John Peter Neu and Juliana Karmenie, Lebanon and Londonderry.

Feb. 23. Nicolaus Heinrich and Catara. Elisaba. Becker, Lebanon.

March 7. Jost Knaegy and Anna Schirck, Bethel.

March 9. Peter Ebersold and Christina Etter, Hanover and Derry.

March 11. Robert Porterfield and Alcey Wallis, Hanover.

March 25. Johannes Weber and Eva Margar. Braun, Hanover.

March 30. Christian Ebersold and Elisabetha Etter, Hanover and Derry.

March 30. John Nicolaus Fertig and Maria Elisabetha Neu, Cumberland and Derry.

April 14. Leonhardt Stroh and Anna Maria Goettel, Hanover.

April 14. Valentin Pannekuchen and Anna Leein, Paxtang.

April 19. John Wilhelm Bohr and Ana Magdal. Boger, Lebanon.

April 20. Johannes Palm and Barbara Bittelion, Londonderry.

April 26. John George Stahlschmidt and Salome Reinhardt, Tulpehocken.

May 2. Rudolph Doerr and Sabina Sauter, Williamsborough.

"The following marriage was after the death of J. C. Stoever:"

May 29. Heinrich Schwab and Elisabetha Stelbzer.

By the Herrn Pfarrer Mindbohner (Melsheimer?)

Nov. 9. Johann Friederich Stoever, Lebanon, and Anna Margaretha Daenschaerez, Hendelberg (Heidleberg?)

--- A ---

Aar, Elisabetha 62
Abmeyer, John Melchior 73
Ache, Johannes 50, 64
  John Heinrich 51, 68
  Maria Catarina 51
  Maria Susanna 50
Achebach, Anna Maria 76
Acker, George Heinrich 6
  Heinrich 6
Ackermann, Michael 61
Adam, Bernhardt 63
  John 63
  John George 20
  Jonas 62
  Juliana 62
  Michael 20
  Samuel 67
Adams, Elisabeth 58
  John 70
  Mary 61
Adlam, John 14
  Mary 14
Adolph, Heinrich 31, 38
  John Heinrich 29
Ainsworth, Benjamin 64
  Jane 69
  Jno. 70
Albert, Anna Barbara 61
  Elizabetha 28
  John 46
  John Adam 38
  John Michael 48
  John Peter 51
  John Wilhelm 43, 54
  Maria Margaretha 48
  Michael (Jr.) 43
  Peter 51
  Wilhelm 19, 38
Albig, Barbara 75
Albrecht, Anna Frantzina 11
  Eva Christina 29
  Heinrich 70
  John 7
  Judith 7
  Leonhardt 72
  Maria 64
  Mattheis 29
  Michael 11
Alexander, Agnes 65
Allen, Agnes 71
  Elizabetha 75
  Margaretha 63
  Sarah 62
  Thomas 72
Alles, Abraham 76
Allgeyer, John Wolf 18
  Maria 18
  Maria Eva 19, 54
  John Wolf 19
Allison, David 70
  Rosanna 69
Alstatt, John 6
Altig, Barbara 75
Altstatt, John 7
  Judith 7
Amborn, Anna Margaretha 8
  Anna Maria 59
  Christoph 8, 54

Amborn (continued)
  John 8
  John Wilhelm 8
Amweg, Sophia Louisa 67
Andereck, Catarina 22
  Christian 22, 54
Anderson, George 56
  Mary 10
  Thomas 10
Andre, Juliana 29, 30, 36, 62
Andrew, James 68
Angst, Anna Elisabetha 71
  Daniel 71
Anspach, Anna Catarina 25
  George 25
  Johann Peter 56
  John Peter 25
  Leonhardt 39
  Magdalena 32
  Peter 32
Anton, Anna Catarina 64
Apfel, Johannes 40
  Peter 23
  Eva Rosina 23
Appel, Anna Elisabetha 69
  Barbara 46
  Catarina 46
  Johannes 46
Aras, Elizabetha Catarina 65
Armbruester, Philipp 64
Armstrong, Andrew 75
Arnold, John George 58
Ashby, Precilla 76
Asherast, William 75
Aston, Mary 72
Atkinson, James 68
  Jno. 70
  Thomas 68, 74
Augenstein, Anna Margaretha 65
Augin, Elizabeth 5
Aulenbach, Margaretha 66
  Magdalena 42
  Maria Mag. 29
  Maria Magdalena 65
Auman, Elizabetha 8
  Jacob 8
Aver, Anna Catarina 37
  Anna Elisabetha 37
  Eva Margaretha 37
  Maria Magdalena 37
  Michael 37, 61
Axer, Barbara 34
  John Michael 35
  Michael 34

--- B ---

Baader, Christoph 8
  Nicolaus 8
Baasz, Philipp 67
Bach, Adam 28, 51
  Adam (Jr.) 73
  Anna Catarina 28
  Anna Maria 28
  Barbara 51
  Eva Catarina 57
Bachman, Heinrich 40
Backer, Dinah 70

Backestoss, Jacob 63
Bader, Catharina 57
Baecker, George 18
  John Jonathan 6
  Jonathan 6
Baerling, Jacob 15
  Jacob Cunradt 15
  John Frederick 15
Baerlinger, Jacob 18
Baetlin, Anna Margaretha 54
Baettle, Michael 24
Baettly, Michael 28
Bahler, John Nicolaus 44
Baker, Adam 11
  Elizabetha 11
Baldwin, Hannah 57
Balm, Wilhelm 76
Balmer, Catarina 66
  Elisabetha 61
  George 61, 70
  John Adam 71
  Margaretha 61
  Michael 50
  Peter 70
  Philipp Adam 45, 63
Balmus, Anna Maria 69
  Peter 65
Balspach, George (Jr.) 45
Baltz, Sabina 72
Balz, Barbara 50
  George 50
  John George 50
Bamberger, Christian 73
Banckauf, Antonius 11
Barbara, Christina 31
Bard, Sarah 68
Barnet, Isabell 72
  James 61
Barnitz, George Carl 14
Bart, Ana 18
  Anna 55
  Justina 75
Barth, John Adam 64
Bartholomae, Michael 74
Bartholomaei, Dominicus 62
Bartholomaey, Maria Magdalena 71
Bartholuss, Lucia Henrietta 70
Bartruff, Andreas 49, 67
  Anna Margaretha 49
Baseler, Agnes 54
  Anna Catarina 36
  Heinrich 26, 34
  John Frederich 17
  Thomas 51
  Veronica 10, 17
Bassler, Catarina 63
  Maria Elisabetha 73
Batdorf, George Peter 27
Batteiger, Catarina 69
Battesteld, Margaretha 63
Battorf, Christian 28
Battorff, Maria Mag. 35
  Michael 76
Batz, Barbara 50
  George 50
  John George 50
Bauck, Anna Catarina 56
Bauer, Anna Eva 23
  Anna Maria 23

Bauer (continued)
Barbara 41, 46
Eva 41
George Thomas 42
Heinrich 59
John Jacob 41
John Martin 23
John Valentin 23
Margaretha 59
Martin 17
Michael 23, 31, 32, 61
Thomas 40, 41, 46
Baulinger, Catarina 17
Baum, Adam 63
Anna Maria 56
Baumaenin, Maria 8, 9
Baumaenn, Barbara 55
Bauman, Catarina 74
George 10
Jacob 58
Maria 10
Baumann, Anna Christina 17
Catarina 16
Elizabetha 9
Emma Maria 9
George 9
George Stephan 55
Johannes 9
John George 9, 12
John Jacob 9
Juliana 67
Maria 9, 11, 12, 13
Maria Chris. 14
Baumgaertner, Anna Catarin 66
Gottfried 43
Heinrich 73
Johannes 21
John Dorst 21
John Jacob 43
Peter 21
Baumgartner, Elisabetha 76
Gottfried 62
Michael 7
Baur, Magdalena 63
Baurin, Margara. 76
Bayer, Adam 68
Andreas 71
Asahel 66
Elizabetha 73
Elizabetha Catarina 74
Heinrich 53
Michael 68
Susanna Maria 74
Beamensdoerfer, Maria Elis-
abetha 72
Beans, Jennet 68
Bear, William 69
Bebeler, Anna Maria 6
John Jacob 6
Beber, Maria Magdalena 56
Becher, Anna Barbara 55
Catarina Barbara 43, 59
Bechtel, Anna Margaretha 64
Christian 28, 45, 63
Eva Catarina 45
George 38
John Nicholaus 45
John Nicolaus 38, 41
Margaretha 28
Maria Elizabetha 5
Nicholaus 45
Bechthold, John Nicolaus 46
Margaretha 46
Beck, Andreas 67
Becker, Anna Catherine 56
Anna Maria 22, 27
Catara. Elisaba. 77
Catarina 69

Becker (continued)
Johannes 43, 63
John Joseph 6
John Michael 19
Margaretha 63
Maria 60
Maria Elizabetha 43, 75
Michael 55
Peter 43, 54
Sara 34
Beckle, John Ulrich 7
Beer, Barbara 54
Catarina Barbara 14
John George 14
Beerling, Anna Margaretha
Euler
Jacob 16
Beetel, Eva 27
Peter 27
Beight, Samuel 62
Beistel, Andreas 74
Philippina 74
Bell, Alice 73
Anna 72
Elizabeth 68
Elizabetha 73
Hanna 72
Martha 71
Samuel 63
Beltz, Johannes 76
Bender, Catarina 60
George Valentine 43
Maria Catarina 66
Salome 76
Valentine 43
Bendig, Wilhelm 69
Bendter, Catarina 67
Benedict, Peter 68
Benin, Anna Eva 72
Benson, Richard 64
Benteler, Christian 63
Bentz, Christian 17
Jacob 15
John George 15
John Jacob 15
Maria Barbara 15
Philipp 17
Valentin 58
Beren, Frederick 17
Joseph 17
Berg, Catarina 56
Berger, George 18, 44
George Wilhelm 43
Heinrich 61
Johannes 66
Simon 67
Bergheimer, Anna Eva 9
Casper 9
Johann Caspar 53
Johann Leonhardt 10
John Ludwig 9
Maria Elisabetha 10
Berghmer, Susanna Catarina
53
Berghoefer, Anna Maria 57
Berghoester, Catarina 17
Berin, Sophia 28
Berlidt, Anna Catarina 6
John Wolff 6
Berlin, Catarina 16
Bernhaeuszel, Susanna Ca-
tharina 5
Valentine 5
Bernhardt, Adam Valentine
John
Bernitz, Elias Daniel 17
George Karl 23
John Leonhardt 9, 10, 14

Bernitz (continued)
Leonhardt 17
Beschel, Anna 55
Beset, Mary 69
Best, Christina Dorothea 63
Bettlin, Anna Maria 55
Beuckert, Margretha Elenora
58
Beuskert, John Jacob 21
Beutelstein, Anna Margaretha
63
Maria Christina 65
Beyer, Albinus 18, 58
Andreas 5, 53
Anna Catharina 31
Anna Magdalena 31
Catarina 34
Elisabetha 58
Eva 34
Eva Elizabetha 59
Heinrich 21, 29, 31, 32, 34,
38
Johann Heinrich 64
Johannes 31
John Jacob 23, 31
Margaretha 23
Maria Elisabetha 29, 38
Maria Salome 31
Maria Sophia Margaretha
18
Martin 59
Michael 48, 49
Philipp 34
Susanna 54
Beyerle, Anna Maria 39
John Michael 14, 39
Michael 32
Beyerlin, Anna Catarina 15
Beyerstall, Dorothea 57
Biber, Magdalena 54
Bich, Jacob 40
Bichszler, John 59
Bickel, Anna Maria 26
Catarina 76
Christian 25, 26
Eliabetha 51
Elisabetha 72
Elizabetha 65
Heinrich 25, 48, 71
Jacob 25, 71
Jno. Jacob 76
Johannes 26, 74
John Jacob 26, 35, 66
John Tobias 51
Magdalena 76
Maria Catarina 51
Maria Margar. 70
Maria Margaretha 26, 34
Rosina 26
Simon 26
Thomas 26
Tobias 26, 28, 34, 51
Biegeler, Anna Maria 18
Marx 18
Biegler, John Michael 58
Maria Catarina 63
Biel, John Freiderich 52
John Nicolaus 52
Maria Elisab. 52
Maria Elizabetha 48
Nicolaus 48, 51
Bienen, Christian 60
Biener, Elizabetha 65
Bier, David 54
Bigham, John 73
Bilgeram, Anna Maria 76
Biliams, Catarina 69
Billmeyer, John. Leonhardt 55

Billmeyer (continued)
John Martin 35
Leonhardt 18, 35
Binckel, Magdalina 58
Bindnagel, Johannes 20
John 29
Regina 20
Bindtnagel, Anna Sabina 23, 62
Johannes 23
John 19, 21, 24, 23
John Martin 23, 68
Regina 21
Sabina 35
Bindtnagle, John 22
Bingeman, John Cunradt 72
Bintz, Michael 55
Biohl, John Nicolaus 71
Birckel, Anna Eva 18
Dorothea 20
Jacob 18, 20, 22
John Jacob 18
Magdalena 56
Maria Dorothea 18
Michael Leonhardt 18
Birckie, Daniel 74
Bird, Andrew 12
Magdalena 65
Rebecca 12
Birdman, Catarina 17
John 17
Birgler, Marx 21
Bischof, Heinrich 14
Bischoff, Elixabetha 13
Heinrich 13, 55
Johannes 32
Maria Dorothea 77
Biscof, Elisabetha 14
Bishoff, Margaretha 76
Bisswanger, Geo. Peter 54
Biszwanger, George Peter 8
Maria Barbara 8
Bittelion, Barbara 77
Black, James 66
Mary 55
Blackburn, Elisabeth 70
Blanck, Christian 10
Jacob 73
Johannes 10
Blaser, Christian 6
Juliana Catharina Margar-
etha 6
Blecher, Dorothea 67
Blessing, Elizabetha Barbara
73
Bleystein, Anna Margaretha 35
Margaretha 31
Block, Patrick 55
Bluem, Maria Eva 57
Blum, Catarina 53
Elizabeth 26
Joanna Catharine 21
John 26
Maria Catharine 21
Bockenmeyer, Magdalena 56
Bockle, Catarina 67
Boebel, Heinrich 70
Boeckel, Margaretha Dorothea
40
Boeckle, Anna Maria 49
Catarina Charlotta 5
Heinrich 49, 51
Margaretta Dorothea 5
Mattheis 60
Ulrich 5
Boecklin, Margaretha 49
Boehler, Johann Frantz 75
Boehm, Johannes 8, 54
John Heinrich 8

Boehmer, Maria Juliana 67
Boeringer, John Philipp 33
Stephen 33
Boesshaar, Anna 34
Balthasar 34, 56, 61
John 50
John George 39
John Peter 39
Maria Catarina 75
Mattheis 39
Boesshaer, Magdalena 73
Boeszhaar, Balthasar 28
Elizabetha 28
Geo. 76
George 28
Friederich 73
Hanna 28
Juliana 28
Peter 73
Boetten, Anna Maria 58
Boetzel, Otillia Margar. 68
Boger, Ana Magdal. 77
Anna Maria 73
Margaretha 74
Maria Elisabetha 72
Mattheis 61
Boggs, John 72
Bohr, Anna Margaretha 76
Burckhardt 51
Johann Adam 65
John Mattheis 51, 62
John Nicolaus 71
John Wilhelm 77
Jno. Burchardt 70
Lucia Henrietta 51
Mattheis 51
Michael 47
Bohrman, Agnes 60
John George 54
Bohrmann, Catarina 58
John George 58
John Jacob 70
Boid, Elizabeth 68
Boile, Sarah 69
Boin, Maria Catar. 57
Bollenbacher, Abraham 34
Boller, Anna Catarina 55
Bollman, John Adam 38
Boltz, Anna Dorothea 21
Anna Maria 76
Catarina 15
Catarina Barbara 21
Dorothea 65
Elizabetha 18
Eva Catarina 61
John Jacob 66
John Michael 21
Maria Barbara 20
Michael 15, 18, 20, 34
Boner, Catarina 65
Bonnet, Jacob 48
Rosina 48
Bontz, John 56
Bopp, Anna Elizabetha 73
Catar. Margar. 52
Catarina 52
Johannes Nicolaus 75
John Nicolaus 52
Borden, George 62
Born, Daniel 24
Bors, Ludwig 18
Borst, Anna Dorothea 21, 67
Barbara 59
Maria Elizabeth 15, 21
Michael 21
Susanna 21
Bort, Andreas 18
Anna Maria 62

Bort (continued)
Maria Barbara 18
Borth, Andreas 56
Bortner, Elisabetha 50
Heinrich 50
Jacob 29, 41
Johannes 50
John George 50
Maria Elisabetha 50
Philipp Jacob 50, 68
Bosch, Michael 73
Bowman, John 72
Boyd, Elenore 58
Jane 72
Boyer, Catarina 70
Mattheis (Jr.) 76
Brachtbill, Dorst 21
Braechbil, John 24
Maria Barbara 24
Braeden, Agnes 65
Brandes, Catarina 64
Brannen, Timothy 68
Bratschisch, Samuel 3
Brauerin, Elizabetha 8
Braumwaehrt, Maria Magda-
lena 57
Braun, Agnes 52
Andreas 76
Anna Juliana 45
Anna Margara. 76
Anna Maria Regina 71
Catarina 60
Catarina Barbara 31
Conradt 73
Conradt (Sr.) 52
Eva Margar. 77
Johannes 7, 58
John Michael 61
John Wendel 57
Maria Catarina 71
Maria Magdal. 76
Martin 31, 56
Michael 45
Braunwell, John Heinrich 52
Mattheis 52
Breaden, William 65
Brecht, Adam 24, 45, 46, 63
Anna Elizabetha 73
Catarina 64
Christian 46
David 49
Elisabetha 67
Elizabetha 67
John Heinrich 41
Maria Elisabetha 45
Maria Margaretha 46
Wendel 41
Brechbiel, Dorst 43, 49
Johannes 44
John 19, 20
Maria Regina 19
Peter 67
Brechbill, John 21
Brechbille, Anna Barbara 21
Brechtbiel, Anna Barbara 75
Johannes 71
John Nicolaus 66
Breckbiel, Dorst 20
Elizabetha 20
Johannes 20
John Peter 20
Breedyes, Hanna 12
James 12
William 12
Brehm, Jacob 46
Margaretha Elisabetha 46
Breit, Catarina 75
Breitenstein, Leonhardt 57

Brendel, Eva Catarina 29
  George 29
  Philipp 60
Brenneis, Margaretha 55
Brenneisen, John 63
  Rudolph 62
Brenneiser, Jacob 61
Brenneiss, Barbara 60
Brenner, Maria Elisab. 32
  Philipp 52
Brians, Daniel 74
Bricker, Anna Maria 60
Brickle, Catarina 50
  Paulus 50, 69
Brickler, Eva Margaretha 35
  John Gottfried 35
  John Jacob 35
  John Peter 35
  Mattheis 35
Brintzler, John Frederick 19
  Maria Elisabetha 19
  Nicolaus 19, 54
Brix, Joseph 65
Broband, Johann 13
  John 13
Broeckle, George 62
Bronner, George Michael 62
  Jacob 74
  Maria Barbara 11
  Wolf Heinrich 62
Bronnerin, Anna Maria 11
Brooth, Elisabeth 62
Brosius, Anna Catarina 45
  Catarina 28
  John George 28, 41
  John Nicolaus 40, 45
  Juliana 40
  Maria Catarina 40
  Maria Elisab. 62
  Maria Elisabetha 24, 40
  Maria Magdalena 40
  Maria Margaretha 36, 45
  Nicolaus 40, 41, 45, 63
  Peter 35, 37
  Sebastian 24, 36, 40, 41, 62
Brown, Agnes 71, 74
  Ana Eva 42
  Anna Barbara 22
  Elizabetha 73
  Isabell 71
  Jacob 22
  John 22, 42, 68, 71
  Margaretha 75
  Maria Regina 22
  Mary 65, 75
  Sarah 73
Brubacher, Anna Maria 39
  Isaac 39
Brubacker, Heinrich 75
  Johannes 75
Brucher, Catarina 3
Bruechen, Maria Barbara 57
Bruecker, Catarina 48
  John Michael 48
  Philipp 48
Bruender, Ana Catarina 25
  Heinrich 25
Brumbach, Maria Gertraudt 56
Brunner, Barbara 12
Bruschel, Samuel 11
Bryan, Elenore 74
Bubar, Lampert 18
  Maria Catarina 18
Buchanon, Margaretha 64
Bucher, Heinrich 75
  Margar. 76
  Martinus 35
  Peter 35, 76

Buchman, Philipp 74
Buchs, Johannes 76
Buchtrueckel, Wentzel 14
Buck, Mary 73
Bucks, Johannes 76
Budinger, Anna Margaretha 16
Buechin, Maria Elisab. 61
Bueckle, Geo. Adam 70
Buehler, John David 56
  Susanna 18
  Ulrich 18
Buenckel, Maria 60
Buengel, Anna Maria 57
Buerger, — 22
  Adam 62
  Carl 70
  Catarina 20, 34
  Eva 34
  George 16, 20, 21
  John George 57
  Ulrich 58
Buettel, Anna Margaretha 20
Buetzer, John Christian 17
  Ulrich 17
Buger, Jacob 9
  John 9
  John Ulrich 9
  Rosina 9
  Susanna Barbara 11
  Ulrich 13
Bumpas, Thomas 56
Bunert, Michael 64
Bung, Paulus 54
Burchhardt, John Jacob 69
Burckard, Simon 64
Burckel, Anna Maria 25
Burckert, Maria 54
Burckhardt, Catarina Elisa-
  betha 72
  Paul 57
Burckhart, Maria Magdalena 15
  Paul 15
Burger, Anna Maria 54
  Barbara 9
  Michael 42
  Sebastian 42
Buringer, Florian 61
Burney, Elizabeth 55
Burringer, Florina 35
  Phillipina Christina 35
Busch, Johannes 67
  John Michael 30
Buschfeld, Catarina 59
Busser, Anna Maria Doro-
  thea Frederica 67
Buwinger, Florian 36
  Johann Leonhardt 36

--- C ---

Caldwell, David 71
Callbreath, John 60
Callus, John 4
Camell, Anne 68
Cammerer, John Andreas 39
  Maria Barbara 39
Campbell, Jane 68
  John 68
Campell, John 74
Camron, Anna 71
Canaan, Anna 59
  Charity 10
  Francies 10, 11
  Lasenbury 10
  Robert 10
  William 10

Canter, Maria 32
Cantz, John Jacob 49
Cantzon, John 69
Carey, Hannah M. 10
Carl, Andreas 21
  Anna Elizabetha 8
  Anna Maria 21
  Jacob 8
  John Frederick 57
  John Michael 21
  Maria Dorothea 8
  Michael 14
  Simon 26
Carnaghan, James 73
Carnill, Anne 68
Carpenter, Elizabetha 74
Carr, James 61
  John 62
  Mary 69
Cars, Elizabetha 59
Carson, Andrew 73
Carstnitz, Anna Regina 28
Cartlay, Elizabeth 55
Cassel, Catarina 21
  John Heinrich 21
  John Jacob 21
  Nicolaus 76
Cassen, Jane 72
Catermaenn, Maria Barbara
  54
Causseler, John 59
Cavet, Gryssel 72
  Moses 70
Chagoin, Margaretha 45
Chagrin, George Philipp 70
Chaguin, Maria Margar. 57
Chambers, Mary 66
Charrin, Anna 75
Cheeck, Hannah 61
Chreesty, Robert 56
Christ, George 30
  Heinrich 4
Christman, Abraham 8
  Anna Maria 8
  Isaac 8
  Jacob 8, 9, 10
  Johannes 9
  Magdalena 10
  Maria 60
  Sara 8
Christoph, Maria Barbara 7
Clarck, Daniel 76
  Elizabetha 44
  Hannah 75
  James 61
  John 75
Clark, Abraham 65
  Benjamin 20, 34
  Elenore 68
  Elizabeth 70
  James 36
  Jane 20, 65
  Laurence 69
  Margaretha 36, 63, 64
  Mary 20, 69
  Matthew 57
  Patrick 56
  Susanna 69
  Thomas 20, 67
  William 64
Clausser, Johannes 33, 37
  Philipp Adam 33, 37
  Simon 33
Cledy, Barbara 55
  Johannes 55
Clellan, Jane 74
Clerck, Elizabeth 70
  Margaretha 76

Cloward, Lyddia 69
Clunty, Robert 71
Codougan, Elisabeth 62
Coerper, Andreas 33
  John Andreas 33
  Margaretha 13
  Nicolaus 13,33,54
Collins, John 68
Collwell, Margaretha 65
Colvert, John 9
  Rebecca 9
Conally, Bridgitte 59
Conner, James 59
  Johanna 61
Conradt, John Michael 75
Cook, Gratia 4
  Thomas 4
Coole, Elisabeth 76
Cooper, John 62,71
Coppels, William 63
Corell, Maria Margaretha 56
Cornelius, Peter 56
Corry, Anna 62
Cowden, John 71
Cowen, Henry 64
Cox, John 59
Crafford, James 69
  Margaretha 70
Craig, William 69
Craigh, Isabell 74
Craighton, John 70
Crain, Ambrosius 72
  William 72
Crampton, James 66
Crautzdorf, Maria Barbara 60
Crawford, John 68
Creesop, —— 54
Cresswell, Mary 59
Creutzberger, Margar. 25
Creutzer, Andreas 35
  John Michael 35
  Peter 35
Crisp, Sarah 11
  William 11
Crist, Cunradt 46
  Maria Catarina 35
Crocker, John 66
Croesman, Felicitas 20
  Philip Balthasar 20
Crogge, William 59
Crow, Catarina 72
Crysop, Daniel 10
  Elisabeth 10
  Hannah 10
  Michael 10
  Robert 10
  Thomas 10,11
Cummins, Jonathan 69
Cumru, Sabina Roth 54
Cuningham, Humphry 63
Cunning, John 75
Cunningham, Hugh 70
  James 57
  Margary 76
  Mary 71
  May 67
  Patrick 73
  Sarah 71,72
  William 76
Cunradt, Anna Elizabetha 27
  Anna Margaretha 27
  Christian 34
  Elisabeth 69
  George Philipp 27
  John George 27
  John Joseph 34
  John Nicolaus 27
  John Peter 27

Cunradt (continued)
  John Stephen 27
  Leonhardt 34
  Maria Magdalena 34
  Stephan 59
  Stephen 27
Cuntz, Anna Elizabetha Ca-
    tharina 13
  John 13
Currey, Agnes 71
  Anna 55
Curt, John Ernst 67
Cypher, Margaretha 57

--- D ---

Daenschaerez, Anna Marga-
    retha 77
Daenscheriz, Margaretha 52
Dambach, Johannes Jacob 55
Daniel, Elias 23
Danin, Hannah 75
Danninger, Jacob Friederich
    69,71
Darby, Patrick 75
Daugherty, Catarina 66
  John 65
Daut, Elizabetha 74
Dauter, Catarina 74
David, John 75
Davies, Benjamin 69
  Els. 64
  Margaretha 62
  Owen 69
  Thomas 63
Davis, Edward 14
Dawbin, Elizabeth 12
  John 12
  Thomas 12
Dea, Sara 5
  Thomas 5
Deabi, Frederick 20
Dean, William 69
Deck, Anna Maria 65
  Friederich 70
  Hieronymus 40
  Johann Nicolaus (Jr.) 69
  Johannes 40,67
  John 47
  John Heinrich 27,30,36,
    40,61
  John Nicolaus 37
  John Nicolaus (Jr.) 47
  Nicolaus 35
Decker, Christina 74
  Michael 74
Deckin, Barbara 40
Deebi, Catarina 20
  Frederick 20
Deeby, John 23
Degen, Anna Regina 28
  Jacob 28
Degreif, Herman 46
Dehm, Elisabetha 26
  Nicolas 26
Deininger, Catarina 64
  Eva Barbara 47
  Margaretha 76
Deiss, Clara 74
Deissinger, Peter 73
Delinger, Jacob 7,11
  Knaben 11
  Maegdlein 11
  Maria Barbara 7
  Maria Catharina 11
Demmen, John Christian 38

Dennam, John Christian 68
Dereb, Mary 64
Derr, Anna Maria 71
Derver, Magdalena 63
Despenet, Rosina Barbara 65
Dettborn, Ludwig Heinrich 22
Detteborn, Ludw. Heinr. 15
Detzler, John Melchior 36
Deutsch, Hartman 76
Devis, Catarina 17
  Heinrich 17
Dieb, Anna Margaretha 66
  Catarina 70
  Catarina Margaretha 64
  Daniel 43
  Johannes (Jr.) 48
Dieben, John 65
Diebentorffer, Michael 33
Diebin, Johannes 52
Diebo, Philipp 54
Diehl, Daniel 16
  John Daniel 58
  Maria Elisabetha 58
Diehle, Moritz 46
Diehlin, Anna Margaretha 12
Diel, Anna Margaretha 55
  John 44
Dielman, Cunradt 45
Dielmann, Andreas 45
  Anna Margaretha 45
  George 45
  Susanna Rosina 45
Diemer, Hans George 47
Dierdorf, Johannes 58
Dieter, Joh. George 10
  John George 10
  Maria 10
  Maria Anna 54
  Maria Susanna 36
  Susanna 10
Dietrich, George Hansz 64,
    65
Diettel, Heinrich 75
Dietz, Ana Margaretha 64
  Catarina 65
  Maria Dorothea 64
  Eva Elisabetha 34
  Jacob 34
  Johann Jacob 62
  Johannes 34
Diewing, Maria 74
Diggy, Sarah 69
Dill, Margaretha 54,59
Diller, Caspar Elias 71
  Casper Elias 36
  Charlotte Barbara 36
  Eleanora 67
  Eva Barbara 33
  Johannes 39
  John Martin 39
  Juliana 66
  Maria Magdal. 66
  Philipp Adam 31,33,60
Dillman, Catarina 75
Dinnies, John Peter 64
Dinniss, Hannah 74
Dirbi, Johannes 21
  John George 21
  Maria Catharine 21
Diren, Esther 56
Dittes, Jacobina 30
  Tobias 30,41
Ditzler, Antonius 66
  Melchior 67
Dixon, Nancy 73
  Robert 68
Dobler, Jacob 65
Doerr, Agnes 58

Doerr (continued)
  Anna Barbara 54
  Johannes 19
  John George 19
  Maria Juliana 19
  Margaretha 63
  Maria Urgina 19
  Rudolph 77
Dohm, Anna Barbara 65
Dollager, George 33
  Maria 33
Dollinger, George Philipp 42,
  56
  John George 72
  Maria 42
Dollmar, Catarina Barbara 31
Donner, Jonas 55
Donntheuer, Jacob 33
  John Christian 33
  Susanna 33
Dontius, John Heinrich 26
Dor, Catarina 37
Dorn, Anna Catharina 13
  Wilhelm 13
Dornbach, Anna Margaretha 30
  John Wilhelm 30
  Maria Elizabetha 30
  Mattheis 30
Dorst, John Casper 54
Dorum, — 37
  Catarina 36
Dotson, Hannah 4
  John William 4
  Richard 4
  Thomas 4
Dotterer, George 8
  John George 8
  John Michael 8
  Rudolph 8
Dougless, Mary 74
Dovies, Edward 14
  Martha 14
Downsen, Anna Margaretha 45
  Thomas 46
Doyel, John 51
Doyle, Elizabeth 51
  Nicolas 51
Drapel, George 66
Drechsler, Catarina 53
Dreher, Daniel 24
  David 24
  John Heinrich 24
  Maria Barbara 24
Dreisch, George Leonhardt 49
  Jacob 49
  John Leonhardt 49
  John Reichardt 49
  Rosina 49
  Susanna 49
Drember, Margaretha 66
Dress, Cornelius 6
Dressel, Gotthardt 59
Druggon, Dennis 61
Drumming, Agnes 72
Dub, Anna Maria 46
  Catarina 76
Dubbs, Heinrich 25
  Jacob 26
Dubs, Heinrich 20
  John Jacob 23
  Philip 22
Duckner, Anna Catarina 66
Duliban, Catarina 71
Dumb, Ursula 54
Dumm, Adam 67
  Anna Sabina 49
  George 70
  Hans George 49

Dumm (continued)
  John George 67
Duncan, Sophia 75
Dunckelberger, Peter 11
Dunckleberger, Anna Catha-
  rina 11
Dunkin, John 69
Dunlap, Moses 72
Dunn, William 71
Dupp, Heinrich 48
Dups, Heinrich 18
  John 49
  Maria Sabina 18
Dupss, Anna Maria Gottliebin
  60
Dyart, John 13
  William 13
Dyx, Rachel 61

--- E ---

Early, Catarina 14
  Daniel 14
Eberd, Jacob 5
  John George 5
Eberdt, John Michael 6
  Tobias 6
Eberle, George 52
  Susanna 52
Eberly, Veronica 72
Ebersold, Christian 77
  Peter 77
Ebert, Anna Maria 60
  Johann 14
  John 29,39
  Maria Elizabetha 65
Eberth, Johannes 62
Ebrecht, Paul 61
Echardt, Anna Barbara 60
Eckel, Herman 45
  John Herman 60
Eckert, Andreas 76
  Anna Dorothea 9
  Casper 31
  Catarina 47
  Cunradt 9
  Engel 38
  Eva Maria 31
  Johannes 9,38
  Jonathan 42,47
  Maria Catarina 42
Ecket, Catarina 76
Eckhardt, George Adam 75
  John Casper 60
Edelmann, Anna Margar. 71
Edwards, John 68
Egis, George 74
Egler, Jacob 69
Egner, Johannes 5
  Mattheis 5
  Mattheis 6
Egnerin, Maria Elizabeth 6
Ehrhardt, Barbara 76
  Carl 10,11
  Charles 12
  Clara 12
  John Michael 58
  Margaretha 58
  Maria Elisabetha 34
  Maria Elizabetha 59
  Theobaldt 11
  Wilhelm 61
Ehrman, John 5
Eichelberger, Anna Marga-
  retha 55
  Elizab. Magdalena 68

Eichelberger (continued)
  George Michael 52, 64
  John Frederick 56
  John George 63
  Maria Barbara 62
  Maria Eva Barbara 66
Eichholtz, Jacob 57
Eigster, Catharina 7
Einert, John George 16
Eisen, Carl 16,58
Eisenhardt, Johannes 63
Eisenhauer, Anna Margaretha
  43,44
  Anna Maria 32
  Barbara 43
  George Martin 43
  George Michael 32
  George Philipp 46
  Johannes 43,46
  John 41,44,46
  John Frederick 32
  John Jacob 32
  John Nicolaus 32,44
  John Peter 43
  John Valentin 43
  Magdalena 32
  Margaretha 74
  Maria Barbara 32,70
  Maria Magdal. 32
  Maria Magdalena 32,66
  Martin 43,61
  Peter 31,71,74
  Petrus 31
  Samuel 32
  Veronica 46
Eisenhaur, Martin 43
Eissenhauer, Catarina Elisa-
  betha 46
Eitlen, John Simon 58
Elder, Dorothea 44
  Elisabeth 64
  John 44
Eli, Christian 31
  Maria Catarina 31
  Nicolaus 31
Ellbrodt, Wilhelm 55
Ellenecker, Antonius 33
Ellet, Ruth 65
Ellinger, Anastasius 73
  Anna Magdalena 68
  Anna Maria 70
  George 28,70
  John George 57
Ellis, Evans 4
  John 4,5
Ellit, Robert 62
Ellradt, Dietrich 17
  Elisabetha 17
  Jeremias 17
Ellmecker, Anna Margaretha
  28
  Antonius 33
  Leonhardt 28
  Maria Magdalena 60
Ellrodt, Anne Catarina 59
  Elisabetha 55
Elser, Christina 64
Elsser, Peter 68
Elszer, Anna Margaretha 52
  Eva 67
  Peter 52
Embisch, Christoph 51
  Johannes 51
  John Friederich 51
Emmerich, Catarina 76
  Magar. Elisabetha 37
Emmert, George 26
  John George 36,37,59

Emmert (continued)
  Susanna Juliana 59
Emrich, Juliana 70
Enderes, Nicholaus 74
Endress, Andreas 73
  Anna Dorothea 72
Endtler, Philipp Adam 57
Engel, Anna 75
  Jacob 49
  Margaretha 49
Engelerdt, Anna Catharina 10
  Christoph 10
Engelmann, Jacob 37
  John George 37
Engelsch, Eva 56
  Heinrich 14
  John Michael 14
Englerd, Christop 8
Englert, Maria Dorothea 57
English, Rachael 72
Ensminger, Ana Catarina 33
  Anna Maria 63
  Anna Catarina 33
  Christina 60
  Heinrich 33
  John Heinrich 59
  John Ludwig 63
  John Nicolaus 64
  John Nicolaus (Jr.) 48
  Maria Margar. 50
  Nicolaus 50
  Peter 32
  Susanna Catarina 59
Enson, Sarah 64
Enssminger, Catarina Elisab. 69
  Johann Heinrich 60
  Maria Catarina 62
Enszminger, Christina 29
  John Heinrich 29
  John Nicolaus 29
Enys, Anna 63
Epprecht, Jacob 76
Eprecht, Jacob 45, 47, 50
Ergebrecht, Anna Catarina 55
  Anna Elisabetha 23
  Anna Maria 31
  Catarina 23
  Hanzs Martin 63
  John George 23
  Maria Catar. 55
Ermentrout, Anna Elisabetha 38
  John 60
Ernst, Anna Margaretha 66
  Christoph 72
  Eva 16
  Johannes 56
  John Wilhelm 57
  Martin 16
Erster, Anna Margar. 60
Eschbach, Anna Elizabetha 44
  Margaretha 75
  Simon 44, 63
Eschberger, Maria Magdalena 24
Eschebach, Maria Barbara 75
Eshender, Esther 58
Espert, Anna Elizabetha 47
  John George 47
  Simon 47
Espy, Martha 71
Essel, Anna Maria 61
Esskuch, Margaret 59
Esskuchin, Anna Maria 56
Etschberger, Jacob 26, 42
  John Philipp 42
Etsschberger, Anna Catarina 39

Etter, Christina 77
  Elisabetha 77
  Peter 74
Eub, Andreas 44
  Christina Barbara 44
  Magdalena 59
Eul, Andreas 58
Euler, Anna Barbara 58
  Anna Margaretha 16
  Catarina 23, 55
  Cunradt 17
  Maria Dorothea 53
Eussminger, Anna Catarina 62
Evans, Anne 75
  Catarina 59
  Daniel 10
  Edward 10
  Rachael 11
  Roger 53
  Samuel 11
  William 53
Ewig, Christian 66

--- F ---

Faber, Adam 20, 31, 42, 60
  Anna Maria 42
  Barbara 31, 72
  Bernhardt 31, 42
  Catarina Agatha 71
  Jacob 60
  Johannes 31
  Leonhardt 62
  Margaretha 42
  Maria Barbara 42
  Philipp 31, 72
Fabian, John Michael 7
  Maria Barbara 7
Falck, Maria Elizabetha 74
Falten, Johann Peter 63
Farrell, John 72
Fauler, Anna Maria 71
Faust, Emma Frantzina 11
  George 30
  John George 20, 30
  John Philip 11
  Magdalena Elizabetha 30
  Philipp 30
Fauth, Balthasar 12, 13
  Balthaser 11
  Catharina 11
  Catharina Barbara 11
  Eva Rosina 11, 59
  Jacob 11
  Jacob F. 12
Fauthin, Susanna 12
Fechter, Susanna 54
Federhoff, Anna Elizabetha 51
  George 51, 70
  John Friederich 51
Feg, Anna Margaretha 58
Fehler, Anna Barbara 26
  Anna Margaretha 25
  Anna Maria 26
  Catarina 48
  Jacob 25, 66, 72
  Johannes 48, 70
  John Jacob 26
  John Nicolaus 72
  John Nicolus 25
  John Peter 26
  Leonhardt 26
  Maria Eva 26
  Peter Jacob 53
Feistenauer, Johannes 70
Fell, William 4

Felleberger, Catarina 73
  Maria Sabina 67
Felt, Anna Catarina 68
  Barbara 68
  Catarina 52
  Catarina Margaretha 75
  Peter 52
Felten, Johannes 50
  Peter 43
Feltin, John George 72
  Maria 74
  Regina 74
Felty, Anna Maria 50
  George 50
Feree, Roass 61
Ferguson, Barbara 63
Fernsler, John Philipp 53
Ferrar, Anna Elisabetha 54
Ferrir, Elizabeth 55
Ferry, Esther 26
  Maria 56
Ferrys, Elenore 67
Fertig, John Nicolaus 77
Feuerbach, Catarina Barbara 72
Fey, John Cunradt 19
Fiedler, Andreas 38
  Catarina 38
  Heinrich 38
  John Gottfried 38
  John Peter 38
  Margaretha 38
  Maria 38
Field, Water 53
Fiess, Anna Maria 48
  John David 48, 66
  John Jacob 48
Filbert, Catarina 51
  Elisabetha 69
  Samuel 51
  Sauel 46
  Susanna 46, 51
  Thomas 42, 51, 69
Filich, Margaretha 58
Finley, Catarina 68
Finney, Rebecca 71
Firnsler, Elizabeth 66
Firnssler, Anna Christina 48
  Catarina 64
  Jacob 70
  Johann Philipp 69
  John Heinrich 70
  John Michael 68
  Juliana 73
  Philipp 48
Firnszler, Barbara 70
  John George 34
  John Philipp 53
  Philipp 34
Fischer, Anna Magdalena 69
  Anna Maria 50, 67, 71
  Barbara 49
  Catarina 62, 66
  Catarina Elizabetha 30
  David 19, 37
  Elisabetha 70
  Elizabetha 55
  George 66, 69
  Hieronymus 38
  Jacob 32, 45, 72, 73
  Johannes 49
  John Adam 75
  John Jacob 37, 49, 60
  John Leonhardt 67
  John Michael 53, 69
  John Nicolaus 8
  John Peter 73
  John Philip 42

Fischer (continued)
Leonhardt 37
Lorentz 65
Magdalena 71
Maria Barbara 35
Maria Elisabetha 32, 38
Mattheis Samuel 45
Michael 5, 8, 66
Peter 42, 49, 67
Philipp 45
Sophia 68
Fischgess, Anna Elisab. 62
Fisher, Christian 40
Ludwig 5
Maria Elisabetha 57
Fix, Adam 43
Eva Margaretha 43
Flannery, Anne 53
Flatsher, John 58
Fleck, Elizabetha 75
Fleming, John 72
Flohr, Barbara 73
George 46
John George 64
Flohry, Engelhardt 58
Flory, Engelhard 30
Joseph 76
Foerster, Anna Elizabetha 40
Barbara 76
Christina 40
Cunradt 40, 46
Jacob 46
Johann Leonhardt 62
John Peter 40
Fohrer, Anna Rosini 61
Folmer, John Michael 45
Magdalena Regina 45
Foltz, John Heinrich 57
Forester, Jane 75
Forgy, Samuel 69
Forr, Susanna 63
Forsett, Jacob 55
Forster, Dorcas 69
Fortunee, Heinrich 12
John Heinrich 12
Susanna Catarina 12
Fosset, Richard 75
Foster, Christian 69
James 69
Foy, Francies 10
Francis 10
Fraelich, Margaretha 59
Francis, Johanna 53
Franck, Catarina 53
Eva Margaretha 61
John Christoph 75
John Nicolaus 63
Maria Barbara 62
Maria Catarina 67
Franckhauser, Eva 33
Peter 33
Frank, John Jacob 55
Frantzina, Anna 25
Frederich, Anna Margaretha 35
Anna Maria 23
George 22, 27
Noah 63
Freiderich, Anna Marg. 7
Fremdling, Christian 75
French, Isabell 64
Frendling, Christian 71
Frey, Anna Eva 55
Anna Maria 59
Catarina 38, 65
Christian 5
George 45
George Michael 45
Gottfrey 59

Frey (continued)
Heinrich 38, 60
Johann Heinrich 73
Johannes 7
John 5
Magdalena 57
Margaretha 62
Maria Barbara 58
Maria Catarina 33
Maria Catharina 5
Maria Margaretha 7, 55
Maria Sybilla 60
Martin 33, 54, 59
Salome 56
Valentin 59
Fried, John Adam 60
Friedel, Bernhardt 24, 36, 37, 46
Dorothea 37
Elisabeth 24
Jacob 24
John Bernhardt 24
John Martin 24
George Ludwig 36
Margaretha 46
Susanna 24
Friederich, Andreas 26, 60
Anna Elisabetha 41
Anna Elizabetha 65
Anna Maria 48
Eva 61
George 29, 42, 47
Gertraudt 60
Johannes 26
John Christoph 48, 68
John George 47
Margaretha 29
Maria Catar. 58
Maria Elizabetha 60
Noah 37, 47
Friedle, Bernhardt 27, 31
Dorothea 31
George Ludwig 16
Martin 75
Friedtel, George Ludtwig 21
John George 21
Maria Magdalena 21
Fringer, John Nicholas 42
John Nicolaus 42
Froehlich, Catarina Barbara 61
Froelich, Anna Catarina 22
Jacob 22
Fromman, Elisabetha 9
Elizabetha 11
John Paul 9
Maria Christina 9
Paul 9, 11
Sarah 9
Frosch, Catarina 5
Johannes 5
John George 5, 11
Maria Elizabetha 5
Fryman, Heinrich 63
Fuchs, Anna Elisabetha 38
Anna Margaretha 38
Anna Maria 38
Elizabetha 65
Eva Catarina 70
Frantz 19
Jacob 38
John Frantz 43
Mara Catarina 63
Fuchz, Johann Christoph 74
Fuechs, Elizabetha Magdalena 66
Fulck, Charles 4
Johanna 4
Fulk, Charles 53

Fulton, Alexander 73
Funck, Catarina 16
John 16
Margaretha 56
Fuss, Christina 61

--- G ---

Gaeiss, Elisabetha 57
Margaretha 57
Gaemling, Sophia Catarina 57
Gaener, Eva Catarina 23
John Dietrich 23
Gaensemer, Catarina Barbara 27
George Daniel 27
Johannes 27
Margaretha 25
Gaert, Peter 18
Gaertner, George 31
Peter 15
Gahus, John 66
Galbreath, William 64
Gall, Johann 74
Gallmeyer, Margaretha 73
Gally, Catarina Barbara 31
William 31
Gambil, John 47
Susanna 47
Ganger, Heinrich 5
Gannemer, Anna Maria 18
Jacob 18
Gansert, Andreas 33
Catarina 61, 67
John Andreas 33
Margaretha 33
Gashens, Mary 75
Gassert, Anna Maria 52
Jacob 40
Jacob John 40
Johannes 40, 52
John Balthaser 40
John Jacob 40
Maria Margaretha 40
Gauger, Nicolaus 34
Gaumer, John Adam 57
Gebert, Frederich 19
Johannes 8
Michael 8
Susanna Catarina 19
Gebhardt, Anna Barbara 33, 35, 46
Anna Catarina 33
Anna Margar. 69
Anna Margaretha 40, 47
Anna Maria 30
Catarina 29
Elizabetha 30
Johannes 30, 33, 35
John 41
John George 30
John Heinrich 29
John Jacob 32
John Nicolaus 27, 30, 32
John Philipp 29
John Phillip 32
Juliana 30, 73
Maria Barbara 65
Maria Eva 29
Nicolaus 74
Peter 29, 30
Philipp 29, 30, 40
Valentine 29
Gebhart, Peter 45
Geblin, Anna Margar. 62
Geelbwicks, Friederich Hein-

Geelbwicks (continued)
  rich 53
Geelwichs, Catarina 23
  Frederich Heinrich 23
  George Karl 23
Geelwuchs, John Frederick 16
Geembel, John 14
Gehrhardt, Magdalena 62
Geiger, Anna Elizabeth 13
  Anna Maria 70
  Catarina 12, 18
  Catharina 11, 13
  Christian 23, 56
  Heinrich 55
  Jacob 13
  John George 12
  John Jacob 12
  Maria Elizabetha 12
  Maria Margaretha 23
  Nicolaus 58
  Wilhelm 61
Geismer, Daniel 26
Geiss, Anna Barbara 41
  Appollonia 52
  Catarina 52
  George Adam 41, 52, 67
  Philipp Jacob 49, 52
Geissemann, Anna Maria 51
  George 51
Geisz, Anna Barbara 48
  Catarina Elizabeth 48
  George Adam 48
  John Michael 49
  Philipp Jacob 49
Gelaspi, Peter 64
  Mary 68
Gemeinhardt, Johan George 56
George, Maria Barbara 53
  Maria Magdalena 72
Gerber, Jacob 54
Gerberich, Dieter 65
Gerbrig, Elisab. 66
Gerhard, Regina 49
  Valentine 21
Gerhardt, Barbara 67
  Catarina 71
  Cunradt 48
  Heinrich 67
  Maria Catarina 48
  Philipp 24
  Regina 69
  Susanna 75
  Valentin 48
Gerhardtin, Anna Margaretha
  6
Gerhart, Philipp 33
Gerlach, Catharine 12
  John George 12
  Theobaldt 10, 11, 12
German, Margaretha 53
Germann, Catarina 72
Gerst, Maria Engel 64
Gesell, Anna Catarina 63
Geyer, John George 18
Gibson, Robert 64
  William 62
Gicker, Jacob 46
  Maria Catarina 46
Giesemann, Wilhelm 41
Giesser, Anna Catraina 62
Gilbert, John 59
Gill, James 12
Gilligham, Clemence 63
Gillighan, Clemens 41
  John 41, 64
Gillighin, Jane 61
Gilliman, Elizabeth 69
Gingerich, Veronica 63

Gingrich, Anna Maria 73
Glantz, Hieronymus 53
Glascow, Nancy 76
Glass, Christian 52
  Eva Elizabeth 52
  George 52
Glassbrenner, Anna Maria 67
  Christina 41
  Elisabetha 50
  George 16, 48, 50
  Johannes George 55
  Freiderich 42
  John Friederich 42
  John George 76
  Margaretha 16
  Maria Christiana Marga-
    retha 16
Glasser, Susanna Maria 75
Glillin, Sarah 69
Gloninger, Catarina 53
  Johann 53
Glover, John 75
Gockel, Elisabetha 70
Goellnitz, Christian 68
Goer, Cunradt 34
Goettel, Anna Maria 77
  Eva 45
  Eva Barbara 72
  Maria Eva 40
  Peter 40, 61
Goetz-Danner, Anna Marga-
  retha 13
Goldman, Cat. Elis. 27
Goldtman, Jacob 34
Gordon, George 43
  Maria Margaretha 43
  Thomas 76
Gossler, Maria Elisabetha 38
Gotteskind, Anna Maria 58
  Catarina 33
Gowdy, Samuel 66
Gowringer, Samuel 11
  Thomas 11
Grace, William 61
Graefin, Maria Barbara 32
Graf, George 22
  George (Jr.) 29
  Michael 32
Graff, Andreas 35, 56
  Anna Barbara 61
  Eva Maria 56, 59
  George 19, 43
  George Michael 63
  John Cunradt 19
  John George 57
  John George (Jr.) 19
  John Michael 19
  Maria Elisabetha 47
  Michael 47
Graham, William 68
Grahem, Alexander 56
  Sarah 56
Grain, Robert 46
Grand, Sarah 53
Grandy, Elizabetha 55
Grass, Andreas 55
Grasser, Anna Maria 65
Grau, Leonhardt 53
Gray, Daniel 60
Grays, Rachel 63
Grayu, Elizabetha 43
Greber, Heinrich 26
Greenlee, Alexander 74
Grehl, Margaretha 51
  Michael 51
Greim, Adam 43
  Christina Cordula 45
  Jacob 42, 45

Greim (continued)
  John George 43
  John Sebastian 42
  Maria Salome 42
  Sebastian 42, 45
Greiner, Maria Cath. 6
Greinerin, Maria Catharina 6
Greinert, John Frederich 6
Greter, Jacob 56
Greuel, Thomas 58
Greys, Grace 71
Griffith, Mary 61
Grimes, Jane 75
  Martha 74
  William 75
Gring, Anna Catarina 65
Grisemer, John Valentine 7
Griszemer, Maria Elizabeth 7
Groh, Valentin 55
Grojean, Margaretha 64
Groll, Christian 11, 15, 18
  Elisabetha 15, 18
  Elizabeth 11
  John Christian 17
Gross, George 61
  John Martin 68
  Margaretha 59
Grossmann, Christina 65
  Susanna 44
Grosz, Barbara 74
  Catarina 50
  Elisabetha 50
  John Martin 50
Groszman, John Michael 28
  John Nicolaus 28
  Maria Barbara 28
  Michael 28
  Sophia 28
Grubb, Cartis 74
Gruber, Anna Kunigunda 39
  Anna Margaretha 38
  Charlotta Frederica 11
  Charlotta Fredericka 10
  Christian 30, 38, 39, 59
  Eva Maria Rosina 38
  Heinrich 29, 38
  John Adam 38
  John Albrecht 38
  John George 38
  Maria Catarina 38
  Philipp Ernst 10, 17
  Phillip Ernest 10
  Susanna 38
Grueber, Maria Elisabetha 13
  Philipp Ernst 13
Gruen, Gertraudt 57
Gruenenwait, Phillip 51
Gruenenwaldt, Maria Marga-
  retha 51
  Philip 51
Gruenewald, Christina Bar-
  bara 39
  Joseph 39
Guard, Francis 52
  Joseph 52
Guellin, Adam 58
Guenther, John 6
  John Peter 6
  Maria Margaretha 6
  Maria Salome 66
  Peter 69
Guenthuer, Maria Catarina 63
Guill, James 12
  John 12
  Mary 12
  Thomas 12
Gump, John George 12
Gundtacker, Johannes Mi-

Gundtacker (continued)
chael 61
Guntrum, Martin 75
Gur, Maria Elisabeth 72
Guschwa, Ana Margaretha 42
Guthman, Catara. Margar. 63
Gutmaennin, Eva Margaretha 13
Gutman, Adam 69
George 44
Peter 63
Stephen 56
Gutmann, Philipp 7

--- H ---

Haag, Anna Barbara 67
Anna Catarina 46
Anna Margar. 46
Appolonia 48
Barbara 39
Catar. Elisab. 42
Catarina Elizabetha 48, 68
Elizabetha 47
George (Jr.) 48
George (Sr.) 48
George Michael 46
Johannes 24
John 46
John George 30, 43, 47, 64
John George (Jr.) 46
John Nickel 43
John Nicalaus 29
John Nicolaus 44, 45, 47, 65
Margaretha 48
Maria Barbara 46
Maria Catarina 47
Maria Susanna 29, 64
Haager, Catarina Elisabetha 61
Eva Maria 61
Haagmeyer, John Michael 58
Haak, John George 36
Maria Susanna 36
Haass, Abraham 34
John Frederich 8
Haasz, Abraham 28
Anna Maria 12
Cunradt 12
John 12
Margaretha 12
Maria Magdalena 28
Maria Susanna 28
Habach, Peter 56
Haberland, Catarina Dorothea 66
Hacker, Anna Maria Barbara 67
Haecker, Barbara 45
Jacob 45
Haeckert, Jacob 40
John Jacob 60
Haedderich, John George 24
Peter 24
Rosina 24
Haeffele, Johannes 43
Margaretha 43
Haeffner, John Jacob 26
Maria Catarina 27
Maria Johanna 26
Nicolaus 26, 35
Haehle, Frederich 18
Margaretha 18
Haehlin, Elisabetha 69
Haehnle, Anna Barbara 22
Anna Margaretha 22
Elizabetha 22

Haehnle (continued)
Eva Catarina 22
Frederich 25, 27, 37, 44
Frederick 27
Freiderich 29
Friederich 22, 43
Jacob Friederich 22
John Michael 22
John Seigmund 20
Margaretha 25, 27, 37
Maria Eva 22
Maria Magdalena 51
Michael 46, 75, 76
Siegesmund 27
Sigmund 22, 23
Sigmund (Jr.) 22
Haehnlein, Johannes 63
Haehnlin, Frederich 57
Magdalena 71
Margar. 52
Maria Elis. 58
Haehnly, Frederich 35
Haeker, Johannes 65
Haepplin, Maria Barbara 70
Haermaennin, Catarina 53
Haessel, Bernhardt 14
Haessler, John George 74
Haffner, Catarina Elisabetha 45
Johannes 45
Hahn, John Michael 16
Michael 16
Hall, Hugh 69
William 75
Halteman, Jacob 57
Hambrecht, Eva Catarina 56
John Adam 1931, 57
Hammann, Maria Catarina 74
Hammon, Susannah 60
Hamspacher, Margaretha 55
Rebecca 58
Hanna, Isaac 71
Hannthorn, John 56
Hanspacher, John George 14
Maria Eva 14
Rebecca 14
Tobias 14
Hansz, Jno. Heinrich 62
Hardt, Wilhelm 48
Harrington, Jacob 11
Sarah 11
Harris, David 68
Jane 56
Harry, Catarina 53
Hart, Maria Barbara 56
Harteich, Eva Catarina 70
Hartman, Anna Maria Apollonia 53
Elisabetha 14
Herman 14
Johann Frederich 54
Michael 42
Ulrich 20
Hartzenbuehler, Elizabetha 9
Hatt, John George 57
Magdalena 56
Hatz, Elizabetha Barbara 31
George 31, 66
Hauck, Anna Barbara 73
Anna Maria 63
Barbara 71
George 20
John George 54
Philippia 56
Hauer, Antonius 71
Haug, Catarina 64
Hausknecht, Anna Catarina 57
Christian 14, 15
Hauss, Philipp 65

Haussahn, Maria Elisabetha 24
Hausshalter, Adam 45
Anna Barbara 60
Elisabetha 45
Elizabetha 59
Johann George 61
John Adam 60
Margaretha 58
Haussman, Cunradt 15
Haussmann, Anna Margaretha 15
Hausswirth, Abraham 57
Hauswirth, Abraham 18
John 18
Hausz, Anna Elizabetha 66
Hautsch, Anna Maria 56
Hautz, Barbara 47
Frantz Hubeler 70
Lorentz 27, 44
Philipp 33
Philipp Lorentz 70
Susanna 60
Wendel 67
Hays, Jane 72
Heard, George 58
Hearken, Eleanora 14
John 14
Hebberling, Johannes 67
Heberling, John Peter 65
Heck, Bartholomaeus 66
Catarina 30
John Jacob 38
Heckendorn, Anna 57
Johannes 74
Heckerdorn, Sara 32
Heckman, Andreas 75
Ana Maria 42
Elizabetha Margaretha 42
John Peter 42
Peter 27, 42
Hedderich, Anna Elisabetha 26
Anna Elizabetha 60
Anna Margaretha 34
Caspar 30
Christoph 34, 37
Johannes 28
John Peter 50
John Peter (Sr.) 50
John Wirner 28
Jost 26
Margaretha 50, 52
Maria Barbara 34
Maria Catar. 68
Peter 40
Peter (Jr.) 50, 68
Philippina 50
Wilhelm 26, 52
Hederling, Johannes 8
John Wilh. 8
Heesze, Eva Catarina 50
Johannes 50
John Michael 50
Matthias 50
Hehnlin, Magdalena 56
Heiliger, Christina Barbara 31
Philipp 31
Heilman, Adam 20
Heim, Frantz Hugo 4
Johannes 14
John Caspar 14
John Casper 14
John Christian 4
Wilhelm 4
Heinrich, Anna Elizabetha 28
Anna Maria 27, 71

Heinrich (continued)
  Anna Maria Elizabèth 71
  Barbara 55
  John 17
  John Adolph 27
  Juliana 75
  Nicolaus 77
  Susanna Rosina 45
  Tobias 17
Heintzmaenn, Susanna 56
Heissmann, Susanna 17
Heiter, Melchior 59
Held, John George 68
  Maria Magdalena 73
Helfferich, John 6
  John Peter 6
Heller, Jacob 54
  Joseph 31
Helm, Frederick 75
  John Frantz 73
Helwig, Adam 59
  Anna Margaretha 59
Hemberlin, Catarina 70
Hemperle, Anna Maria 29
  Antonius 29, 67
  Martin 29
Henckel, Anna Catharina 55
  George 12
  Gerhardt 6
  John Balthasar 12
  Philipp Christoph 12
Henckelin, Anna Catharina 6
Henckle, Anna Catharina 5
Henderson, John 62
  Martha 60
Hendricks, Henry 14
  Jone 14
Henne, Conradt 70
Hennicker, John Nicolaus 64
Henning, Catarina 64
Henninger, Anna Elisabetha 70
  Anna Maria 11
  John Michael 4
  Michael 11
  Maria Rosina 4
Henry, Anne 74
Heorkin, Bregille 11
  John 11
Herbert, Catarina 51
  Catarina Margaretha 44
  Eva Margaretha 51
  John 44
  John Adam 37, 44, 51
  John Thomas 51
  Susanna 44
Herbster, Anna Maria 49
  David 47, 49, 67
  Rosina 49
Herburger, Johannes 19
  Juliana 19
Herchelrodt, Valentin 61
Herger, Andreas 9, 16
  Anna Margaretha 9, 51
  Catarina 9
  Eva 16
  Johannes 9
  Leonhardt 51
Herman, Anna Maria 20
  Catarina 72
  Jacob 5, 20
  Johannes 72
  Leonhardt 7
  Maria Elisabeth 20
  Maria Magdalena 7
  Martin 67
Herr, Anna 72
  Hanna 72
  Johannes 64

Herr (continued)
  John 24
Hertle, John Heinrich 66
Hertz, John Philipp 60
Hess, Martin 51
  Matthias 67
Hesser, John George 8
Hesset, Anna 15
  John George 15
Hessner, John Frederich 8
Hetzler, Anna Christina 66
  Anna Margdalena 71
  Balthaser 65
Heus, Marx 17
Heuser, Catharina 56
Heussler, Caspar 64
  Casper 48, 49
  Rosina 49
Heuszler, Casper 49
  Maria Eva 49
  Maria Magdalena 49
Heuteler, Antonius 17
  John Mattheis 17
Heuter, Melchior 23
Hey, Johannes 65
Heydt, Abraham 36, 67
  Anna Margaretha 66
  Anna Maria 8, 9, 13
  Catarina 67
  Isaac 8
  Jno. 9
  Johannes 8, 10
  John 8, 9, 13
  John Jost 8
  Jost 9, 13
  Jost. 8
  Magdalena 36
  Margaretha 67
  Peter 36
  Sara 9
Heyer, Barbara 60
  Maria 76
Heyl, Anna 22, 25, 36, 43, 47
  Anna Barbara 25
  Anna Maria 19
  Barbara 19, 73
  Catarina 60, 76
  Christina 25, 73
  Elisabetha 20
  Elisabetha Barbara 19
  Elizabetha 25
  Elizabetha Barbara 57
  George Adam 19, 54
  Jacob 25, 55
  Johannes 25
  John 57
  John Adam 18, 19
  John George 54
  John Jacob 23
  John Wendel 23, 59
  Margaretha 25
  Maria Eva 73
  Wendel 22, 25, 36, 43
  Wendell 47
Heylman, Anna Elizabeth 20
  Anna Elizabetha 73
  Anna Maria 15
  Catarina 20
  Catarina Elizabetha 74
  Peter 15, 56
Heylmann, Anastasius 15, 71
  Anna Christina 74
  Hans Adam 28
  Johannes 16
  John Adam 15
  John Martin 8
  John Peter 15
  Magdalena 71

Heylmann (continued)
  Maria Magdalena 15
  Peter 15, 16, 28
  Sabine 28
Hicks, John 71
Hiesner, Adam 64
Hildebrandt, Anna Catarin 54
Hilden, Catarina 7
  Peter 7
Hill, Abigail 72
  Andreas 18
  Anna 35
  Anna Catarina 14
  Anna Maria 14
  Annie 72
  Catharina 11
  Jacob 14
  Jane 68
  John 14
  John Christian 14
  John Jacob 14, 57
  Robert 71
Hillis, Anna 75
  Jenny 75
Hinckel, Caspar 67
Hinds, Antony 59
  James 58
Hinnen, Anna Catarina 41
  Heinrich 41
Hinszler, Maria Magdalena 49
Hiszler, Casper 49
  Rosina 49
Hitze, John 68
Hodge, David 12
  Elizabeth 12
  John 12, 55
  Rohamy 12
Hoeffner, John George 6
Hoeg, Anna Margaretha 65
  Magdalena 70
Hoegel, Anna Margaretha 39
  Maria Margar. 40
Hoeger, George 30
  Martin 72
Hoegie, George 55
Hoegien, Eva Catarina 67
Hoehmann, Johannes 56
Hoellen, Dennis 71
Hoells, Hansz George 62
Hoerauf, Andreas 51
  John Heinrich 51
Hoerchelradt, Margar. 68
Hoerchelrodt, Anna Barbara 66
  Elisabetha 67
Hoerdter, Elisabetha 54
  Maria Barbara 54
Hoerner, Dorothea 24
  John Michael Ernst 24
  Maria Christina 61
  Michael 74
Hoester, Anna Catara. 58
Hof, Leonhard 55
Hoff, Anna Barbara 62
Hoffert, John George 7
Hoffman, Andreas 22
  Anna Maria 28
  Catarina Margar 58
  Elizabetha 28
  Eva Catarina 28
  Jacob 28, 33, 34
  Johannes 36
  John Andreas 22
  John Christian 28
  John Peter 35
  John Philipp 54
  Juliana 28
  Maria Elisabetha 55
  Maria Margaretha 39

Hoffman (continued)
Martin 39
Peter 26,36
Hoffmann, Daniel 39
Egidius 18
John Egidius 19
Martin 22
Hofman, Cartarina 40
Friederich 39
Jacob 45
John Jacob 26
Margaretha 74
Maria Eva 47
Martin 23
Rosina 35
Hofmann, Christoph 18
John Christoph 18
Maria Margaretha 18
Philipp 66
Hohmann, Johannes 21
Maria Magdalena 21
Holder, Andreas Hugo 4
Anna Maria 59
Catarina 48
Johannes Nicolaus (Jr.) 64
John 4
John Nicolaus 27,38
John Nicolaus (Jr.) 46,48
Maria Barbara 66
Nicolaus 39
Holderbaum, Ana Maria 68
Catarina 73
Elisabetha 71
Holderin, Maria Barbara 4
Holinger, John Philipp 60
Maria Barbara 28
Philip 28
Hollenbach, Anna Maria 37
Jinny Maria 37
Johannes 37
John 76
John Mattheis 37
Maria 37
Holtz, Anna Margaretha 70
Elisabetha 72
Holtzapfel, Erasmus 55
Holtzbaum, Susanna 54
Holtzeder, Anna Maria 6
David 6
John David 8
Holtzinger, Jacob 29,58
John 29
Holtzman, Heinrich 43
Heinrich Friederich 43
Holtzwart, Catarina 62
Holzapfel, Erasmus 17
Homann, Magdalena 22
Homes, Mary 60
Honig, John George 57
Nicolaus 57
Hoof, Anna Barbara 18,54
Emma Maria 11
Jacob 11
John Jacob 11,18
Hoolman, Daniel 12,55
Isaac 12
Rebecca 12
Hopkins, Sarah 58
Hornberger, Conrad 71
John Bartolomeus 53
John Carl 55
Horsebrough, Sarah 57
Hortle, Heinrich 64
Hoster, Catarina 59
Houck, John George 21
Hough, Anna 65
Elizabeth 64
Mary 62

Hough (continued)
Sarah 61
Houtz, Philipp Lorentz 22
Howard, Anna 56
Hubel, Anna Catarina 57
Hubele, Anna Maria 27
Jacob 43
Hubeler, Abraham 36
Anna Barbara 40
Anna Margaretha 34
Eva Catarina 65
Eva Maria 62
Jacob 34
Maria Barbara 36
Huber, Abraham 28
Anna Barbara 60
Anna Elisabetha 55
Anna Maria 67
Barbara 56
Daniel 44,60
Elisab. 52
Elisabetha 76
Elizabetha 74
George 45
HanszUlrich 66
Jacob 64
Johannes 52,54,64
John George 24,59
John Jacob 52
John Michael 43
John Wilhelm 30
Maria 76
Maria Margaretha 59
Michael 45
Rosina Margaretha 45
Salome 70
Sebastian 30,60
Sophia 44
Veronica 55
Wilhelm 27
Huck, Stephan 74
Huckenborger, Magdalena 60
Hudchinson, John 69
Huebscher, Lorentz 70
Ulrich 57
Huengerer, Elizabetha 39
John George 39
Melchior 39
Huens, James 67
Hueston, Andrew 11
Esther 56
Robert 11,66
Sarah 11
Huggens, James 57
Hui, Thomas 10
Hume, John 67
Hummel, Johann Friederich 73
Rosina 45
Humphreys, Samuel 72
Hundsraecker, Elizabetha 75
Hunter, Robert 73
Hurter, Susanna 63
Hurtzel, George 57
John Ludwig 20
John Mattheis 20
Hyde, Mary 61
Hylman, Agnes 13

Iauch, Anna Margaretha 75
Conradt 69
Ierg, Dorothea 55
Ietter, Eva Catarina 65
Eva Margaretha 66
Igsin, Ana Johanna 17

Ilin, Anna Margaretha 72
Imbode, Anna Christian 76
Immel, Johannes 25
John 59
John Leonhardt 54
Jonh 20
Immler, Anna Marie 13
George 61
Ingerham, Elisabetha 57
Innboden, Johann Schweick-
hardt 67
Innis, James 73
Iotter Iost 65
Irbin, Abraham 63
Irving, Margaretha 63
Irwin, Samuel 75
Iserlin, Eva Catarina 17
Israel, Eva Catarina 15
Iuengling, Johannes 58

Jacob, Philipp 31
Jacobi, Adam 45
John Nicolaus 45
Jacobs, H.E. (Rev.) 3
Jaeger, Barbara 32,61
John Adam 7
Maria Margaretha 7
Maria Philipena 10
Philipp Carl 10
James, William 64
Jameson, Elizabetha 74
Jeager, Barbara 33
Jeckel, Ulrich 34
Jeffreys, James 63
Jensel, Friederich 51
Maria Agnes 51
Jergan, John George 6
Mattheis 6
Joakles, Anna Sara 23
John 23
Joeckel, Ulrich 49
Johnson, James 65
Johnston, Sarah 72
Joho, Eva Catarina 14
Johannes 14
Maria Christina 14
Jones, Amos 74
Anna 13
David 12,13,50
Emma 4
Henry 13
John 35,36
Jonathan 50
June 12
Margaretha 36,57,72
Phillipina Christina 35
Rees 4
Robert 36,60
Samuel 62,73
Jordan, Anna 74
Josee, Nicolaus 10
Josie, Anna Johanna 58
Josin, Anna Barbara 9
Jost, Anna Maria 40
Casper 40
Hannah 17
John Nickel 28
Jung, Anna Catarina 54
Anna Maria 9
Catarina 9,55
Catharina 9
Daniel 5
Jacob 5
Johan Theobaldt 9

Jung (continued)
Johannes 5
John 53
John Theobaldt 9
Ludwig 5
Margaretha 5
Maria Barbara 9
Sybilla 5
Theobaldt 9
Jungblut, Caspar 73
Daniel 71
Hanna 17
Jacob 17
John Jacob 17
Nicolaus 58
Junf, Anna Maria 5

--- K ---

Kachel, Jno. Cunradt 76
Kaemmerling, John Jacob 22
Kaempf, Magdalena 39
Mattheis 39
Kaempfer, Mattheis 61
Kaempffer, Anna Barbara 39
John Philipp 39
Maria Appollonia 39
Mattheis 39
Kaercher, Justina 59
Kaercherin, Elizabetha 6
Kaerchner, Elisabetha 54
Kaeufer, Elisabetha Catar. 53
Kaiser, Elisabetha 19
Kalliah, Anna 66
Kally, John George 36
John Heinrich 36
Michael 64
Sarah 22
William 22, 36
Kampf, Christian 14
Kanely, William 10
Kanter, Maria 26
Kanterrmann, Jacob 61
Kantner, George 41
John Jacob 41
Kapf, Gertraudt 22
Veit 22
Kapp, Andreas 58
Anna Barbara 27
Anna Catarina 27
Eva 27
George Veit 27, 60
Gertraud 40
Gertraudt 42
Johann Friederich 56
John Veith 27
Margaretha 27
Margaretha Elisabetha 27
Maria Magdalena 27
Martin 29
Veit 40, 42
Kappler, Anna Maria 58
Barbara 23
Catarina Barbara 19
Christina Magdalena 31
John Jacob 19
Margaretha 16, 18
Martin 16, 19, 24, 31, 37
Susanna 31
Kappy, Erdtmann 41
Karcher, Anna Barbara 60
Barbara 28
Kare, Abernie 58
Karg, Andreas 71
Karger, Anna 61
Karmenie, Antonius 66

Karmenie (continued)
Juliana 77
Michael 75
Karnoughan, William 71
Karr, Martha 68
Robert 68
Kasey, Richard 75
Kastnitz, Andreas 43, 70
Catarina Elisabetha 37
Christina Johanetta 37
Elisabetha 37
Johann George 37
John Frantz 43
John George 60
Katterman, Anna Catarina 35
Jacob 35
Katz, Ludwig Heinrich 27
Michael 27, 60
Kau, John Nicolaus 18
Kauffeld, Christoph 18
John Cristoph 18
Maria Elisabetha 18
Kaufman, Anna Maria 46, 66
Barbara 47
Catarina 50, 65
Christian 46, 57, 64, 70
Eva 7
Jacob 47
Johannes 38
John 7, 47
Magdalena 46
Maria Appollonia 47
Veronica 46
Kaufmann, Jacob 73
Maria Magdalena 68
Kauth, Eva Rosina 23
Kautzmann, Eva 63
Kayser, John Michael 39
John Wilhelm 30
Justina Catar. 57
Justina Catarina 38
Wilhelm 43
Kaysser, Christoph 33
Kearsen, Elisabeth 70
Keeper, William 61
Kees, Thomas 69
Kehl, Catarina 46
John Michael 46
Keim, Heinrich 72
Keller, Anna Barbarina 65
Anna Margaretha 35
Anna Maria 54, 64
George Wendel 50, 64
Jacobina Rosina 50
John 37
Joseph 35
Valentine 43
Wendel 50, 65, 66
Kellerin, Anna Maria 5
Kemp, Anna Margaretha 53
Kendel, Anna Maria 65
Kennedy, Alexander 72
Gilbert 73
Kenny, Catharine 59
Kent, Samuel 65
Kepner, Andreas 7
Benedict 7
Catharina 7
Johannes 6, 54
John 6
Kepnerin, Barbara 7
Kerlinger, Catarina Agatha 60
Kern, Abraham 33, 34
Anna Catarina 14, 33
Anna Maria 50
Johann Christoph 67
John Adam 50
Leonhardt 61

Kern (continued)
Margaretha 30
Thomas 30
Kessinger, Anna Margar. 72
Johann Michael 65
Ketterle, Andreas 59
Kezey, Anne 77
Kichler, Heinrich 29
Juliana 29
Kiebing, Anna 54
Kiefe, Eleonore 64
Kienen, Philomey 64
Kilimer, Nicolaus 70
Killgore, Joseph 68
Killhoeffer, Maria Eva 63
Killis, John 10
Kinkead, Jane 70
Kintz, Anna Magdalena 58
Johan George 59
Philip 14
Kintzel, Anna Maria 25
Catarina 73
Elizabetha 32
Jacob 32
Johannes 32
Magdalena 74
Maria Elizabetha 74
Thomas 68
Kintzer, Anna Elizabetha 36
Jacob 35, 37
John Jacob 36
John Nickel 30, 45
John Nicolaus 8, 40
Juliana 30, 36, 39, 40, 45
Maria Margaretha 36
Nicolaus 30, 36, 39, 40, 58,
60
Walther 35
Kintzel, Catarina 75
Charlotta 75
Kintzor, Juliana 26
Nicolaus 26
Kirber, Anna Margaretha 66
Michael 68
Kirchhoefer, Anna Maria 54
Kirckwood, William 74
Kirn, Susanna 55
Kirschner, Dinnes 39
Kirstaetter, Dorothea 21
Johan Michael 64
Johann Martin 65
John 16
John Leonhardt 72
John Martin 60
Julianna 16
Margar. 63
Maria Dorothea 15
Martin 15, 16, 21
Sebastian 63
Kirstetter, Elisabetha 67
Juliana 67
Kissecker, Anna Engel 75
Kissinger, Andreas 43
Anna Maria 33
Johannes 63
John Philipp 60
Michael 33, 59
Kissner, Anna Sabina 49
Johann Wolf 62
John 37
John Wolf 46, 49
Sabina 37, 46
Kistler, Johannes 60
John 25
Maria Magdalena 25
Kittler, John Adam 11
Kittner, Christina Catarina 41
George Adam 41

91

Kittner (continued)
George Michael 58
Heinrich 41
Johanna Catarina 41
Johannes 55
John Jacob 41
John Nicolaus 41
Kittring, George Michael 20
John Adam 20
Maria Margaretha 20
Rosina Barbara 20
Kitzmiller, John Jacob 53
Philippina Christian 61
Kitzmueller, Andreas 37
Ann Maria 38
Anna Margaretha 37
Anna Maria 32, 37
George Adam 37
Jacob 37
Jno. Jacob 69
Johannes 21, 37
John 30, 37
John (Jr.) 53
John (Sr.) 53
John Caspar 37
John George 21
John Jacob 21, 32, 37, 38
John Jacob (Sr.) 21
John Leonhardt 30
John Martin 21
Maria Catarina 37
Klauer, John George 8
Susanna 54
Klauser, Barbara 26
John 26
Kleber, Anna Maria 16, 36
Barbara 16, 36
Elizabetha 27
George Ludwig 16, 36
Heinrich 36
Johann Ludwig 68
John Bernhardt 36
John Martin 36
Michael 16, 27, 36, 73
Susanna 16, 36
Klebsaddel, Andreas 7
Klebssaddel, Frantz 14
Maria 14
Klee, Anna Margaretha 16
Nicolaus 16
Kleeman, Christian 18
Kleesin, Anna Maria 9
Kleesz, John George 9
John Philipp 9
Maria Barbara 9
Paulus 9
Klein, Adam 40, 43
Anna 23, 24, 32
Anna Barbara 40, 56
Anna Maria 16, 36
Christina Sophia 67
Elizabetha 57
George 24, 32
Heinrich 16, 20, 24, 36, 55
Johannes 71
John George 23, 24
John Gottlieb 43
John Wilhelm 49
Maria Barbara 24
Maria Elizabetha 56
Michael 39
Peter 44
Regina 57
Sabina 24
Kleinfelter, George 65
Kleinhaus, Dorothea 5
John George 5
Klesmann, Jacob 74

Klestmann, Catarina Barbara 45
Nicolaus 45
Kline, Anna Maria 20, 36
Heinrich 20, 36
Kling, Anna Elisabetha 53
Klingel, Frederich 64
Kloosz, Johannes 64
Kloss, Johannes 45
Kloter, Anna Maria 57
Klund, John Adam 17
John Jacob 17
Knabel, — (Herr) 3
Knaegy, Jost 77
Knauer, Anna Elisabetha 21
Christoph 21
Knedy, Isaac 17
Leonhard 17
Knemmerling, Jno. Martin 71
Knertzer, Balthasar 14
Kneuget, Leonhardt 24
Kneussel, Antonius 54
Kniesz, Catarina Elizabetha 65
Knobel, Anna Maria 54
Knoll, Johannes 27
Knopf, Anna Elisabeth 66
Hannah 58
Ludwig 59
Maria Elisabetha 57
Peter 57
Susanna 42
Knopff, Philipp 55
Kober, Anna Elisabetha 18
Anna Margaretha 19
George 19
John Dietrich 18
John Egidius 18
John Michael 19
Margaretha 37
Peter 70
Kobnar, Maria Margaretha 71
Koch, Adam 66
Anna 73
Christian 72
Christina 76
Elizabetha 73
George Michael 55
John George 10
Martin 71
Melchior 8
Peter 75
Kochdorfer, Andrew 33
Geo. Philipp 33
John Christoph 33
Kochenderfer, Andreas 38
Kochendoerfer, Andreas 66
Kochendoerffer, Andreas 57
Kock, John Christian 49
Koebel, Maria Sybilla 54
Koeblinger, Catarina 5
Johannes 5
John Martin 53
Martin 5
Koehler, Elizabetha 8
Heinrich 6
John Heinrich 8
Maria Catharine 6
Maria Christina 6
Koehrer, Jacob 24
Koelchner, George Adam 5
John George 5
Koeller, Heinrich 70
Martin 55
Koellicker, Rudolph 72
Koellmer, Margaretha 58
Koemmet, Veronica Barbara 66
Koenig, Anna Magdal Sophia 64

Koephenhoefer, Anna Bar. 54
Koerber, Johann Michael 57
Koerner, Maria Barbara 74
Koester, John Dieterich 73
Koger, John Jacob 18
Nicolaus 18, 54
Kohl, John George 54
Kohlmann, Catarina Barbara 24
Sebastian 24
Kolb, Christina 34
Cunradt 7
John Christoph 40
Maria Barbara 7
Philip 40
Philipp 34
Koller, John Adam 44
Kolmar, John Martin 71
Maria Margaretha 71
Konnoway, Arthur 36
Catarina 36
Charles 36
Kopf, Michael 55
Kopfenhoefer, Anna Rosina 54
Catarina 19
Koppenheffer, Thomas 51
Koppenhoefer, Anna Maria 23
Catarina 56
Elizabeth 28
Eva Margar. 37
Eva Maria 70
Jacob 28, 34
John George 34
Michael 37
Thomas 23, 44, 77
Kornmann, Anna Appolonia 74
John Ludwig 35
Korr, — 33
Anna Barbara 41
Barbara 76
Casper 40
Christian 71
Kraeht, Catarina 76
Kraemer, Andreas 16, 56
Anna Margaretha 71
Anna Maria 32
Frederick 61
Friederich 32, 35
Johannes 69
John Adam 52
John George 16, 35
Margaretha 52
Maria Catarina 35
Maria Magdalena 20
Maria Margaretha 75
Peter 52, 63, 66
Kraemerin, Maria Ursala 53
Kraeuser, Elisabetha Catar. 53
Krafft, Andreas 37, 38
Anna Elisabetha 38
Anna Margaretha 38
Anna Maria 38
Elisabetha 38
John 37
John Michael 38
Justina Catarina 38
Maria Catarina 38
Maria Elisabetha 38
Maria Magdalena 38
Susanna 38
Kraft, Andreas 29, 37
Anna Margaretha 64
Maria Elisabeth 64
Valentine 3
Kramer, Friederich 47
John Jacob 47
Krampf, Carl 8

Krampf (continued)
Maria Dorothea 8
Krauel, Catarina 38
Krauss, Albertina 53
Heinrich 8
Kreamer, John George 15
Kreber, John Philipp 40
Philipp 40
Krebs, Christian 33
Christiana Margaretha 8
Heinrich 8
John Heinrich 53
Krehl, Carolus 50
John Michael 50
Michael 50
Kremlich, Solomon 55
Kress, John Eberhard 31
Kretscher, Maria Agnes 57
Kreuber, Anna Maria 62
Kreuel, Ana Maria 24
Anna Catarina 24
Johannes 24
John Adam 24, 25
Margaretha 20
Maria Margaretha 25
Thomas 20, 24, 25
Kreugel, Margaretha 17
Thomas 17
Kreuter, Anna Margaretha 17
Frederich 17
Friederich 58
Kreutzer, Maria Magdalena 56
Krevel, Thomas 19
Krim, Maria Barbara 53
Kroeber, Johann Adam 62
Kroh, Abrahnm 68
Magdalena 76
Margaretha 56
Krohbiel, Magdalena 59
Krueger, Casper 7
Elias 17
George Valentine 7
Johannes 66
Michael 17
Krum, John Heinrich 62
Ktaepper, Elisabetha 57
Kucher, Anna Barbara 12
Anna Catarina 19
Barbara 17
Christoph 19
Eva Barbara 71
John Frantz 19
John Peter 19, 20, 23, 54
Maria Barbara 23
Peter 12, 15, 17, 19, 22
Rosina 15, 19
Kue, Patrick 56
Kuefer, Ana Margaretha 28
Anna Barbara 23
Anna Maria 48
Barbara 18, 24, 25, 51
Elisabetha 48, 52, 71
Elizabeth 7
Elizabetha 48
Johann Martin 66
John Frederich 48, 68
John Martin 48
Maria Elisabetha 52
Maria Elizabetha 48
Martin 52
Peter 68
Valentin 18, 23, 25, 34
Valentine 23, 31
Vincens 25, 28, 62
Kueffer, Ana Margaretha 28
Andreas 72
Anna Catarina 62
Barbara 71

Kueffer (continued)
Catarina 20
Elizabetha 28
Eva 58
Margaretha Barbara 6
Maria Barbara 28
Leonhardt 6
Valentine 28
Vincens 20
Kuehler, John Heinrich 4
Valentine 4
Kuehn, Catarina 66
Kuehner, Caspar 14
Casper 16
Frederick 20
Kuehnle, John Mattheis 20
Kuehny, Johannes 61
John 59
Kuehports, Jacob 58
Kuemmerlin, Jacob Friederich
45
John Michael 45
Kuemmerling, Anna Magar. 52
Anna Maria 73
Christoph Freiderich 52
Johannes 47, 66
John Martin 67
Martin 52
Kuemmerly, Johannes 64
Kuenig, Anna Catarina 57
Anna Maria 24
Catarina 33
Eva 62
George Jacob 18, 24
Jacob 50
John George 18, 24
Kuerschner, Anna Barbara 60
Kuertzel, Andreas 43
Dorothea 43
Kuhbauch, Johann Friederich 68
Kuhn, Adam Simon 11, 32
Eva 4
Eva Barbara 15
John Jacob 54
Kuhny, Mary 64
Kulin, Elisabetha 63
Kuntz, Anna Catar. 63
Anna Catarina 17
Anna Cath. 10
Anna Elizabeth 36
Anna Eva 9, 23
Cat. 14
Catarina 5, 9, 18
Geo. 14
George 6, 9, 71
Jacob 5, 11
Jno. Geo. 12
Joh. George 17
Johannes 56
John 21
John Adam 8
John Geo. 10
John George 5, 8, 9, 11, 14,
15, 53
John Nicolaus 36
John Philipp 12
Maria Catarina 14
Maria Eva 57
Kuntzlemann, Maria Barbara
76
Kuppenhoefer, Elisabetha 26
Thomas 26
Kupper, Catarina 69
John George 65
Kurtz, Lorentz 65
Kutz, Jacob 35
Johannes 35

Labengeiger, Anna Barbara 65
Christoph 57
Labengeiyer, Anna Barbara 23
Christoph 23
John Jacob 23
Maria Catarina 23
Laber, Balthaser 73
Laed, Margaretha 75
Laedin, Rosina 73
Laey, Catarina Barbara 68
Sybilla Margaretha 7
Mathias 7
Laney, Samuel 70
Lang, Anna Christina 69
Anna Margaretha 30
Anna Maria 39
Barbara 33, 66
Catarina 75
Christina Catarina 48
Conradt 19
Cunradt 33
Elizabeth 67
Jacob 30, 50
Johannes 30, 39, 50, 69
Johannes Jacob 50
John 40, 49
John Adam 48
John George Thomas 30
John Martin 52, 74
John Urban 53
Maria Catarina 50
Nicolaus 39
Langenecker, Anna 76
Lard, Elizabetha 74
Lathly, George 11
Rachael 11
Lattur, Barbara 42
Herman 42, 62
Susanna Margaretha 42
Latz, Elizabeth 21
Lau, — 16
Anna Kunigunda 15
Laub, Johannes George 55
Lauck, Andreas 8
John David 8
Laucks, Peter 60
Lauckster, Maria Elizabetha
68
Laudenbusch, Isaac 17
Lauer, Adam 6
Catharine Barbara 23
Christian 27
Johann Christian 59, 56
John Michael 23
John Nicholaus 29
Michael 23, 24, 58
Peter 6
Thomas 31
Laughlin, Elizabetha 74
John 69
Laumann, Catarina Sophia 44
Stephen 44
Laurie, Michael 50
Lautermilch, Gottfried 58
Lawleer, Michael 69
Lay, Andreas 74
Anna Barbara 59
Anna Margar 27
John George 13, 14
Layblin, Rosina 70
Layenberger, John George 17
Nicolaus 17
Leacock, John 58
Leadsoorth, Wiliam 60
Lechner, Catarina 55

Lechner (continued)
George 27
Ledig, Benedict 67
Leein, Anna 77
Leenwill, John 12
Lewis 12
Leewill, John 9
Lehman, Anna Elisabetha 32
Barbara 77
Christian 70
Johannes 9
Rosina 35
Lehmann, Elisabetha 25
Lehn, Johannes 45
Johannes Jacob 44
John 44
John Herman 60
Lehnherr, Jacob 61
Lehnich, Dietrich 11
Leidyn, Magdalena 63
Lein, Magdalena 11
Leininger, Jacob 45
Johannes 45
Leiter, Regina 53
Leitner, Ana Maria 26
Catarina 26
George Daniel 26
John Jacob 26
John William 26
Juliana 26
Magdalena 55
Simon 26
Susanna 56
William 25
Leng, Daniel 74
Lentz, Anna Maria 61
Jacob 45
John George 73
Maria Elisabetha 45
Michael 65
Philipp Jacob 45
Leonhardt, Anna Barbara 57
Barbara 72
Isaac 4
Martin George 75
Leppo, Christina 25
John Abraham 59
Maria Magdelena 25
Maria Susanna 25
Peter 25, 34
Susanna 34
Lerch, John 12
John Michael 12
Lerkin, John 67
Lerter, Maria Eva 67
Lesch, Adam 32
Catarina Elisabetha 58
Sophia 32
Lescher, Johannes 67
Lessle, Peter 62
Leutz, Michael 76
Levan, Anna Elizabeth 4
Anna Maria 4
Levandt, Anna Elisabetha 54
Lew, Maria Justina 57
Lewers, Robert 75
Lewis, Stephen 12
Welsh 62
Leydig, Johannes 49
John Jacob 49
Maria Catarina 49
Leyenberger, John Frantz 27
John Nicolaus 42
Nicolaus 37
Lichtenwallner, John 7
Margaretha 7
Lightel, William 55
Likens, Susanna 66

Lindemann, Mar. 54
Lindenmuth, Michael 68
Linn, Anna Elizabeth 59
Margaretha 59
Philipp 59
Linnenburger, Friederich 54
Lintner, Elizabetha 57
Lintzenbechler, Paulus 7
Lips, Juliana 53
Lischeer, Abraham 5
Johannes 5
Liske, Sarah 69
Litsch, Magdalena 75
Little, Henry 69
Litz, Eva Catarina 47
Wilhelm 47
Litzenbechler, Johannes 7
Lochmann, Elizabetha Dorothea 55
Lock, James 74
Mary 74
Loefel, Christian 17
Loeffel, Anna Margaretha 16
Christian 16, 55
John Peter 16
Loeffler, George Ludwig 22
Johannes Philipp 75
John Adam 22
Loefner, Peter Riedtin 25
Loescher, John Nicolaus 6
John Vincentz 6
Loesh, Anna Christina 59
Loewe, Casper 59
Loewengut, Anna Barbara 26
Catarina 26
Jacob 25, 26, 34, 45
John Jacob 27
Margaretha 25
Loewenstein, Catarina 16
George 16
John George 55
Maria Elizabetha 16
Lohman, Tobias 70
Lohmueller, John 32, 47
Long, Abraham 4
Christian 73
Cunradt 30
Elizabeth 4
Jacob 76
James 75
Nicolaus 30
Peter 4
Loodenton, Elizabeth 60
Loos, George 66
Looser, Catarina 75
Jacob 69
Lorentz, Anna Johanna 25
Anna Maria 66
Heinrich 25, 26
Loresch, Jacob 22, 44
Margaretha 44, 74
Maria Barbara 44
Maria Catarina 71
Losch, Daniel 70
Loughlin, Alexander 73
Jane 70
Louis, Anna 55
Low, Anna Margaretha 36
Casper 36
Daniel 10
Elisabetha 10
Elizabeth 10
Frances 56
James 64
John 10
William 10, 11
Lucas, Adelheit Elisabetha 24
Daniel 24, 40, 63

Lucas (continued)
John Adam 43
Maria Catarina 24
Maria Elisabetha 43
Maria Magdalena 24
Philipp Adam 24
Luct, Anna Eva 62
Ludwig, Johann George 65
John George 41
John Michael 11
Maria Christina 41
Lueckenbuehl, John Adam 5
Luecker, Anna Johanna 64
Lusk, Mary 72
Lutz, Christian 35, 50, 61
Christoph 41
Elisabetha 41
Leonhardt 12
Maria Margar. 62
Wilhelm 64

--- M ---

Maag, Catarina 71
Elizabetha 11
Johannes 13
Peter 13, 57
Rudi 11
Macarty, Cornelius 62
Machon, George 76
Mack, Erna Barbara 53
Margaretha 53
Philippina Christian 53
Mackey, Thomas 61
Mader, Anna Magdalena 66
Madern, Adam 44
Anna Margaretha 60
Catarina 66
Elisabetha 49, 62
John Adam 50
John Daniel 49, 67
John Nicolaus 44
John Thomas 32, 49
Magdalena 50
Maria Eva Rosina 49
Michael 49
Vernica 49
Veronica 49
Madinger, Anna Elisabetha 54
Maennerin, Maria Sara 60
Maennig, John Adam 70
Maercker, John Mattheis 17
Maess, Anna Margaretha 45
George 45, 62
Maria Magdalena 6
Maessner, Casper 25
Christian 49
Maeuntzer, Anna Catarina 16
Anna Dorothea 17
Elizabeth Catarina 16
George Jacob 16
John George 16
Magham, Mary 68
Maghen, Mary 76
Mahorder, William 72
Makee, Agnes 75
Makintyer, Alexander 56
Malfair, Anna Maria 48
Michael 48
Malfir, Magdalena 76
Michael 65
Malvir, Anna Maria 63
Man, Samuel 75
Manck, Gottfried 15
Mann, Bernhardt 46
Catarina Elisabetha 46

Mann (continued)
George Bernhardt 20
George Stephan 59
Manningham, Mary 72
Mannsperger, John Martin 58
Marcker, Catarina 22
Julianna 22
Maria Elizabetha 22
Mattheis 56
Peter 21, 22
Marcket, John Heinrich 24
Markley, Martha 56
Marret, Nicolaus 59
Marreth, John Nicolaus 39, 44
Michael 39
Nicolaus 39
Marshal, John 57
Marstaller, Frederick 20
Margaretha 54
Philip Balthasar 20
Philipp 51
Marstellar, Jno. George 12
Martin, Alexander 74
Engel 76
Isaac 68
John 52
John George 48
John Heinrich 41
Mary 68
Nicolaus 59
Rebecca 52
Samuel 69
Sarah 52
Martzeloff, John Philipp 60
Mast, Anna Catarina 23
Jacob 23
Mattern, Catarina Elisabetha 70
Mattheis, Anna Margaretha 18
Catarina 18
John George 18
John Jacob 13, 18
Magdalena 18
Margaretha 13
Philipp 73
Matthias, John Jacob 11
Margaretha 11
Matz, John Jacob 64
Maul, Juliana 65
Maurer, Anna Catarina 71
Anna Margaretha 75
Catarina Margaretha 27
Eva Margaretha 27
Geo. 71
George Michael 27
John George 27
John Jacob 27
John Philipp 27, 58
Maria Elisabetha 27
Peter 65
Philipp 27, 42
Rosina Barbara 71
Mausser, Jacob Mattheis 19
Maxell, Rebecca 70
Mayer, Anna Margaretha 15
Dieterich 15
Heinrich 61
Mayhew, Anna 13
Joseph 12
William 12
Mayhuw, Joseph 55
Mays, Andrew 71
Margaretha 70
McCaddoms, Rebecca 64
McCafferty, Sarah 64
McCall, James 56
McCardy, Daniel 63
McCarthy, Laurence 64

McCarthy (continued)
Margaretha 69
Peter 68
Thomas 59
McCaughlin, Sarah 65
McCellan, Robert 64
McChees, Isaac 12
James 12
McCleere, Michael 70
McClunnighen, Elisabetha 73
McClunty, Alexander 72
McClure, Susannah 75
William 72
McCnely, Margaretha 56
McCord, Margaretha 75
McCrabbord, William 69
McCraight, Anthony 72
McCrannighan, Patrick 66
McCrory, Joseph 61
McCullock, Hannah 69
McCurry, John 72
McDowel, Elizabeth 56
McDuff, James 57
McElhanny, John 75
McElhenny, Mary 73
McEntyre, Margaretha 67
McFarling, Walther 75
McGill, Andrew 10, 11
Mary 10, 11
McGomery, John 69
McGregor, Duncan 77
McGuill, Andreas 13
Andrew 14
James 13
Mary 14
McKay, Elisabetha 23
Thomas 23
McKee, Thoas 68
McKentzie, Benjamin 76
McKiney, Matthew 74
McKnees, Henry 12
James 12
McKue, Patrick 23
Sarah 23
McKut, Mary 73
McLean, Jane 63
McLinty, Susannah 76
McLoughly, Daniel 11
John 11
McLung, Robert 70
M'Clunty, Abraham 68
McLyntie, Joseph 74
McManus, Mary 73
McMollen, Elisabetha 71
Jane 72
McMollon, Jane 63
McMurphey, Cornelius 74
McNealy, Mary 61
McNees, Elenore 70
McNeese, James 63
McNeess, James 23
McNight, Patrick 76
McNitt, Thomas 70
McNut, Martha 69
McNutt, Jane 71
William 71
McQuien, Margaretha 74
McRentzie, Benjamin 76
Meben, Mary 61
Meck, George Michael 5, 7
Maria Barbara 5, 7
Michael 75
Meetch, Agnes 70
Meeth, Anna Maria 39
Johanna Maria 33
Johannes 39
John 33, 39
John Philip 42

Meeth (continued)
John Philipp 39
Maria Christina 39
Philipp 29, 33, 38, 60
Meihel, Anna Maria 54
Meipel, Anna Eva 62
Meissner, Caspar 60
Meivel, Anna Maria 37
Melsheimer, Pfarrer 77
Merans, Mary 64
Merck, Heinrich 24
Maria Barbara 24
Merckel, John Peter 25
Merckir, David 75
Merckling, Anna Frantzina 11, 32, 60
Anna Maria 61
Christian 3
John George 35
Maria Appolonia 57
Maria Catarina 3
Mercklingen, Anna Maria 14
Merkling, Anna Franzina 8
Mert, Maria Barbara 43
Mertz, Johannes 43
Mery, Catarina 53
Samuel 53
Messerschmidt, Johannes 69
Messerschmidtin, Johanna Maria 10
Messersmidt, Johannes 4
Metz, George Jacob 46
John Jacob 46
Metzger, Anna Maria 46
Philipp 46
Meuerle, David 68
Meusser, Elisabetha 61
Meyer, Ana Maria 24
Anna 75
Anna Barbara 19, 50, 59, 63
Anna Catarina 21
Anna Margaretha 58
Anna Maria 23, 25, 31, 40, 50, 62, 65
Anna Rosina 16
Anna Sabina 19
Anna Sophia 60
Catarina 28, 29, 30, 34, 47, 75
Christian 28, 30, 31, 34, 41, 47, 74
Christoph 16, 19, 23, 24, 29, 48, 54, 60, 72
Christopher 15
Egidius 35
Elisabetha 19
Elizabetha 66
Eva Magdalena 71
George 20, 21, 22, 35, 50, 55, 56, 68, 72
George Peter 21
Heinrich 16, 52, 70
Johannes 29, 31, 61, 64, 67, 75
John 25, 31, 40
John George 19, 23, 33, 52, 61, 63
John Heinrich 21
John Jacob 21
John Ludwig 35
John Vincentz 6
Maria Barbara 23, 62
Maria Catarina 73
Maria Elisabetha 50
Maria Elizabetha 47
Maria Eva 35, 71
Maria Margar. 63
Michael 21, 76

Meyer (continued)
  Rosina 15, 24, 48
  Ursula Margar. 54
  Valentin 35, 43
  Veronica 19, 21, 63, 64
Meyers, George 20
Meyle, Anna Sabina 23
  Elisabetha 24
  Heinrich 24
  Johannes 24
  John Martin 23, 24
Meylie, Barbara 63
  Catarina 63
Meyly, Anna Sabina 49
  Heinrich 60, 76
  Martin (Jr.) 49
Michael, Anna Maria 12
  Christian 70
  George 6
  Heinrich 12
  Susanna 72
Miess, Elisabetha 77
Miley, James 75
Miller, Heinrich 76
  Sebastian 4
Millighan, James 68
Mindbohner, Pfarrer 77
Minier, Christina 63
Mintz, Mary Margaretha 61
Mittag, Johannes 11
  Susanna 11
Mittelkauf, Maria Salome 14
Mittelkauff, Catharina 9
  Leonhardt 9
  Peter 9
Mohr, Adolf 54
  Anna Maria 60
  Eva Catarina 17
  Johannes 73
  John Frederich 25
  John Geo. 57
  John George 25
  Jost 17
Moll, Johannes 56
Mollen, Arthur 72
Montgomery, Robert 65
Moor, Elisabeth 58
  Jacob 12
  James 10
  Jane 76
  John 12, 70
  Moses 61
  Rilie 12
  Sarah 12
  Terkis 12
  Theodota 10
  Thomas 12
Mooser, Anna Barbara 41
  Christina Catarina 41
  Erdtmann 41
  Eva Barbara 69
  John Michael 54
  Michael 41
  Regina 69
Morgan, John 53
  William 11, 57
Morgenstern, Eve 14
  Johann 10
  Johannes 14, 18
  John 5, 9, 14
  Juliana 14
  Juliana Catarina 18
  Maria Elisabetha 10, 23
  Maria Elizabetha 14
  Philip 16
  Philipp 14, 57
Morgensternin, Juliana Catharina 6

Morgon, Elisabetha 17
  William 17
Morphew, Henry 16
  William 16
Morr, Andreas 47, 64
  Anna Catarina 47
  Catarina 47
  Christina 47
Morris, Hugh 76
  Jane 15
  John 15
  Mary 14
  William 15, 62
Morton, Agnes 71
  James 72
  Sarah 66
Moseler, Anna Maria 26
Moser, Anna Maria 68
  Christina 40
  Eva 7
  Jacob 40
  John 7
  John Jacob 26
  John Martin 7
  John Michael 7
  Margaretha 7
  Maria Catarina 29
  Regina 26
  Tobias 6, 7, 54
Mosser, Adam 46
Motz, Anna Maria 58
  Bernhardt 35
  Catharina 54
  Eva Maria 35
  Margaretha 75
  Maria Catarina 64
Mountgomery, John 56
Mt. Gommery, Margaretha 56
Mourdagh, John 70
Mueller, Adam 13, 14
  Agnes 73
  Andreas 56
  Anna Catarina 25
  Anna Christina 13
  Anna Maria 14, 70
  Anna Maria Appolonia 7
  Appollonia 32
  Barbara 58
  Catarina 13, 60, 61, 63, 73, 74
  Catarina Esther 67
  Catharina 13
  Christian 14, 25, 39, 68
  Christina 14
  Christoph 72
  Cunradt 25
  Daniel 75
  David 47, 75
  Frantz 73
  George 22, 25, 49, 65
  Hans Adam 25
  Heinrich 45, 50, 65, 68
  Jacob 5, 7, 8, 54
  Jacobina 50
  Jno. Jacob 53
  Johannes 31, 54, 58, 66
  Johannetta 37
  John Bernhardt 50
  John Heinrich 25
  John Melchior 31
  John Michael 39
  John Peter 25
  John Thomas 47
  Leonhardt 40, 62, 63
  Magdalena 13
  Margar. Magdal. 68
  Margaretha 73
  Maria Agatha 31

Mueller (continued)
  Maria Catarina 25, 59
  Maria Christina 30
  Maria Margaretha 39
  Michael 57, 59
  Moritz 57
  Nicolaus 31, 55
  Nicolaus (Jr.) 35
  Sebastian 7
  Simon 14
  Susanna 66
  Theobaldt 69
  Thomas 39
  Ursula 57
  Valentin 55
  Valentine 13
Muench, Anna Margaretha 44
  Anna Maria 48
  Catarina 30, 43, 52
  Catarina Margaretha 44
  Christina 38, 41, 44
  Christina Barbara 41
  Christoph 48
  Geo. Michael 68
  George 44, 63
  Heinrich 71
  John Christoph 66
  John Cunradt 19
  John George Michael 48
  John Michael 19
  John Peter 41
  John Philipp 48
  Maria Appolonia 68
  Mattheis 49
  Peter 19, 29, 31, 38, 41, 44, 65
  Simon 43, 44, 76
  Susanna 76
Muentz, Nicolaus 3
Murhead, Robert 75
Murr, Andreas 25
Myer, Michael 12, 20
Myle, John Martin 18

--- N ---

Naess, Anna Catarina 59
  Anna Margaretha 57
  Barbara 57
  Elizabeth 24, 68
  Heinrich 51
  Heinrich 73, 76
  Sebastian 18, 24, 59
Naesz, Mattheis 54
Nagel, Anna Maria Barbara 49, 66
  Antonius 44
  Elizabetha 66
  Eva 65
  Eva Catarina 44
  Johannes 49
  John Christian 49
  Juliana 45
  Maria Barabara 47
  Maria Barbara 44
  Maria Dorothea 44
  Maria Magdalena 49
  Sebastian 49, 66
Nagle, Barbara 44
  Johannes 7
  John 7
  Margaretha 6
  Maria Margaretha 7
Neal, Agnes 73
Nef, Anna Maria 25, 48
  Michael (Jr.) 25
Neff, Abraham 59

Neff (continued)
   Anna Catrarina 5⅞
   Jacob 52,59
   John Heinrich 52
   John Jacob 32
   Margaretha 57
Negele, Peter 60
Neiss, Christoph 73
Nelson, Andrew 62
Neu, Elizabetha Catarina 51
   John Adam 66
   John Michael 75
   John Nicolaus 74
   John Peter 76,77
   John Wilhelm 73
   Joseph 62
   Maria Catarina 63
   Maria Elisabetha 72,77
   Maria Elizabeth 62
Neuman, Seidel 25
Neumeister, Christoph 55
   John Wilhelm 30
Neuschwanger, Jacob 13
   John Jacob 56
   Maria 13
   Peter 73
New, Adam 48
   John Nicholaus 73
   John Philipp 75
Newman, Seideler 35
Nicolaus, John 15
   Ludwig Heinrich 15
Niesz, Maria Barbara 47
   Peter 47
Noecker, Maria Eve 68
   Maria Magdalena 35
   Martin 35
Nold, Michael 54
Noldt, Cornelius 6
   John Michael 6
Noll, Johannes 56
   Philipp 34
Nolld, Balthaser 44
Nosseler, Christina 14
Nuesch, Margaretha 58
Nufer, Ana Elizabetha 73
Nunnenmacher, Christina 74

--- O ---

Oar, Mary 64
Oberfeld, Elizabetha 74
Oberholtzer, Jacob 72
Oberholzer, Anna Elisab. 63
Oberkehr, Charlotte 36
   Peter 36
Oberle, Christina Barbara 32
   John 30
   Michael 32
Oberlin, Christina Barbara 39
   Eva 66
   Eva Margaretha 48
   John 62
   John Adam 57
   John Martin 57
   John Michael 59
   Margaretha 63
   Maria Catarina 58
   Martin 44,65
   Michael 39
Obermann, John Caspar 65
Obermeyer, Anna Barbara 34
   Geo. 68
   George 34
   Johann George 64
Obold, Joseph 59

Obold (continued)
   Sebastian 42
Ochs, Catarina 53
   John Adam 8
   John Leonhardt 7
   Leonhardt 7
   Matheis 53
Oehler, Catarina 72
Oehrle, Johannes 51,65
   John 51
   John (Jr.) 76
   Regina 51
Oesterlin, Margaretha 57
Ogle, Joseph 10,13,14
   Mary 14
   Sara 10
   Sarah 13
Ohler, Andreas 9
   Peter 9
Ohlerin, Ursala 9
Ohlinger, Johann Ulrich 73
Ohnselt, Frederick 24
   John 24
Ohr, Elizabetha Gertraudt 6
   John George 6
Ohrendorf, Christian 33
Ohrendurf, Anna Margaretha 60
Old, Anna 62
   James 62
Olig, Catarina Elisabetha 57
Olin, Anna Elisabetha 21
Olinger, Barbara 70
Oliphants, Rebecca 62
Ollinger, Catarina 73
   Christoph 6
Opp, Friederich 28
Optograef, Elisabetha 53
Ort, Anna Margaretha 54
   Balthasar 15,21
   Barbara 15
   Catarina 31
Osborn, George 63
Otlinger, Jacob 58
Ottinger, Jacob 17
   John Jacob 17
Ouir, Christina 59
Owen, John 16
   William 16
Owens, Nolly 55
   Thomas 74
   William 70

--- P ---

Packwood, Samuel 62
   William 61
Paffenberger, Adelheit 62
Palm, Jacob 77
   Johannes 77
Pannekuchen, Johann Peter 65
   Valentin 77
Pannel, Elizabetha 59
   Mary 62
Parry, Thomas 10
Partemer, Johannes 69
Paterson, Hannah 60
Pattison, Agnes 11
Patton, Mary 60
Patty, Margaretha 63
Patz, Andreas 71
Paul, Robert 10
Paxtang, Anna 62
Penssinger, Wilhelm 35
Peter, Catarina 69
   George 72

Peter (continued)
   Heinrich 76
   Johannes 70,76
   John 5
   Magdalena 70
   Ulrich 21
Petry, Anna Catarina 31,38
   Catharina Elisabetha 38
   Johannes 72
   John George 38,54
   John Jacob 38
   John Nicolaus 38
   Philip 38
   Philipp 31,59
Pettigrew, James 69
   Martha 71
Pfaffenberger, Adelheit 28
   Christian 44
   Johannes 44,68
   John 44
   John George 31
Pfaffman, Antonius 3
Pfautz, Anna Barbara 54
Pflantz, Anna Catarina 67
   Christina 74
   Elisabetha 42
   Mattheis 42,61
Pflautz, Anna Elisabeth 70
Pfleuger, Maria Barbara 54
   Maria Catarina 59
Pfostberger, Adelheit 36
Pfrang, Anna Maria 66
   John Michael 65
   Maria Agnes 66
   Maria Eva 70
Phaghon, Mary 73
Philbel, John Adam 4
Philbert, Anna Elisabetha 38,46
   Anna Elizabetha 44
   John Peter 38
   John Philipp 38
   John Thomas 47
   Maria Catarina 38,46,68
   Maria Christina 38
   Mattheis 45
   Samuel 29,38,42,46,50
   Susanna 38,42,46,50
   Thomas 42
Philipp, Eva Christina 63
Philippe, Casper 29
Philippin, Christ. Elisab. 64
Philippy, Anna Maria 48
   Christian 48,63
   Johannes 66
Phillippe, John Heinrich 29
Pickerstaff, Samuel 58
Pickets, Margaretha 53
Pilgrum, Margaretha 75
Pits, Sarah 75
Pitts, David 62
   Welshburn 69
Plattner, Maria 54
Pleure, Isabell 57
Pohin, Juliana 58
Pokin, Anna Margaretha 59
Pontius, Johannes 26,36
   John 59
   John Peter 26
Popp, John 45
Porcks, Mary 4
Porterfield, James 75
   Robert 77
Post, Samuel 73
Potts, Anna Barbara 43
   Ludwig 43
Praello, Edward I. 71
Preece, Mary 69

Preece (continued)
Thomas 70
Preiss, Elizabetha 75
Presby, Leonard 75
Preschinger, Jacob 24
Pressel, Valentine 10
Pressler, Anna Margaretha 47
Anna Maria 47
George 47
Maria Elisab. 67
Pretz, Anna Maria 65
Pretzius, Jacob 65
Prey, Anna Maria 11
Catarina 11
Elizabetha 11
Henry 11
Sarah 11
Susanna 11
Priess, Maria 75
Probst, Johann Michael 54
Proops, Michael 56
Prossman, Anna Magdalena 60
Frantz 42
Just. Catar. 42
Prossmann, Justina 41
Pruess, Maria 75
Puder, Christina 54
Puls, Catharine Elizabeth 5
Purviance, David 67

--- Q ---

Queer, Thomas 10
Quickel, Anna Catarina 23
George (Jr.) 23
John George 15, 57
John Michael 16, 58
Maria Elizabetha 59

--- R ---

Rack, Laurence 68
Radebach, Anna Catarina 44
Anna Elizabetha 44
George 44, 47
Heinrich 44
John Nicolaus 44
Maria Margaretha 44
Maria Margaretha 44
Peter 44
Raetelsperger, Anna Maria 63
Rafler, James 63
Raisch, Jacob 72
Ralph, Zacharias 75
Ramberg, Anna Christina 67
Christian 67
Ramberger, Anna Maria 73
Rameler, Catarina 58
Ramler, Anna Margaretha 31,
65
Anna Maria 59
Eva Margar. 62
Jacob 27, 61
Johannes 21, 32
John Jacob 27
Leonhardt 21, 24, 27, 30, 31,
36
Margaretha 27, 30
Rammage, Margaretha 76
Rammler, Eva Margaretha 37
Jacob 37
John Michael 37
Martin 37
Rampton, Richard 55

Ramsey, Jane 72
Ranek, Anna Barbara 23
Michael 23
Rasch, Anna Barbara 31
Anna Magdalena 31
Elizabetha 31
George Casper 31
Johannes 31
Rathfang, Anna Margaretha 27
Frederich 27
John Friederich 25
Maria Elisabetha 25
Rathgeber, Balthasar 31
Rattenauer, Gottfried 39
John George 39
Rauch, Anna Margaretha 28
Bernhardt 28
Elisabetha 71
Elizabetha 28
Sabina 28, 72
Rauh, Philipp 71
Raup, Eva Catarina 70
Johannes 71
John Michael 18
Michael 54
Peter 18
Rausch, Anna Eva 42
Daniel 42, 53
Elisabetha 18, 70
John Daniel 42
Magdalena 74
Michael 15, 17, 18
Stephan 58
Rautenbusch, Isaac 57
Maria Drusiana 56
Rea, Sarah 70
Read, Nels 63
Peter 72
Reber, Anna Margaretha 15
John George 15
Leonhardt 15
Rebmann, Elizabetha 74
Redebach, Anna Maria 65
Redman, Conradt 70
Reed, Elenore 67
George 37
John George 37
Margaretha 69
Samuel 65
William 69
Reess, Jacob 37, 61
John George 37
John Nicolaus David 37
Reffior, —— 10
Refior, Cunradt 8
Maria Appolonia 8
Rehm, Anna Margar. 60
John Jacob 38
Maria Magdalena 60
Rehwald, Anna Maria 75
Reiber, Abraham 47
Anna Maria 72
Anna Rosina 73
Catarina 72
Reich, Eva Kunigunda 44
Mattheis 44
Reichenbach, Johannes 70
Reid, Johannes 67
Reidt, Leonhardt 26
Reiff, George John 8
Peter 8
Reiffen, Anna Elisabetha 53
Reimer, Ana Magdalena 29
Anna Magdalena 39
Maria Magdla. 61
Rein, George 65
Reindzel, Andreas 50
Reinhardt, John Casper 6

Reinhardt (continued)
Salome 77
Reinholdt, Christoph Heinrich
67
Reinier, Anna Margaretha 60
Reinoehl, George Heinrich 29
Reiss, Anna Margaretha 34,
35
Anna Maria 25, 72
Johannes 25
John Ludwig 25
John Michael 35
Magdalena 25
Maria Catarina 25
Maria Elisabetha 25
Michael 25, 34
Renin, Anna Maria 6
Retnel, Margaretha 38
Reuger, Mattheis 7
Reugerin, Barbara 6
Reusch, Mary Regina 76
Reuscher, Susanna 58
Reush, Elizabetha 74
Reusner, Anna Elisabetha 15
Catarina Barbara 15
Michael 15
Reuss, Johannes 35
Reusser, Jacob (Jr.) 41
Reuter, Elisabetha 26
Jacob 26, 31, 59
Magdalena 31
Reyer, Johannes 72
Maria Catarina 63
Reynolds, Bridgitte 23
Elisabetha 23
Francis 23, 53, 56
John 23
Jos. 10
Joseph 10, 23
Rebecca 23
Sarah 10, 23, 62
Rheinhardt, Emma Christina
13
Michael 13
Rheinhart, Juliana 57
Rheinoehl, John Heinrich 73
Rice, Molly 75
Richard, William 5
Richardson, Abraham 61
Richter, Michael 6
Peter 4, 6
Ried, Anna Maria 76
Catarina 71
Elizabeth 68
Eva Elisabetha 27
Eva Elizabeth 27
John George 30
Rieder, Anna Maria 52
Michael 52
Riedt, Andreas 42
Anna Catarina 26
Anna Susanna 42
Casper 64
Catarina 75
Christina Barbara 40
Eva Margaretha 40
Eva Maria 40
George 40, 42
Jacob 40, 63
John George 58
John Jacob 40
Margaretha 67
Maria Dorothea 60
Peter 63
Riedtin, Anna Catarina 25
Riegel, Catarina Elisabetha
26
Catarina Elizaba. 67

Riegel (continued)
Daniel 29
Johannes 26, 29, 36, 55
John 26, 28
John Geo. 54
Maria Catarina 26
Philipp Adam 26
Riehl, Catarina 55
David 29
Riehm, Maria Elisab. 62
Riem, Balthasar 32
Maria Appollonia 32
Riess, Jacob 40
Johann Martin 73
Justina Elis. 54
Riesz, Adam 65
Ringel, Catarina Barbara 60
Ringer, Catarina 33
Ritscher, Anna Margaretha 40
Johannes 29, 40
John Peter 66
Maria Elisab. 64
Ritschor, Maria Sara 68
Ritter, Adam 45
Barbara 74
Catarina 33
Elizabeth 6
Joseph 33
Philipp Adam 45
Ritzman, Margaretha 35
Ritzmann, Eva Maria 65
John Peter 66
Robinson, James 74
John 69
Joseph 69
Roeder, Caspar 49, 69
Roehben, Anna Margaretha 6
Catarina Barbara 6
Nicolaus 6
Peter 6
Roeher, Anna Margaretha 41
Jacob 40, 41
John Jacob 41
Maria Catarina 41
Roehrer, Anna Catarina 39
Anna Elizabetha 39
Anna Maria 39, 62
Dorothea 39, 41, 67
Gottfried 34, 39, 41, 43
Jacob 37, 39
John Gottfried 35
John Jacob 39, 62
Juliana 39
Magdalena 35, 41
Maria Magdalena 34, 39
Roenninger, Catarina 25, 64
Cunradt 43, 46, 64
Maria Margar. Barbara 43
Maria Salome 43
Susanna Margar. 46
Wendel 43
Roesal, Mattheis 18
Roeser, Anna 64
Christiana 59
Roesnner, Werina 57
Roessel, Catharina 11
Maria Barbara 12, 13
Matheis 12, 13
Matthias 11
Roesser, Catarina Barbara 62
Roesshorn, Adam 7
John Adam 7
Roessle, John 52
Roessler, John George 65
Roeszle, John 52
Susanna 52
Roeszlin, Catarina 73
Roetelstein, John Heinrich 36

Roger, William 65
Rogers, Elenore 70
Elizabetha 66
Margaretha 64
Martha 61
Robert 67
William 70
Roht, Lucia 54
Roils, Nicolaus 58
Roland, Catarina 59
Romich, John Adam 53
Ronning, Wendel 37
Roof, Magdalena 31
Roolfert, John 31
Maria Agatha 31
Roomer, Michael 30
Roop, Johannes 62
Rorber, Herman 30
Rosenbach, Maria Magdl 64
Rosenbaum, Antonius 22, 55
Mary 21
Salome 22
Susanna 22
Rosenberger, Erasmus 66
Peter 64
Ross, James 73
Margaretha 62
Rotch, Jane 76
Rotenbach, Christian 58
Roth, Anna Margaret 33
Gottlieb 73
Jacob 5, 74
John Cunradt 5
John George 65
John Heinrich 40
John Jacob 5, 6
Joseph 34, 40, 62
Margaretha 62, 73
Sabina 54
Rothermel, Anna Elizabeth 7
Peter 7
Rothrock, Anna Margaretha 56
Rough, James 69
Rounner, Cunradt 42
Margaretha 42
Rousch, Peter 15
Ruch, Michael 60
Rudesilie, Elizabetha 11
Jacob 11
Rudiesiehl, Eva Catarina 74
Rudiesiel, Anna Johanna 17
Weirich 17
Rudiesielin, Susanna 19
Rudiesile, Philipp 54
Rudolph, Anna Margaretha 65
Rudy, Catarina 76
Ruecker, Magdalena 75
Melchior 74
Rueger, Elizabetha 58
Jacob 24
John Jacob 24
Ruehfeld, Adolph 3
Ruesel, Catarina Barbara 14
Ruesser, Agnes 13
John George 13
Ruhi, Sebastian 19
Ruhl, Geo. Philip 33
Ruhlmann, George 31
Maria Catarina 60
Rul, Anna Catarina 53
Elisabetha Catarina 53
Rupert, Anna Barbara 16
John Adam 16, 17
Ruscher, Catarina 55
Christina 55
Margaretha 57
Russell, James 57
Jane 57

Ruth, Anna Catarina 20
Barbara 20
Catarina 21
Maria Catarina 20
Peter 20, 21
Rutherford, Mary 71
Rutt, Sebastian 42

--- S ---

Saber, Margaretha 54
Saeger, John George 57
Saenger, John 8
John Christian 8
Saladin, Anna Catarina 50
Elisabetha 50
Nicolaus 50
Saltzer, Jacob 67
Sauebert, John Jacob 58
Sauer, Dorothea 35
Frederick 14
John Heinrich 35, 57
Sauermilch, Catarina 63
Saur, Ana Eva 55
Maria Elizabetha 65
Saurin, Maria 58
Sauszer, Catarina Elizabetha 49
Michael 49
Sauter, Anna Elizabeth 61
Barbara Margaretha 61
George 39
Heinrich 28, 36
Jacob 74
Sabina 28, 36, 47, 76, 77
Sawer, Johannes 55
Sawyer, William 76
Scannel, John 73
Schaack, Anna Elizabetha 51
Barbara 51
Elizabetha 51
Jacob 51
Schaaf, Anna Dorothea 71
Schaat, Andreas 64
Schaber, Christoph 69
Schack, Catarina 63
Schade, Catarina Barbara 33
John George 33
Schadt, Andreas 46
Anna Elisabetha 46
John Jacob 46
John Michael 46
Maria Catarina 46
Maria Susanna 46
Samuel 46
Schaefer, Andreas 45
Anna 45, 64
Anna Margaretha 73
Anna Maria 61
Caspar 60
Catarina 46
Christina 30
Elizabetha 44
George 27
Johannes 25, 30, 44, 46
John Adam 44
John Philipp 33, 60
John Nicolaus 46, 47
Peter 57
Philipp 30
Serenius 44
Susanna 30
Schaeffer, Abraham 67
Andreas 64
Anna Barbara 62, 63
Anna Margaretha 16

99

Schaeffer (continued)
Elisabetha 55
Elizabetha Catharine 56
George 42
Heinrich 16
Johannes 35
John David 59
John George 71
John Heinrich 35
John Nicolaus 64
John Philipp 33, 42
Magdalena 70
Maria 68
Maria Catarina 63
Maria Magdalena 59
Maria Margaret 33
Philipp 33
Schaetterle, Christina 41
George 41
Schaeufle, Michael 17
Schafer, Andreas 45
Catarina 45
Schaffner, John Caspar 54
Schaiteler, John George 57
Schally, Carl 20
John Peter 20
Lucas 72
Schantz, Elisabetha 71
F.J.F. (Rev.) 3, 4
Scharf, Appollonia 19
Cunradt 19
Johannes 72
Scharff, Catarina Margaretha 45
Cunradt 45
Schaub, Anna 14, 57
Jacob 60
Martin 14
Schauer, Adam 29
Anna Maria 36
Catarina 60
Catarina Elizabetha 29
Eva Rosina 38
Michael 29, 38
Schauffcler, Christian 77
Schauffle, Eva Dorothea 4
Michael 14
Schauffler, Barbara 71
Valentin 76
Schaum, Christian 47
Christoph 47
Schaurer, Michael 36
Schedt, Carl 50, 51, 52
Eva 52
Eva Maria 76
Margaretha 51
Scheetz, Maria Elisabetha 46
Scheidin, N. 4
Scheidt, Andreas 33
Carl 42
Carolus 67
Catarina 69
Eva Maria 31
George 44
Maria Margar. 61
Scheidter, Maria Barbara 8
Schell, Christina Regina 21
John Albrecht 21
Peter 33
Schenck, George 66
Schenk, Jacob 73
Scherb, Elizabetha 60
Scherer, Johannes 74
John Jacob 56
Scherertz, Arnold 47
Cunradt 75
Daniel 73
Scheretz, Christoph 74

Scheretz (continued)
Jacob 70
Scherff, Isaack 44
John Heinrich 44
Schierisser, Mattheis 56
Schifler, George 32
John George 32
Schill, George 51
John Peter 51
Schillich, John Adam 54
Schilling, Barbara 36
Jacob 36
Schindel, Christina 76
Schirck, Anna 77
Johannes 74
Schirman, Anna Maria 36
Elisabetha Catarina 26
George 36
George Jacob 44
Joh. Simon 36
John George 26, 30, 31
Philipp Adam 26, 33, 36
Simon 26, 33, 36
Schirmann, Anna Maria 28
Catarina Elizabetha 55
George 28, 37
John Simon 28
Philip Adam 28
Philipp Adam 25, 37
Simon 27
Schirmer, George Jacob 28
Schlaegel, Catarina 16
Christian 14
Christoph 10, 16
Daniel 16, 23
Heinrich 10
Maria 14
Schlatter, Anna Maria 68
Schlauch, John Jacob 21
Ursula Elisabetha 21
Schless, Philipp 9
Schlessmann, Maria Eva 47
Nicolaus 47
Schlosser, George Ernst 35
Peter 35
Schmeiser, John George 58
Schmeisse, John Michael 15
Schmeisser, Barbara 15
George 15
Mattheis 15
Schmeltz, John 19
Schmeltzer, Jacobina 40
Johannes 17, 24, 40
John 16, 17
John Jacob 40
John Peter 17
Peter 69
Sabina 17
Schmetter, John 44
Schmidt, Agnes 14
Andreas 42, 46
Anna Catarina 54, 60
Anna Catharina 10
Anna Elizabeth 6
Anna Magdalena 66
Anna Margaretha 51, 61
Anna Maria 56
Carl 44
Caspar 23
Casper 18
Catarina 73
Catarina Ursula 3
Christian 22, 25
Cunradt 51
Elis. Magdalena 55
Elisabetha 25
Elizabetha 51
Eva 44

Schmidt (continued)
Eva Margaretha 56
George Heinrich 25
George Jacob 18
Gertraudt 25
Heinrich John Peter 25
Henry 10, 61
Isabel 65
Jacob 51, 62, 67
Johannes 74
John 25
John Adam 5
John Caspar 57
John Christian 8, 58
John George 22, 46, 48, 55
John Heinrich 25
John Jacob 51
John Martin 64
John Mattheis 5
John Nicolaus 66
John Peter 59
Juliana 51
Margareth 12
Margaretha 51, 55, 69
Maria Barbara 75
Maria Catarina 5
Maria Elisabetha 23, 74
Maria Eva 63
Maria Ursula 6
Martin 48, 66
Mattheis 6
Michael 5
Peter 19, 26
Robert 53
Susanna 44
Thomas 56
Schmutz, Mattheis 66
Schnabele, Barbara 16
Ottmar 16
Schnaebel, Anna 67
Johannes 26
Schnaebele, Barbara 28, 36, 50
Caspar 47
Casper 28
Jacob 48, 63
Johannes 73
John Heinrich 8
John Jacob 47
Lutheran 47
Magdalena 64
Maria Barbara 28, 48
Ottmar 38, 46, 48, 49, 54
Sophia Sabina 47
Schnaebelin, Anna Elisabetha 70
Catarina 74
Schnaeppin, Barbara 9
Schnaetterle, Philip 19
Sabina 19
Schnatterle, Adam 20
Barbara 49
Heinrich 20, 48, 49, 69
John George 20
John Jacob 20
John Michael 20
Martin 20
Philip 20, 28, 31
Philipp 21, 24, 50
Phillip 46
Sabina 20, 24, 39, 50
Sabina Elisabetha 50
Schnauber, Johannes 13
John Christoph 13
Schnebele, Appolonia 7
Heinrich 7
Schneber, Anna Margar. 64
Schneid, John Heinrich 19

Schneider, Abraham 40, 42, 46
  Adam 51, 62
  Agnes 73
  Anna Catarina 61
  Anna Margaretha 30
  Balthasar 54, 57
  Catarina 53
  Catarina Margar. 58
  Daniel 24, 36, 40
  Eva 48
  Eva Margaretha 48
  George Daniel 26
  George Martin 42
  Heinrich Adam 41, 64
  Johannes 32, 48, 66
  John Abraham 32, 40, 41, 42
  John Christian 59
  John George 41
  John Heinrich 41
  John Nicolaus 40
  John Peter 6
  John Philipp 32, 34
  Juliana 60
  Magdalena 24, 40
  Margaretha 61
  Maria Catarina 40
  Maria Elizabetha 40
  Maria Magdalena 51
  Philipp 48
  Valentin 54, 74
Schneidter, Abraham 40
Schnelb, Barbara 64
Schnellbecker, Jacob 26
Schnepf, Anna Catharina 9
  Barbara 13
  Christina 9
  Johannes 9, 13
  Lorentz 13
Schnepp, John 9
  Thomas 13
Schneppin, Barbara 9
Schnock, Christian 47
  Frederich 66
  John Kissner 47
Schnuerer, George Jacob 58
Schnug, ── 47
  Anna Eva 65
  Anna Margar. 71
  Christian 70
  Dorothea 71
  Eva Elizabetha 65
  Johannes 74
  John 71
  John (Jr.) 76
Schober, Jacob 29, 61
Schock, Jacob 71
  Jno. George 71
  Johannes 64
Schoeffle, Martin 54
Schoenberger, Balthasar 58
Schopf, Jacob 30
Schopff, Anna Maria 27
  Frantz 27
  Jacob 27
  John 27
  Maria Catarina 27
Scholl, Elizabetha 56
  Michael 59
  Sophia 59
Schollmeyer, George Michael 60
Schomm, Christoph 66
Schrack, Andreas 8
  Rosina 8
Schreiber, Andreas 9, 12
  Anna Margaretha 12
  Anna Maria 7
  Catarina 12

Schreiber (continued)
  Johann Cunradt 7
  John Ludwig 9
  John Theobaldt 9
  Ludwig 12
  Maria 9
Schreier, Catharina 56
Schreiner, Anna Catarina 61
  Johann Philipp 39
  John Michael 39, 57
  John Philipp 61
  John Valentin 63
  Margaretha 35
  Martin 35
Schrellbecker, Rosina 64
Schreyack, Anna 55
  Johannes 55
Schreyak, Jacob 55
Schreyer, Augustus 13
  Catarina 13
  John George 13
Schrielecker, John Valentine 11
Schudy, Michael 75
Schueler, Anna Margaretha 59
Schuett, Carl Valentine Michael 7
  Margaretha Elizabeth 7
  Maria Barbara 7
Schuetz, Anna Margar. 49
  Carl Valentin Michael 53
  Catarina 68
  Elisabetha 50
  George 40
  Jacob 45, 46
  Johannes 45
  John George 72
  John Leonhardt 40
  Leonhardt 74
  Margaretha 54
  Maria Elisabetha 46
  Susanna 58
Schuhehn, John Heinrich 41
Schuhen, Heinrich 37
Schui, Daniel 18
  Ludwig Heinrich 27
Schuler, John Adam 53
Schultz, Anna Catarina 16
  Catarina 17
  Christian 3
  Frederich 18
  Fredericka 15
  George Peter 57
  Heinrich 15
  Johannes 76
  John Heinrich 56
  John Peter 16
  Julia Catarina 18
  Maria Catarina 34
  Maria Eva 14
  Peter 17
  Valentin 14, 54
Schumacher, George 27
  John George 53
  Maria Eva 27
  Peter 71
Schumacker, George 47
Schunck, Anna Barbara 13
  Elizabeth 4
  Frantz 4, 13
  John Casper 4
  John Christian 4
Schupp, Anna Catarina 69
  Christoph 45
  Jacob 31
  Johannes 45
  John Christoph 59
  John Martin 31

Schuppinger, Anna Barbara 58
Schuy, Johannes 47
  Peter 43
Schwab, Anna Eva 57
  Eva Margaretha 32, 65
  George (Jr.) 15
  Heinrich 77
  Johannes 32, 62
  John Jost 60
  Margaretha 76
Schwartz, Esther 51
  Johannes 51, 67
  John Jacob 53
  Margaretha 37
  Michael 37
Schweickert, Philipp 33
  Susanna 33
Schweickhardt, Andreas 63
  Johann 67
Schweinhardt, Elisabeth 57
  Gabriel 13
  George 11, 12, 13
  Johan George 56
  Magdalena 13
  Maria Elizabetha 11
  Susanna 13
Schweitzer, Christian 76
Schwenck, Adam 50
  Jacob 73
  Marx 50
Schwertzel, Jost 52
  Mattheis 68
  Susanna 52
Schwitzer, Jacob 5
Scot, Chryssil 70
  Joseph 66
  Susanna 73
Scott, John 75
Sebastian, Andreas 53
  Eva Maria 8
Sedelmeyer, George 49
  Magdal. 49
Seemahr, Anna Margaretha 65
Seibert, Cunradt 8
  Elizabetha 8
  Frantz 28
  Jacob 25, 36
  John Heinrich 25
  John Jacob 26, 56
  Margaretha 28
Seidelmeyer, Anna Rosina 49
  Heinrich 49
  John Caspar 49
  John George 67
  Maria Elisabetha 49
Seidenbinder, Catar. Margr. 67
Seiler, Christoph Friederich 74
Seip, Frantz 14
Sell, Catarina 58
Seltzer, Ana Christina 20
  Anna Christina 13
  Christian 74
  John Heinrich 19
  John Ludwig 19
  Maria Catarina 19
  Mattheis 19
Seltzerin, Anna Christina 13
Selzer, Maria Eva 67
Sensebach, Jacob 29
Seubler, Magdalena 65
Seyboldt, Maria Elizabetha 55
Seydelmeyer, Johannes 70
Shaaf, Peter 31
Shade, Andreas 29
Shadwell, Anna 57
Sharp, Anna 59

Sharp (continued)
Anne 73
Catarina 68
Elenore 69
John 56, 74
Shealds, Margaretha 69
Sheals, Jane 70
Shepherd, Mary 10
Shlaughter, Margar. 57
Shmidt, Elisabetha 57
John 53
Mary 71
Rebecca 69
Shoerck, Elizabetha 60
Shuel, Juliana 65
Shupp, Christoph (Jr.) 51
Sichle, Jacob 76
Sieber, Elisabetha 54
Siechele, Albrecht 19
Eva Barbara 22
John Albrecht 22
John Peter 22
Siechelin, Maria Elizabetha 66
Regina 65
Siechle, Albrecht 36, 75
Anna Catarina 36
Siechlin, Anna Catarina 72
Anna Margaretha 72
Catarina 51
Eva Barbara 69
Sieg, Elisabtha 67
Siegmann, Regina Sophia 58
Sier, Anna Catarina 70
Sierer, Jacob 60
Sigrist, Barbara 63
Sikles, Jacob 8
Zacharias 8
Simon, Adam 43
Andreas 43
Anna Catarina 59
Anna Maria Elisabetha 58
Catarina 74
Elisab. Catarina 36
John Adam 58
John Nicolaus 35
John Peter 35
Juliana 70
Maria Elizaba. 68
Simons, Susanna 53
Simple, Anna 62
Simson, John 71
Simund, Heinrich 72
Sinken, Sarah 63
Sinn, Heinrich 19
Jacob Mattheis 19
Susanna 19
Sip, Emma Margar. 69
Eva Maria 67
Sirer, Maria Barbara 67
Skarl, Margaretha 58
Skullin, Maurice 59
Snodgrass, William 73
Snyder, Anna Catarina 23
John George 23
Soerer, Ana Eva 64
Anna Magdalena 33
Eva Catarina 47
Jacob 40, 46, 66
Jacob (Jr.) 47
Johannes 33
John Cunradt 33
John Jacob 33
Maria 33
Maria Veronica 70
Soldner, John George 13
Soll, John Adam 17
Solomon, Adam 70
Sommer, Elisabetha 64

Somner, Anna Maria 53
Sonntag, John Adam 31
Maria Catarina 31
Sowder, Henry 50
Sabina 50
Spaller, Catarina Barbara 18
Spanhauer, Heinrich 59
Spannseiler, Catarina 16
Jacob 16, 55
Sparen, John George 31, 33, 37
Philipp Adam 31
Spat, John Peter 43
Maria Salome 43
Spatz, Anna Martin 54
Wilhelm 61
Specht, John George Martin 41
Justina Margaretha 43
Maria Philippenia 41
Martin 41
Speck, Anna Maria 22, 27
Dorothea 73
Eleanora 27
Johannes 22
John Jacob 27
John Michael 27
Margaretha 24, 37, 43
Maria Catarina 22
Martin 16, 22, 24, 27, 36
Susanna 16
Spengel, Catarina Elizabeth 17
Geo. 9
George 13
Johanna 13
Michael 23
Spengele, George 14
Margaretha 14
Spenglein, Maria Elizabeth 5
Spengler, Ana. Margar. 10
Anna Maria 58
John Michael 29
Michael 29
Speugel, Daniel 17
Spicker, Margar. Barbara 72
Spickler, Barbara 62
John Martin 44
Martin 39, 42, 44
Spiegel, Anna Eva 23
Eva Christina 31
Gottfried 31
Michael 23, 31, 41
Spieler, Maria Barbara 65
Maria Eva 66
Spiess, Anna Elisabetha 37
Anna Elizabetha 44, 64
John Jacob 36
Maria Barbara 61
Maria Dorothea 34
Maria Eva 37
Ulrich 34
Spitaler, Veronica 60
Spon, Johann Adam 5
Maria Barbara 5
Michael 5
Sprecher, Dorothea 51
Elizabetha 65
Eva Margaretha 32, 51
George 51, 65, 74
Jacob 51, 67
Johann George 32
John Christoph 6, 51
John George 6
Margaretha 51
Maria Elizabetha 68
Spring, Caspar 46
John Frederick 46
Sshuetz, Susana Margr. 64
Stachler, Anna Elisabetha 61
Staehlin, Anna Barbara 59

Staehly, Johannes 76
Staengel, Maria Magdalena 57
Staengele, Johannes 63
Stahl, Augustus 73
Stahlschmidt, Anna Catarina 59
John George 77
Stambach, Barbara 58
Jacob 14
Maria Catharina 14
Stammgas, Balthaser 40
Elizabetha 40
Stammgast, Balthasar 62
Stanbury, Elisabetha 76
Stang, Elisabetha 70
Johann George 65
Starret, Frances 75
Staub, Mattheis 68
Stauch, John George 47
John Nicolaus 47
Staufer, Magdalen 74
Staug, Elisabetha 70
Staut, John Michael 8
Stautzenberger, Andreas 53
Steans, Edward 68
Steel, Elisabeth 70
Isabell 71
Thomas 71
Steffer, Johan Casper (Jr.) 4
Johan Casper (Sr.) 4
Steg, Maria Elizab. 68
Stehrer, John 76
Steig, John Peter 6
Stein, Abraham 41, 42
Anna Catarina 33, 41
Anna Magdalena 41
Anna Maria 41, 42
Christian 41
Elisabetha 43
Heinrich 62
Jacob 41, 47
Johann Friederich 56
Johannes 41, 47, 65, 71
John 41
John Abraham 46, 62
John Adam 42
John Heinrich 41
John Jacob 41
John Sebastian 41
Ludwig 19, 32
Maria Catarina 32, 41
Peter 40
Sebastian 33
Wilhelm 46, 47, 69
Steinbach, Christian 7
Maria Magdalena 7
Steinbrennerin, Sybilla 7
Steingrau, Johannes 45
Steinmanerin, Maria Eliza-
betha 7
Steinmann, Anna Maria 73
Steitz, Anna Maria 53
Catarina 53
George 35
John George 21
Margaretha 35
Stelbzer, Elisabetha 77
Stempel, Gottfried 45
Maria Ottilia 60
Stephan, Adam 66
Anna 54
Anna Christina 9
John Heinrich 8
Ludtwig 9
Maria Christina 9
Peter 8, 9
Stephanin, Anna Christina 8
Stephens, Isabell 68

Sterf, Anna Catarina 56
Sterneberger, Elisabetha 62
Sterret, Benjamin 69
Steuber, John Balthasar 6
  Maria Barbara 6
Steuer, George Simon 11
  John George 11
Steupel, Eva Catarina 48
  Gottfried 49
  John Davíd 49
  Rosina 49
Steutz, Anna Maria 58
Steward, Anne 56
  John 57
Stewart, David 63
  Lazarus 71
Stieb, Jacob 52
Stiebich, Salome 74
Stiegeler, John Jacob 67
Stiegler, Johann Sebastian 67
Stiess, George Adam 54
Still, Benjamin 73
Stober, Anna Eva 20
  Barbara 73
  Catarina 72
  Catharina Agatha 57
  Christina 59
  Eva 23
  Eva Barbara 61
  Eva Catarina 67
  George 67
  Jacob 73
  Johann Wilhelm 61
  John 76
  John Jacob 59
  John Peter 20
  John Valentin 23
  Valentin 59
Stobler, Maria Catar. 67
Stocker, Maria Eva 54
Stoecklin, Anna Elizabetha 13
Stoehr, Johann Adam 65
  Maria Elisabetha 72
Stoer, John Heinrich 57
  John Philipp 59
  Margaretha 56
Stoever, Adam 53
  Anna Christina 32, 48, 69
  Anna Eva 48
  Anna Margaretha 32, 48, 68
  Anna Maria 32, 48
  Barbara 53
  Caspar 13
  Catarina 48, 52
  Cattarina 53
  Elizabetha Catherine 56
  Frederick 52
  Gertraudt 3
  J.C. 77
  Johan Casper (Jr.) 3, 4
  Johann Casper 32
  Johann Casper (Jr.) 66
  Johann Casper (Rev.) 3, 4
  Johann Casper (Sr.) 3
  Johann Frederick 52
  Johann Friederich 77
  Johannes 32, 53, 75
  John 53
  John Adam 32, 48, 74
  John Caspar 32, 37, 49
  John Caspar (Jr.) 47
  John Casper 48, 52, 53
  John Casper (Jr.) 48
  John Casper (Sr.) 48
  John Frederick 32, 53
  John Frederick 48
  John Jacob 53
  John Philipp 53

Stoever (continued)
  M. L. (Prof.) 3
  Maria Catarina 3, 32, 35,
    36, 37, 48, 52
  Maria Catarina (Sr.) 48
  Sophia Magdalena 32
  Tobias 32, 48, 74
  W.C. (Esq.) 3
  William 53
Stofenberger, Adelheit Elisa-
  betha 24
Stohler, Johannes 67
Stoll, John Adam 54
Stoltz, Maria Elizabetha 74
Stoppelbein, Anna 74
Storm, Jacob 58
Stout, Elizabehta 55
  Joseph 63
  Peter 57
  Samuel 65
Stover, Eva 59
Straghorn, Elizabeth 66
Strahl, John Peter 62
Strain, Agnes 68
  John 69
  Sarah 68
Strattel, Brigitta 68
Straup, Barbara 58, 64
Strauss, —— 48
  Albrecht 29, 30, 38, 49
  Anna Elisabetha 29, 39
  Anna Magdalena 29, 39
  Anna Margaretha 49
  Barbara 45
  Caspar 39
  Catarina 49
  Christian 39
  David 49
  Elisab. 42
  Elisabetha 47, 49
  Jacob 42, 46, 49, 67
  Johann 67
  Johannes 49
  John Jacob 29, 39
  John Matthias 39
  John Nicolaus 5, 8
  John Philip 29, 39, 60
  John Samuel 29
  Maria Barbara 29, 43, 64
  Maria Catarina 29, 69
  Maria Catharina 39
  Maria Christina 29, 39
  Maria Elisab. 67
  Maria Elisabeth 29
  Maria Eva 29, 49
  Maria Eva Rosina 69
  Maria Susanna 29
  Philip 29
Stricker, Barbara 52
  Johannes Wilhelm 52
  Lorentz 52
Stroeher, Mattheis 75
Stroh, Ana Elisabetha 72
  Anna Maria Elizabetha 75
  Johann 67
  John Daniel 69
  Leonhardt 77
  Michael 72
Stroher, Anna Catarina 72
  Margaretha 72
Strohfuss, Dorothea 74
Strubel, Clara 19
  John Frederick 19
Stuart, James 11, 76
  Jane 68
  Mary 11
  Robert 72
Stuck, Barbara 31

Stuck (continued)
  Catarina 71
Stucker, Barbara 59
Stucky, Anna Maria 52
  Christian 52
Stueber, Barbara 13
  George Philipp 7
  John Balthaser 7
  Maria Catharina 7
  Maria Catharina Eliza-
    betha 7
Stuebich, John 76
Stuep, Christina 30
  Dorothea 44
  Elisabetha 54
  Friederich 40
  Johannes 40
  John Heinrich 34
  Maria Elisab. 41
  Maria Elizabetha 40
  Martin 30, 31, 33, 34, 38,
    58
  Susanna 31, 33, 38
Stuepp, Anna Christina 66
Stuertzer, Philipp 56
Stulp, Anna Kueningunde 59
  John Frederich 60
Stump, Michael 57
Stup, Catarina 60
Sturtzen, John 67
Stutzmann, Christian 76
Suess, Anna Margaretha 61
  Barbara 66
  Emanuel 66
  Johan Christoph 61
  John Leonhardt 14
  Ludwig 14
  Maria Salome 14
  Salome 64
Suesz, Johann Ludwig 56
Sultzbach, John Jost 17
Sumi, Anna Margaretha 42
  Michael 42
  Peter 42
Suni, Maria Magdalena 55
Superiores, —— 16
Suter, Geo. Thomas 37
  John 40
Swaller, Samuel 56
Swan, Mary 70
Swaney, Henry 63
Swinehardt, Elisabetha 55
Sydebueger, George 49
Syllaben, John 62

--- T ---

Tabernien, Elizabeth 8
Taefeler, Melchior 31, 36
Taefer, Melchior 31
Taeffeler, Anna Catarina 35
  Anna Elizabetha 35
  Christian 35
  Maria Barbara 35
  Mattheis 35
Tanner, Clara 61
Tate, Edward 71
Tauber, Philipp Christian 70
Tauth, Susanna 11
Taylor, James 76
Teafersbiss, Anna Barbara 18
Teep, Isabel 56
Tegin, Anna Margaretha 38
Teiss, Elisabetha 70
  Maria Elizabetha 56
Tempelmann, Barbara 62

Tempelmann (continued)
John Cunradt 61
Templemann, Barbara 62
Elisabetha 32
Tennewald, Anna Christina 64
Maria Appollonia 64
Tennin, James 58
Terrin, Elizabetha 30
Teuber, Anna Barbara 27
Teufersbiss, Anna Barbara 19
Barbara 11
Elizabeth Barbara 11
Teufersbissen, Catharina Bar-
bara 11
Teuss, Susanna Barbara 20
Thani, Jacob 36
John George 36
John Jacob 44
Thany, George 72
Thau, Catarina 69
Thiel, Carl 59
Thistle, Elenore 56
Thomas, Anna Magdalena 26
Ludwig 26
Mary Elizabeth 65
Peter 67, 74
Thome, John 72
Thompson, Andrew 73
Margaretha 66
Nancy 68
Thonteur, John 33
Thontheur, Christian 34
John 34
Thornton, William 70
Thorum, Susanna 42
Thranberg, Frederick 57
Thrennin, William 66
Thuerner, Agnes Magdalenea
45
Gottlieb 45
John Wilhelm 45
Thurm, John Gottlieb 43
Thurnbury, Edward 55
Tiffenbach, Johann Adam 54
Tigh, Jacob 55
Tittel, George 44
Tittle, Elisabetha 26
Johannes 44
John 20, 22, 26
John Adam 44
John George 44
John Peter 44
Peter 22, 62
Rachael 62
Tomson, Anna 53
John 60
Tondith, Elizabetha 13
John 13
Traber, Catherine 56
Johann Ludwig 68
Trabern, Elisabetha 54
Traenckel, Catarina 16
John Christoph 58
John Stephen 19
Stephen 16
Tranberg, Christina Barbara
17
Frederich 17
Tranckel, Johann Stephan 56
Traner, Michael 73
Tratter, Margaretha 61
Traut, John Heinrich 56
Wendel 56
Treese, William 61
Triessler, Joseph David 56
Trippner, Anna Elizabeth 41
John George 41
John Peter Leonhardt 41

Troester, Anna Elizabetha 34
Anna Margar. 70
Frederich 36
Friederich 34
John Heinrich 36
John Jacob 36
John Michael 35
Maria Dorothea 34
Martin 35
Trostel, Bernhardt 11
Trott, Herman 22
Trotter, Anna 10, 59
Elizabeth 10
James 10
Margaretha 64
Mary 10
William 10
Truckemueller, Margaretha
Elisabetha 72
Truckenmueller, Anna Maria
67
Tscheill, Wilhelm 53
Tucker, Agnes 70
Tunsteld, Anna Catarina 12
John Jacob 12
Turner, Antony 5
Rebecca 75
Susanna 5
Turnur, Thomas 5
Tusser, Esther 55
Tussing, Maria Barbara 28
Peter 28
Tuszing, John Philip 30
Peter 30
Tweed, Jane 66

--- U ---

Uhler, Anastasius 15, 16, 18,
20, 21, 23, 44, 47, 55
Anna Barbara 15, 29, 69
Anna Catarina 48, 49
Catarina Barbara 69
Christoph 44
Christopher 15
Dorothea 16, 21, 23, 47
John Christoph 72
John Michael 75
John Martin 15, 72
Michael 15
Uhrich, Anna Barbar. 66
Christoph 27
Elisabetha 71, 76
Johannes 33, 50, 55
John Christian 50
Maria Appollonia 27
Maria Catarina 27
Ulandt, Johann 57
Ulrich, Adam 22, 34, 35, 37
Ana Maria 33
Christoph 35, 72
Eva Margaretha 63
George 68
Johannes 26
John 29
John Deitrich 57
John Dietrich 16
John Geo. 58
Juliana 22, 35
Margaretha 29
Martin 74
Peter 21
Rosina 16
Umbehag, Balthasar 41
Umbehauer, Anna Catarina 62
Umberger, Catarina 63

Umberger (continued)
Elizabeth Dorothea 21
Johannes 21 ⁻
John Leonhardt 24
Juliana 60, 72
Julianna 16
Leonardt 28, 59
Leonhard 21
Michael 24, 59
Unbehagen, Appolonia 42
Balthasar 42, 46, 47
Catarina 42
Elisabetha 42
John Thomas 42
Jonas 42
Justina Catarina 42
Samuel 42
Unruh, Hans George 32
John George 32
Valentin 27

--- V ---

Vadis, Heinrich 17
Varner, Benjamin 67
Jane 62, 64
Veit, Carl 40
Veitheim, Sophia Catarina 61
Velt, Maria Elizabetha 68
Velten, Anna Maria 50
George 50
Veltey, Anna Barbara 34
George 34
Johannes 34
John Cunradt 34
John Heinrich 34
John Ulrich 34
Juliana 34
Maria Barbara 34
Sebastian 34
Veltin, John George 18
Maria Elisabetha 18
Velty, George 28, 62
Verdriess, Catarina 17
Hartman 60
Jacob 17, 23, 55
Johannes 17
John Valentin 17
Viel, Johannes 36
Wilhelm 36
Vierling, Johann Jacob 63
Vieruhr, Anna Barbara 56
Voelcker, Daniel 26
Jacob 26
Vogel, Andreas 8, 52
Andrew 73
Anna Catarina 56
Anna Maria 52
Johannes 8
Vogt, Anna Barbara 68
Volck, George 72
John Peter 58
Karl 4
Ulrich 65
Volckman, Johannes 55
Volemer, Catarina 66
Vollmar, Adam 18, 55
Anna Maria 20
Geo. Adam 68
George Adam 20
Jacob 41, 59
John Jacob (Jr.) 28
John Michael 28
Maria Appollonia 41
Maria Eva 67
Maria Magdalena 20

Vollmar (continued)
  Sabina 68
  Susannah Margaretha 60
Vollmer, Jacob (Sr.) 27
Voltz, John Jacob 76
Von Beber, Anna 10
  Joseph 10
  Peter 10
Von Huss, John 61
  Valentin 61
Vornwalt, Jacob 43

--- W ---

Wacker, Elizabeth 66
Wagener, Michael 15
Wagner, Ana Maria 68
  Anna Catarina 47
  Anna Elizabetha 22
  Appollonia 49
  Cunradt 48, 63
  Elizabetha 74
  Frantz Caspar 63, 67, 69
  George 22
  George Ludwig 41
  Gertraudt 43
  Jacob 48, 49, 62, 68
  Jacobina 68
  Johannes 47, 72
  John Martin 75
  John Mattheis 54
  John Michael 62
  Justus Simon 56
  Lazarus 56
  Ludwig 30, 38, 41, 42
  Ludwig Adam 38
  Magdalena 41, 58, 67
  Margar. 64
  Maria Catarina 67
  Maria Elisabetha 38
  Maria Eva Rosina 38
  Maria Margaretha 38
  Maria Magdal. 68
  Mattheis 47, 49
  Susanna Catarina 49
  Tobias 32
Waibel, Anna 68
Waible, Anna 52
  John Adam 52
Waite, James 59
Walborn, Maria Catarina 53
Walck, Michael 15
Walcker, John 75
  Thomas 65
Walker, Agnes 69
  Chrysy 65
  John 65
  William 69
Wallace, Isabella 65
  James 64
  William 69
Wallbort, Anna Susanna 58
Wallis, Alcey 77
Walmer, Christina 52
  George 52
  Johannes 52
  John George 72
  Peter 44
Walter, Magdalena 56
Walther, Anna Maria 48
  Catharine 68
  Cunradt 13
  David 48
  Jacob 48, 66
  Johannes 39
  Johannis 39

Walther (continued)
  John David 48
  John Jacob 48
  Margaretha 54
  Margaretha Barbara 13
  Susanna 62
Wampler, John Peter 60
Wampsler, Anna Magdalena 61
  Anna Veronica 61
Wamsser, Maria Magdalena 46
  Nicolaus 46
Wance, Jane 75
War, Maria Margaretha 50
  Thomas 50
Warren, George 10
Wartman, Adam 5
  Catarina 5
Waters, Isabel 73
  John 58
Watson, Catarina 73
  Hugh 74
  Margaretha 72
Weackly, Nancy 63
Weaker, Catharine 53
Weaver, John Adam 33
Webber, Heinrich 44
Weber, —— 50
  Anna 67, 69
  Anna Maria 51, 69, 76
  Casper 43
  Christiana 76
  Cunradt 45
  Daniel 72
  Eva 73
  Heinrich 69
  Jacob 49, 51
  Johann Wendel 68
  Johannes 73, 77
  John Adam 32, 33, 43, 61
  John Friederich 75
  John George 32, 33
  Laurentz 54
  Maria Catarina 43, 51
  Michael 45, 47
Webert, Elizabetha 51
  Heinrich 51
  John 51
  Melchior 65
Weegman, Christoph Friede-
    rich 64
Wegman, Anna Maria 32
  Christoph Freiderich 32
  Christoph Friederich 70
Wegner, Barbara 44
  Heinrich 44
Weidelblech, Elisabetha 50
  John 50
Weider, Catarina 56
  Johanna Dorothea 56
Weidman, Anna Maria 72
  Eva Frederica 58
  John 58
  Magdalena 64
  Maria Catarina 60
  Maria Elizabetha 60
Weidner, Johannes 66
  Ludwig 64
Weidtmann, John Heinrih 63
  Margaretha 32
  Martin 32
Weifin, Maria Barbara 7
Weigandt, Philipp 63
Weiland, Eva Catarina 47
Weiler, Maria Otilia 53
Weill, Anna Maria 59
Weimer, Anna 67
Weinmar, Bernhardt 13
  John Bernhardt 13

Weinmar (continued)
  Mattheis 66
Weipent, Susanna Margaretha
    7
Weipentin, Susanna Margare-
    tha 7
Weisenkind, Elisabetha 64
Weismaenn, Susanna 9
Weismannin, Susan 13
Weiss, Anna 66
  Anna Margar. 63
  Heinrich 70
  John Adam 71
  Maria Sybilla 17
Weissman, Abraham 8, 13
  Anna Christiana 8
Weissmann, Abraham 13
Weiszmaenn, Susanna 9
Weitz, Martin 52
Weitzel, Elizabetha 76
  Wirner 28
Weller, Barbara 17, 18
  Johann Jacob 56
  John Jacob 18
Wells, Edward 57
Welsch, Jacob 16, 17, 56
  John Jacob 57
Welsh, John 55, 59, 63
  John Peter 16
  Samuel 62
  Thomas 65
  William 16
Weltz, Andreas 16
  Jacob 65
Wendel, Abraham 58
  Anna Elizabeth 13
  Valentin 13
Wendelwirbel, John 8
  Sarah 8
Wendrich, Balthasar 56
  Elisabetha 42
  Frantz 42
  Maria Magdalena 69
Wentz, Jacob 44, 47, 49
  John Jacob 47
  Maria Catarina 47
  Rosina 73
Wepner, Johannes 74
Werner, Johannes 65
Weschenbach, Elisabetha 25
  Heinrich 25
Weszner, Martin 65
Wetzel, Maria Barbara 13
  Martin 13
Weyer, Eva Margaretha 55
Weyhmueller, Catarina 21
Weyhrich, Anna Maria Cata-
    rina 70
  George 69
  Wilhelm 68
Weyman, Christoph Frede-
    rich 52
  Eva Maria 52
  John Jacob 37
Weynandt, John Jacob 54
Weyrich, Eva Barbara 72
  Peter 74
White, Benjamin 12
  Charity 12
  Mary 55
  Robert 71
  Ruth 12
  William 12
Whitehill, Robert 67
Whiteside, Ralph 47
Whitehead, Thomas 57
Whitside, Elizabeth 55
  Else 68

105

Whitside (continued)
William 70
Widder, Christina 35
Christoph 35
John Michael 35
Wiehmar, Margar. 45
Mattheis 45
Wieland, Anna Eva 46
Johann Friederich 64
John Frederick 46
Wielandt, Friederich 46
Geo. Peter 63
Maria Catarina 46
Wier, Elenore 75
Wild, Elizabetha Catarina 75
Wildensinn, George Carl 14
Johannes 14
Wildfang, Elisabetha 46
George Michael 29, 61
Johannes 37
Peter 45
Sebastian 45, 46
Wildt, Theoboldt 76
Wildtfang, Elizabetha Cata-
rina 37
George Michael 37
Maria Margaretha 37
Wilhelm, Heinrich 22, 60
John Heinrich 58
John Philipp 22
Maria 22
Wilheut, Maria Magdalena 54
Wilkinson, William 76
Will, Michael 54
Willheut, Elisabetha 54
William, George 21
Isaac 21, 74
Jacob 21
Mary 5
Mary Elisabetha 21
Williams, Abraham 20, 26
Benjamin 34
Christian 20
Christina 34, 73
Elizabeth 26, 68
George 68
James 26, 34, 51, 71
Johannes 34, 51
John 4
Margaretha 26, 69, 75
Maria Catarina 69
Ruth 69
William 64
Willich, Maria Magdal. 68
Willis, Rachael 73
Willson, Thomas 55
Wilson, Adam 65
James 72
Jane 65
John 16
Mary 72
Sara 69
Sarah 47
William 16, 62
Winckelmann, Melchior 63
Windelblech, Catarina 34
Peter 34
Windseeth, Elisabeth 55
Winger, Anna 55
Winter, Andreas 43
Justina Margaretha 43
Salome 70
Winterbauer, Magdal 17
Maria Susanna 17
Sebastian 14, 17
Sybilla 17
Wintermuth, Christopher 13
Wintermuthin, — 12

Wipert, Anna Maria 5
Wirnss, George 33
Wirschumer, Dorothea 65
Wirth, Adam 46
Cunrandt 43
George Wilhelm 43
Johann Adam 65
Johannes 46
John Adam 46
John Christian 47
John Jacob 47
Wirtz, Elizabetha 67
Wissenandt, John Peter 34, 55
Maria Magdal. 61
Witter, Christoph 59
Wittman, Adam 61
Christoph 61
George Michael 5
John George 60
Wittmann, Christoph 5
Wittmer, Maria Eva 57
Michael 55
Wittmeyer, Maria Veronica 58
Wittmyer, Anna Maria 50
Christoph 50
Maria Barbara 50
Wittner, Maria Barbara 55
Wohlfahrdt, Ludwig 65
Wohlfahrt, Anna Catarina 67
Wohlfarth, Michael 64
Wohlleben, Anna Maria Elisa-
betha 34
Johannes 39
John 34, 45
John Peter 34
Philipp Jacob 34
Wolandie, Jacob 76
Wolf, Andreas 22, 57
Anna 71
Anna Elisabetha 63
Anna Margaretha 43
Anna Maria 22
Anna Maria Eva 62
Carolus 42
Elisabetha 52
Elizabetha 16, 40, 56
Friederich 63
George 43
Hanna 59
Jacob 16, 17, 43, 52
Johann Wendel 72
Johannes 4
John 16, 17
John Adam 4
John George 56
John Heinrich 4, 15, 57
John Herman 22
John Jacob 22, 71
John Jacob (Jr.) 47
John Peter 17
Jonas 22, 56
Juliana Barbara 76
Maria Eva 29
Maria Magdalena 68
Maria Margaretha 42
Nicolaus 42, 50
Peter 59
Simon 22
Wolfart, Catarina Agatha 25
Elizabetha 28
John 25
Michael 28
Wolfert, George 61
Michael 46
Wolff, Barbara 55
Wolffert, John 28
John George Philip 28
Wolffinger, Anna Elizabeth 6

Wolffinger (continued)
Bernhardt 6
Wolfkiel, Anna Margar. 72
Wolleben, Johannes 60
Wollenweber, Johannes 35
Margaretha 35
Wood, Margaretha 57
Woodside, James 64
Worley, Rebecca 58
Worst, Jacob 33
Wott, Balthasar 6
Maria Ursula 6
Wriedner, John George 6
Wuchtel, Janeslaus 14
Wuerst, Anna Margaretha 60
Wuertz, Anna Margaretha 10
Jacob 10, 54
Johannes 45
John Cunradt 10
Maria Catharina 10
Wuest, Barbara 33
Eva Margaretha 33
Jacob 33, 60
Wunderlich, Daniel 51, 69
Eva Barbara 51
Johannes 66

--- Z ---

Zartman, Jacob 60
Zeh, Anna Maria 25
George 25
John Friederich 60
Zehrung, Anna Elisabetha 72
Zeller, David 61
Heinrich 36
John Heinrich 30
John Heinrich (Jr.) 30
John Heinrich (Sr.) 30
John Nicolaus 34
Margaretha 34
Zemmeral, Rhoda 63
Zerbe, John Jacob 29
Martin 29
Zerfass, Samuel 72
Zerv, Maria Barbara 29
Zerve, Barbara 56
Zerw, Elisabetha 58
Zerwe, Anna Christina 30
Anna Elizabetha 30, 37
Catarina 30, 39, 47, 61
Catarina Elizabetha 30
Christian 30
Elisabertha 53
George Peter 30
Jacob 30
Jacob (Jr.) 64
Johannes 30, 39, 40
John 30, 38, 47, 60
John Jacob 30
John Michael 30
John Valentin 30
Maria Barbara 61
Maria Catarina 30
Maria Margaretha 30, 62
Peter 37
Ziebold, Anna Maria 52
Barbara 52
Catarina 52
Christoph 52
Zieffle, Joseph 63
Ziegeler, Christina 18, 55
Eva 40
George Andreas 60
Jacob 67
John George 55

Ziegeler (continued)
  Philipp 55
Zieger, Anna Maria 29
  Anna Maria Elisabeth 29
  Dorothea 74
  George Heinrich 29
  Jacob 29
Ziegler, Anna Barbara 32
  Anna Christina 14
  Anna Dorothea 58
  Anna Margaretha 15
  George Andreas 32
  George Heinrich 71
  Hans George 32
  Jacob 14
  Jacob (Jr.) 52
  John Philip 14
  John Thomas 32
  Judith 52
  Philip (Jr.) 15
  Philip Jacob 52

Zimmer, Anna Catarina 24
  Christoph 22, 24
Zimmerman, Catarina 50
  Christoph 19
  Elisabeth 61
  Elizabetha 65
  Eva 50
  Gehrhardt 58
  George 44
  George Adam 58
  Hannah 52, 74
  Johann Frederich 62
  Johannes 71
  John Adam 76
  Maria Dorothea 61
  Michael 50, 62
  Sebastian 4, 54
Zimpfer, Jacob 66
Zint, Anna Maria 54
Zoeller, Anna Catarina 59

Zoeller (continued)
  Frantz Paul 42
  Johannes 60
  John (Jr.) 42
  John Heinrich 26
  Michael 75
Zoll, John Christoph 72
Zorn, Jacob 58
Zoth, Margaretha 15
Zuber, Heinrich 5
  John Michael 5
  John Peter Hugo 5
  Maria Elizabetha 5
Zwecker, Christina 59
Zwerontzor, Regina 66
Zweysich, Christian 30
  John Cunradt 30
  John George 30
  Maria Christina 30
Zwickel, Anna Margar. 58